CH'OE PU'S DIARY:
A RECORD OF
DRIFTING ACROSS THE SEA

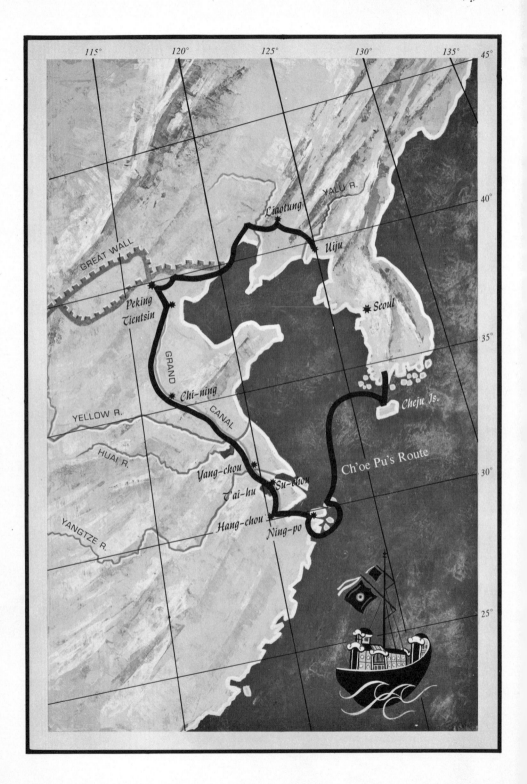

115° 120° 125° 130° 135° 45°

40°

YALU R.

Liaotung

GREAT WALL

Uiju

Seoul

Peking
Tientsin

35°

GRAND

Chi-ning

CANAL

YELLOW R.

Cheju Is.

HUAI R.

30°

Yang-chou

Ch'oe Pu's Route

Su-chou

T'ai-hu

Hang-chou
Ning-po

YANGTZE R.

25°

The Association For Asian Studies: Monographs and Papers, No. XVII

CH'OE PU'S DIARY:
A RECORD OF
DRIFTING ACROSS THE SEA

translated with introduction and notes

by

JOHN MESKILL

Published for The Association For Asian Studies by
The University of Arizona Press, Tucson, 1965

The publication of this volume has been made possible by a generous grant to The Association For Asian Studies by the Ford Foundation.

For
Ichisada Miyazaki
and
Chi-chen Wang

ACKNOWLEDGEMENT

Several scholars have given more thought and time to helping with this book than any student would have cause to expect. Professor Ichisada Miyazaki of Kyoto University brought *P'yohae-rok* to my attention, had it photographed for me, talked over innumerable difficult points that I found in translating it, and criticized the entire manuscript after it was completed. Not only for that but also for his unfailing kindness, I am grateful. Professor Chi-chen Wang of Columbia University patiently read the whole translation through with me, correcting mistakes, explaining syntax, and improving the style. His help in this has been only the most recent of many benefits that I have received from him. I am also grateful to Professor L. Carrington Goodrich of Columbia not only for guiding this work as I prepared it for a dissertation but also for introducing me to Chinese history in the first place. To Professors Wm. Theodore de Bary and Donald Keene I am indebted for the most incisive criticism and compelling suggestions for a sound approach to the study of the diary and to Professors C. Martin Wilbur and Franklin Ho of Columbia for their useful criticisms of detail in the manuscript.

So many other people have made my work easier in direct and indirect ways that I cannot list them all with an adequate description of their assistance. I should like at least to mention a few people in universities and libraries, the generosity of whose help could only be accounted for by their devotion to scholarship: Mr. Key P. Yang of the Library of Congress, Professor Suematsu Yasukazu of Gakushūin University, Professor Takahashi Tōru of Tenri University, Professor Yamamoto Tatsurō of Tokyo University, Dr. Sudzuki Osamu of Tenri University, and Mr. Howard Linton and Miss Miwa Kai of Columbia. To all of them I am warmly grateful.

Barnard College
Columbia University   John Meskill
September, 1964

Contents

ABBREVIATIONS

BD	H. A. Giles, *A Chinese Biographical Dictionary*
CG	W. H. Wilkinson, *The Corean Government*
CJM	*Chōsen jimmei jisho*
CKJM	*Chung-kuo jen-ming ta-tz'u-tien*
CS	*Chōsen-shi*
FSJW	*Pen-ch'ao fen-sheng jen-wu k'ao*
HJAS	*Harvard Journal of Asiatic Studies*
KCLC	*Kuo-ch'ao lieh-ch'ing chi*
Hucker	Charles O. Hucker, "Governmental Organization of the Ming Dynasty"
KC	Key P. Yang and G. Henderson, "An Outline History of Korean Confucianism"
KSG	Hazard, *et al., Korean Studies Guide*
KT	*Kyŏngguk taejŏn*
LCLK	*Ming Ch'ing liang-ch'ao li-k'o t'i-ming pei-lu*
LTFC	*Lan-t'ai fa-chien lu*
MS	*Ming shih*
SIK	*Huang Ming ssu-i k'ao*
SPTK	*Ssu-pu ts'ung-k'an*
SRCY	*Shina rekidai chimei yōran*
SYC	*Shu yü chou tzu lu*
TDC	*Tōyō dokushi chizu*
TGYJ	*Sinjŭng tongguk yŏji sŭngnam*
TH	*Tz'u hai*
THM	*Ku-chin t'ung-hsing-ming ta-tz'u-tien*
TMHT	*Ta Ming hui-tien*
TRD	*Tōyō rekishi daijiten*
TY	*Taedong yŏjido*
Wagner	Edward W. Wagner, "The Recommendation Examination of 1519"
WPC	*Wu pei chih*

INTRODUCTION

P'yohae-rok, A Record of Drifting across the Sea, is the diary of a Korean official who, caught in a storm off the coast of Cheju, Korea, drifted in his boat to the coast of China. Arrested there, he travelled under escort through much of east China to Peking, where his adventure received the attention of the highest authorities, who after deliberating provided the means to return him to the border of his homeland at the Yalu River. The diary, which he completed immediately after returning home in 1488, records the adventures of a castaway, at first at the mercy of sea and wind and later in a foreign land where, unknown and unwelcome, he must win his way to safety. In that sense the story is one not only of adventure but of endeavor as well, since hope of returning safely home lies partly in the ability and courage of the man himself. That he meets the test with strength to spare lets him add to the record another element, that of discovery, for like other castaways who have lived to tell their tale, Ch'oe Pu (1454-1504) seizes the opportunity to note what is remarkable and wonderful along the way.

CH'OE PU

Men of the past, however interesting they have found this diary as a story, have read it for other reasons as well. Ch'oe's grandson remarks, in a passage to be quoted later, that the diary gives some indication of the author's abilities and that reading it has seemed to some men a way of broadening their knowledge. It is still so today, for Ch'oe has recorded something both of himself and of the history of China. The facts of his life suggest that the fateful wind that drove him to China had swept up an unusually capable man.

Ch'oe[1] was born in 1454 in Naju, a prefectural town in Chŏlla Province, on the southwest tip of the Korean peninsula. His father, T'aek, had achieved the scholarly rank of *Chinsa,* but, according to his son, rather than take office, to which his learning might lead him, had stayed at home to care for his parents.[2] In 1477, Ch'oe, too, passed the *Chinsa* examination, winning third place. In

---

[1]The fullest biography of Ch'oe Pu appears in *Chōsen jimmei jisho* (Chōsen Sōtokufu Chūsūin, Keijo, 1937), pp. 1400, 1401, which contains most of the information given here. Other sources consulted include *Yŏnsan'gun ilgi* 56, Yŏnsan'gun 10:10 *wu-yin, hsin-ssu,* and *jen-wu; Yu-mun soe-rok* (Ch'oe Pu); *Haedong chamnok* (6 *chüan,* in *Taetong yasŭng,* Chōsen Kosho Kankō-kai, Keijo, 1910), *ch.* 1; *Yŏllyŏsil kisul* (Yi Kŭng-ik, Chōsen Kosho Kankō-kai, Keijo, 1912), *ch.* 6; *Yŏnsan-jo kosa ponmal muo tang-jok;* and *Chŏmp'ilje sŏnsaeng munjip* (Kim Chong-jik, 1892 edition, 3 fascicles), *Munin-rok.*

[2]The *Chinsa* degree, unlike its Chinese namesake *Chin-shih,* did not qualify one for official employment. For that there were civil service examinations.

1482, five years later, he passed the Civil Service Examination in first place in the second category. He then served successively as Writer and Doctor of Learning in the Printing Office, Auditor in the Military Supplies Commission, Archivist in the National Academy, Supervisor in the Office of the Inspector-General, and Assistant Writer and Writer in the Office of Special Counselors. He is said to have contributed over one hundred articles to *Tongguk t'onggam* (1484), a history of Korea from ancient times.[3] In 1486 he passed the Civil Service Second Examination and was selected to study in the Hodang Library, after which he was successively Junior Fifth Counselor in the Office of Special Counselors and Lieutenant and Assistant Captain of the Yongyang Garrison. He was appointed Commissioner of Registers for Cheju in 1487, soon after *Yijo sillok* records a complaint that important houses on the island were acquiring extraordinary numbers of slaves.[4] Soon after going there, he heard of his father's death, set sail for home, was caught up in a storm and driven to China. His diary tells what happened to him in the nine months that followed.

Returning eventually to the capital, he stayed only long enough to write *P'yohae-rok* at the King's command and then went home to mourn. He came out of mourning in 1492. Soon opponents brought the accuracy of his diary into question, and he had to defend himself before the King. He is said to have recounted the whole story, and he must have impressed the King, for he received a gown as a gift. The highest office of his career was Director of the Ceremonies Office.[5]

In 1498 a political purge banished him to Tanch'ŏn, a remote northern settlement. A second purge in 1504 condemned him to death, to which he is said to have gone bravely after spending the night drinking with friends. He was returned to honor posthumously in 1506.[6]

In an official career of only eighteen years he had gained considerable experience in government. Even by his thirty-fifth year, his age when he went to China, he had passed the highest competitive examinations, contributed to an important scholarly work, and held several offices. His talents must have already begun to earn him the reputation for learning and administrative competence for which he was to be remembered.

In addition, he distinguished himself by outspoken defense of principles. One incident is said to show his salient traits. He and a friend happened to have gone to their home villages, which were fifteen *li* (approximately five miles) apart, at the same time. When later the friend visited him, Ch'oe asked how he

[3]*TRD*, VI: 442.

[4]*Sŏngjong sillok* 206 Sŏngjong 18 (1487), 8, *kuei-ch'ou* 206, 18, 8. The two events are not necessarily related, but Ch'oe himself refers to the island as a troublesome place to govern. The assignment may have been a difficult one.

[5]*Sŏye sŏnsaeng munjip* (Yu Sŏng-nyong, 1633, 7 fascicules), *ch.* 17, *Suhyŏn-jip pal. Pu Muo tangjŏk*, 25r., 25v.

[6]*Sinjŭng Tongguk yŏji sungnam* (Yang Sŏng-ji and others, Chōsen-shi Gakkai edition of 1930, Keijo, 4 vols.), *ch.* 35. p. 352.

His writings, other than the diary, were collected and published under the title *Kŭmnam-jip*, but I have not found a copy of the book and cannot say whether it contains anything of special interest. See, for example, *Chōsen tosho kaidai* (Chōsen Sōtokufu, 1919, 708 p.) p. 380.

had come. The friend said that he had taken an official relay horse. Ch'oe said (in effect), "The state provides transportation only to your house. From your house to mine is a private trip. By what right did you come on a relay horse?" When they went back to Court, Ch'oe told the King what had happened, and his friend lost his job. Nevertheless, he came to Ch'oe and apologized to him. Ch'oe said, "It's all right. Only remember this later."

The story, reminiscent as it is of dozens in formal Chinese biographies, is no doubt largely conventional. Yet it puts Ch'oe in the category of men to whom ideals were important and establishes the honor later attached to his name.

It is a story that also suggests the kind of cultivation that his native talent had received. Ch'oe's education, like that of all Korean men of his time and station, had been Confucian. More broadly, he had been brought up to think of China as the center of civilization; it was as if all his training had gone to prepare him for his journey. Yet he was a Korean, not Chinese, Confucianist, whose point of view deserves attention since it helps to shape the diary.

Most immediately, he was at first unwelcome in China. He had no official duty there, he was an unknown intruder and suspected of being a pirate, and his explanation of how he had come conflicted with the report of a Chinese coast guard who had observed his boat at sea. In the hostile atmosphere about him he had almost no tangible proof of his respectability. All that he could depend on was a display of cultivation, which would show him and his party to be civilized in the Chinese manner and so, presumably, peaceable. He was obliged, therefore, to be on his best behavior, and we may expect to discover in his book a model of Korean propriety. In that sense, the man himself becomes as interesting as what he says about China.

Of less direct influence on his fortunes in China but perhaps more pervasive in his recording of them was what might be called the state of Confucianism in Korea, especially in Korean government. No attempt can be made here to discuss so large a question as a whole, since I have neither studied Korean history systematically nor felt that this introduction should wander so far afield. A brief and tentative description of certain conditions, however, may help to explain attitudes Ch'oe takes in his diary.

When Yi Sŏng-gye (1335-1408) founded the kingdom he named Chosŏn (1392-1910), not all the important Confucianists of his day supported his revolt. Some considered it immoral and the new regime lacking in legitimacy; stung by their opposition, a son of Sŏng-gye killed Chŏng Mong-ju (1337-1392), their leader.[7] For some time after that, the Yi rulers were especially sensitive to the question of legitimacy. Their choice of the archaic name Chosŏn may itself have been made partly to emphasize their legitimate succession to the rulers of old, and their sacrifices to past rulers, even those of Koryŏ, may have

---

[7]Key P. Yang and Gregory Henderson, "An Outline History of Korean Confucianism. Part I, *Journal of Asian Studies,* XVIII: 1 (November, 1958), p. 88.

had the same purpose.[8] One sign of their sensitivity perhaps, was the abhor-
rence they felt of notices in Chinese records that Sŏng-gye had murdered
members of the Koryŏ royal house. For years they asked to have the notices
removed, as was finally ordered.[9]

Confucian colleagues of the murdered man, for their part, did not forget the
issue, either. Several of them refused to support the new government, and one,
Kil Chae (1353-1419), retired to Kyŏng-sang Province and opened a school
where he taught students Chu Hsi's Confucianism, stressing personal integrity.
Though later his students took office with great distinction when conditions
favored it, a tradition of retirement from government had been established.
Even when his successors, as in Ch'oe's time, included many of the most prominent figures of the country and took part in government, the tradition of
withdrawal remained. The men of that academic line came to be called the
Sallim hakp'a, the "Mountain-grove School," connoting the removal of the
school from the busy center of government to rustic retirement.[10] Ch'oe
belonged to the school, and he was not far removed from its beginnings. He
was the pupil of Kim Chong-jik (1431-1492), a high official under Sŏngjong and
the son of Kim Suk-cha (fl. 1414), the most famous student of Kil Chae.

In general terms, therefore, Confucianism in Korea until Ch'oe's time had
not achieved the domination it enjoyed in China. Ch'oe's school, hardly more
than four generations old, rested on no long, native development. Confucianism was far from being the pervasive substance of Korean thought that it
later became; it may still have seemed something of a cult. A fact that must
have kept its adherents sharply aware of being separate was strong opposition,
which, coming from Buddhists and others, challenged, disturbed, and sometimes defeated them. Much about such a position might impart to the Confucianists, even in the improved atmosphere of Ch'oe's time, the fervor of
evangelists. Such fervor in part characterizes Ch'oe Pu, for one, and its roots
may lie in the Confucianists' sectarian past.

Cho'e's attachment to Confucian ethics flavors the whole diary. As he sees
it, much of his hope for gaining the respect and aid of the Chinese depends on
making clear his knowledge of those ethics and his party's adherence to them.
That, in fact, very likely helps to save them all. Even before landing in China,
he makes clear the strength of one moral conviction. As his boat drifts into
sight of land men sail out to meet him. His subordinates beg him to put
on his official dress and thus impress the strangers, but Ch'oe is in mourning
and, despite the danger that his party may be ill-treated, refuses to show dis-

---

[8]*TRD,* VIII: 373.

[9]*SYC, ch.* 1: 8*v.,* 9*r.* See also L. Eul sou Youn, *Le Confucianisme en Corée* (Paris: Paul Geuthner, 1939, 198 pp.),
pp. 145-146; L. C. Goodrich, "Korean Interference with Chinese Historical Records," *Journal of the North China
Branch of the Royal Asiatic Society,* LXVIII (1937): 28-34.

[10]*Cf.* KC, I: 88; Seno Makuma, *Chōsen-shi taikei (kinsei-shi)* (Chōsen-shi Gakkai, Keijo, 1927, 318 pp.) p. 75;
Hatada Takashi, *Chōsen-shi* (Iwanami Zensho 154, Tokyo, 1951, 299 pp.), p. 126

respect toward his dead father by taking off his mourning clothes. Such courageous adherence to filial piety becomes all the more striking when, after the first experience ends unpleasantly, Ch'oe again refuses to change into finery to meet a second group of suspicious strangers. Even the threat of death itself, it would seem, could not shake his convictions, as he himself later affirms when he says, "I would rather die than oppose filial piety and sincerity." The firmness of his filial piety when it is at issue might even be called rigidity, for there were accepted precedents that could release him from his position. The precedents centered around the idea that for all rules there were exceptions, and that certain circumstances made expediency acceptable. His own subordinates argue with him from that point of view, and later Chinese do, too, without success. The measure of his commitment to the principle of filial piety becomes clear at Peking, where he opposes the decision of the Board of Rites itself to set aside his filial obligations. He resists to the last moment those officials who make him dress for Court. "For the time being," the Board says, "mourning for a parent will be unimportant and Heaven's graciousness important," but Ch'oe relents only when a Chinese reaches up and relieves him of his mourning hat.

Though his deep concern over his filial predicament is one of the strongest moral strains in the book, it is not the only one. Ch'oe is anxious to prove himself and his country Confucian stalwarts. Almost from the moment of landing, he instructs his men to be on their best behavior. He says, "We ought . . . to . . . let the people of this land know that the formality of our country is as it is . . . The secondary officials should bow to me . . . the troops . . . to the secondary officials. There should be no skipping over ranks." With this admonition he puts his faith in Confucian decorum, and with good sense. Not only do the Koreans impress the Chinese with their behavior, but they are also well on the way to proving that they are respectable people. Good manners and Ch'oe's Confucian learning save their lives.

In his respect for propriety, Ch'oe incidentally reveals a rather international aspect of Confucianism. He is careful to address Chinese officials of lower rank than his through a subordinate. He does not hesitate, either, to scold Chinese of lower rank when they behave badly toward the Koreans.

Other incidents illustrate his loyalty to his sovereign, his reverence for the Emperor and his sense of justice. Always his Confucianism is apparent, and in many a conversation he impresses the Chinese with his understanding. At one point he banteringly lectures his Chinese escort on the inadvisability of calling Confucius the "Criminal Judge of Lu," because that demeans him before the Emperor; and at another he explains how eunuchs are kept in their place in Korea. In all his verbal victories his self-consciousness as a Korean and Confucianist is evident. He is determined to prove himself a good Confucianist and Korea a great Confucian state. In doing so he must resort to a certain eager pedantry, arising no doubt from the compulsion he feels to

maintain high Confucian standards. It is also evident that in writing the book
he was mindful of the fact that his Korean king would read it and be interested
to discover how his minister measured up abroad. As a result Ch'oe always
seems more Confucian than the Chinese.

In addition to fervent adherence to some Confucian morals, Ch'oe and other
Koreans in the book hold rather surprising views on metaphysical power.
Much has been written about the inadequacy of early Confucianism to explain
the unknown with as much comfort, hope, or beauty as Buddhism or Taoism.
Both of these religions made statements about cosmological principles or the
nature of ultimate reality that Confucianism had said little about. A gradual
recognition of the importance of some of these speculations played a part in
the formation of Neo-Confucianism. Unlike early Confucianism, the new
synthesis had an elaborate theory of reality, including the Great Ultimate,
Principle, and Heaven, discussions of which were meat and drink to some
philosophers in the Yi period.

No one in Ch'oe's diary speculates about any of these concepts, which may
only mean that there are no metaphysicians in the book. One of them, however,
Heaven, is referred to frequently enough to indicate how many educated
Koreans must have regarded it. For Ch'oe and some of his colleagues, Heaven
wills men's fate and other events in the world. It is to Heaven that Ch'oe's
injuries are attributed, and he, therefore is not to blame. According to one
Korean envoy, Heaven set Ch'oe adrift and rescued him, and according to
another, Heaven saved Ch'oe through the virtue of the King, apparently an
intervening influence. When Ch'oe is particularly impatient to continue on his
way in China, Heaven sends rain, good for the farmers and not to be resented.

Under Heaven's auspices though they be, however, men are not powerless.
They have a role of their own. "Let each of you be diligent in the things that
are within the power of men and accept the fate [decided] by Heaven," Ch'oe
tells his frightened men. Heaven assists men to do the things in their power and
can be influenced by prayer. In the drifting boat, Ch'oe says a long prayer,
in the course of which it becomes apparent that Heaven's judgment may be
disputed. Ch'oe accepts the fact that he should be punished if he has sinned,
although he can think of nothing he has done wrong, but points out a chance of
injustice being done. He asks, "Will you, Heaven, presume to be so unmerciful as to let over forty innocent men drown with me?" If the ability to cope with
"outrageous fate" was the strength of Buddhism and Taoism, it would seem
that the Korean Confucianists were strong in that sense, too.

Curiously enough, for Ch'oe, Heaven has its place. He offers no objection
to the remarks of Korean ambassadors that Heaven saved him, but when a
Chinese official observes that Heaven must have made dangers from which to
save him and calamities to bring him through them, Ch'oe answers that his
safety was entirely a gift of the Imperial graciousness. Perhaps there were
times when diplomacy overshadowed Heaven.

Ch'oe's attitude toward poetry is so much that of a Confucian gentleman that it shows even the customary incongruity. In the familiar Confucian manner, he professes a scorn and suspicion of poetry and poets. "Poetry (*shih-tz'u*)," he says, "is something by which the frivolous moan about the wind and moon and not a thing indulged in by sincere men devoted to the Way. I take as my study the investigation of things, extension of knowledge, and pursuit of truth." Po Chü-i, when he decried poetry that was mere "sporting with the wind and snow, toying with grasses and flowers," sounded the same.[11] Yet Ch'oe writes poems frequently when the occasion seems appropriate. He refuses, it is true, to write a poem in exchange for a book, for that would be like selling poetry, but when a pleasant meeting or a test of cultivation, such as his interview at the Ministry of War, calls for a poem, he is willing. No doubt he would, like Po Chü-i, whose work he apparently knew well, profess to attach little importance to such "miscellaneous poems"; but when a hat box is stolen from him in Manchuria, the loss he regrets is the poem that was in it.

Although the firmness with which Ch'oe takes his stand on Confucian ground demonstrates his trust in that school of itself, the excitement of politics at home reinforced his intellectual fervor. That a Neo-Confucianist should be concerned with government is axiomatic, but for Ch'oe and others the very justification of their offices seemed to lie in Confucian principles, at a time when their right to occupy their offices, and even to live, as Ch'oe's fate makes clear, was contested. For that reason as well as from personal conviction, the diary he wrote to show the King leaves no doubt of his Confucian stand.

Chosŏn was less than one hundred years old at the time of Ch'oe's youth and education. The founder, Yi Sŏng-gye, who had died less than fifty years before Ch'oe was born, had laid down policies meant to avoid the woeful fate of his predecessors. One policy was firm allegiance to the Ming dynasty of China (1368-1644). It had not been easy to gain Chinese recognition of the policy, for the early relations between the countries had been strained. It took such signs of Korean sincerity as an immediate request for recognition and pledge of loyalty; a deferring to Ming in the choice of a name for the country and the suggestion of Chosŏn, which had pleasant historical connotations for the Chinese;[12] and eventually regular tribute to make it successful.

Another policy, primarily aimed against subversion, but incidentally probably pleasing to Ming, was the creation of a civil government with Confucian ideals. Two of the hindrances to good government in Koryŏ, the previous kingdom (918-1392), had been private armies, which stood outside the Court's control, and Buddhist clergy who, abusing the Court's patronage, helped to

---

[11]Arthur Waley. *The Life and Times of Po Chü-i*. London: George Allen and Unwin, 1949, p. 108.

[12]Chosŏn was also the name of the dynasty (1122-194 B.C.) founded by Ch'i-tzu (K. Kija), supposedly an uncle of the last Shang ruler, who fled to the North (Hazard, Hoyt, Kim, and Smith, *Korean Studies Guide*, University of California, 1954, pp. 177 *et seq.*). Ming T'ai Tsu, when consulted about the name, is quoted as having said, "For a name for the Eastern Barbarians, Ch'ao-hsien (K. Chosŏn) is the most beautiful and enduring." (Tung Yüeh, *Ch'ao-hsien fu, Chōsen Shiryō Sōkan*, No. 15, 11r.)

impoverish its treasury and morals.[13] The new Yi government planned to prevent their revival, and to that end the King and his successors abolished private armies and destroyed their registers[14] and gradually suppressed Buddhism, at first by such restrictive measures as confiscating lands, removing tax exemptions, imposing new taxes, and limiting the number of temples, their fields, serfs, monks, and nuns;[15] and later by exclusive measures, such as banning the building of monasteries at royal graves, forbidding monks to attend funerals, and closing Seoul to them.[16] As an alternative source of thought and institutions, the early Yi rulers chose Neo-Confucianism, declaring it the basis of national policy, establishing Confucian schools, including a University at Seoul, and selecting officials by means of examinations based on Chinese subjects.[17] The founder, however, who first took steps, moved deliberately and perhaps reluctantly, prodded, it would seem, by Confucian counselors. On the one hand he recognized the force of his supporters' opposition to Buddhism and the usefulness of their own ideas of government, and he did much that they proposed. On the other hand he did not do all. He himself was favorably disposed toward Buddhism, keeping a Buddhist adviser during his reign and retiring to a Buddhist monastery at the end of it. The Confucian proposals that he put into effect seem to have satisfied him as being politically prudent. It is not certain that they represented for him the whole of wisdom.[18]

Ch'oe's attitude toward Buddhists and worshippers of native gods is everything that knowledge of the recent Korean past would lead us to expect of a purposeful Confucianist. With a fervor that he tells us impressed Chinese—certainly it surprised some of them—he decries Buddhists. Throughout the diary he disparages their influence on Korea. Consistent with his description of Korea as a great Confucian state, he names mainly Confucianists and no Buddhists when asked about great Koreans of the past, even though it is inconceivable that Koryŏ, for example, should not have produced great Buddhists. Meeting a Buddhist monk of Korean descent in Manchuria, he rebukes him in solid Confucian phrases. He is happy to hear that the monks are being defrocked, for, he says, "That way, the abolished temples become people's houses, the destroyed bronze Buddhas become vessels, and the heads that once were bald and now are hairy fill the army ranks." He sends the monk on his way with a neat demonstration of the futility of Buddhist prayer.

While still at sea, he uses the same argument—the ineffectiveness of his men's prayers—to question the part Korean gods played in what happened to the group, and later he refuses to pray at a Chinese river shrine, despite the

---

[13]KC, I: 86.

[14]*TRD* VIII: 372-376.

[15]Hatada, *Chōsen-shi,* pp. 115-117.

[16]Cornelius Osgood, *The Koreans and Their Culture,* New York, The Ronald Press Company, 1951, 387 pp; p. 249.

[17]*Cf.* KC, I: 85-91.

[18]*Cf.* Youn, *Le Confucianisme,* pp. 141-145.

urging of his escort. The only unseen aid that he refers to besides that of Heaven is that of his father's spirit.

One of the first reasons for the Yi's patronage of Confucianism had been political advantage, but that in turn raises the question how effectively the government could promote a generally "Confucian" social order. Would the practical implications of Neo-Confucianism, for instance, be compatible with indigenous views about society and politics? The evidence suggests that by Ch'oe's time attitudes and practices prompted by Confucian education were stirring political issues to the point of violence.

As an orthodoxy proposed to be made pervasive, Confucianism was young in Korea. It had attracted the general attention of the educated classes in only relatively recent times. True, it had long been known and studied but apparently by a rather small number of scholars. One official Confucian academy had existed from 682, but in the eleventh century even that was closed for lack of students. For long the dominant and pervasive schools of thought — leaving aside the unknown influences of earlier Korean beliefs — had been Buddhist. Not that individual Confucianists were unknown in the period or without influence; but it was only when Chu Hsi's commentaries were brought to Korea in 1291 and the Academy reopened that Confucianism began to exert the extensive intellectual attraction that later made it preeminent in ruling circles.[19] It is unlikely on the face of the matter, then, that by Ch'oe's time, within two hundred years of its introduction, Neo-Confucianism as a consolidated school of thought had achieved an undisputed dominance. More to the point, it is even less likely that educated Korean society had reached a consensus on the social and political implications of the Confucian teaching. While Confucian education had made most upper-class Koreans Confucianists academically, it had not imposed upon them a single view of their political obligations, as the period of factional disputes that began in Ch'oe's lifetime shows. The parties to the disputes may have argued by means of a common Confucian vocabulary, but their view of the proper political order differed. For that reason, to distinguish one party as "Confucianist," as I shall below, following earlier historians, is merely a convenient expedient, not an assertion that one party was wholly Confucian and the other wholly not.

Historical signs abound that Confucian action as Ch'oe understood it was contested. Of the three major kings to rule Chosŏn in Ch'oe's lifetime, for example, the first, Sejo (r. 1456-1468), attained the throne by forcing his nephew to abdicate, after which he put a number of Confucian officials out of the way and espoused Buddhism. He became well-versed in Buddhist scriptures and had temples rebuilt, one with a colossal Buddha in the capital.[20] The second, Sŏng-jong (r. 1470-1494), for whom Ch'oe wrote his account, restored Confucian government (as the later Confucian historians put it), but again the third,

[19]KC, I: pp. 83-86.
[20]KC, I: 91; Seno, *(Kinsei-shi),* p. 64.

Yŏnsan'gun (r. 1495-1506), deranged it. The distaste which the historians have held for him is indicated by the fact that he is referred to by the title he was given when removed from the throne and not by a reign-name. A headstrong man, he so resented certain Confucianists and their insistent remonstrances that he threw his weight to the side of their opponents.

The composition of the forces that grouped officials into factions at this time is uncertain. Ch'oe's party included many who spoke as vigorous Confucianists, as has been suggested, and were, moreover, younger men not far removed from their examination days.[21] Many, too, had been pupils of Kim Chong-jik, the late, great figure of the *Sallim hakp'a* school. In addition to a common intellectual outlook, they may have felt certain regional interests, since about half of Kim Chong-jik's pupils came from Kyŏngsang Province.[22] In government they were most conspicuous in offices of remonstrance.[23] Ch'oe had held several appointments in two such offices, the Office of the Inspector-General and the Office of Special Counselors, by the time he went to China. Outstanding among the faction in opposition to Ch'oe's party, on the other hand, were higher, older officials who were administrators and advisers of policy.

In 1498, a decade after Ch'oe's adventure in China, the rivalries in government incited the first of four great "Literati Purges," (the others occurred in 1504, when Ch'oe was executed, 1519, and 1545) in which dozens of Confucian ministers lost their positions and lives and thousands of people were affected throughout the country. Although the Purge of 1498 certainly could not be foreseen when Ch'oe was in China, it illustrates the temper of Korean politics in his time and helps to explain the concerns he reveals in the diary. In the usual telling of it, the purge began from two originally unrelated grudges. Kim Chong-jik, the high and influential minister and leader of the *Sallim* faction, who had taught many officials and had a large following in the government, had once refused to give office to the son of a concubine. The son had once been exiled for conspiracy. Independently, a historian who happened to be a follower of Chong-jik wrote honestly into the records that a certain provincial official had misbehaved when the late King, Sŏngjong, died. That made, then, two men with grudges, the concubine's son and the provincial official. Looking about for means of revenge, the latter found that he could see in a funeral valedictory written by Chong-jik an allusive charge of usurpation against Sejo, the King of three reigns before. He showed the text to the concubine's son, who agreed completely with the interpretation and felt that the pupil of such a man could be expected to put slanderous remarks into history.

The two men busied themselves priming the indignation of others. The news reached the King, a tempestuous man who resented the Confucianists for

[21]See Edward W. Wagner, "The Recommendation Examination of 1519: Its Place in Early Yi Dynasty History," *Chōsen Gakuhō* 15, April, 1960, pp. 1-80; p. 4.

[22]See the native places noted in the list of followers, *Chŏmp'ilje sŏnsaeng munjip, Munin-rok*.

[23]See for example, Wagner, *loc. cit.*

harping on his duties, and he ordered that all Chong-jik's followers be arrested. The concubine's son followed the investigation closely, discouraged leniency, made available copies of the damning valedictory, and carefully annotated one for the King's easier understanding.

The investigators found all the members of Chong-jik's party guilty. The minister himself had died in 1492, but his body was exhumed and beheaded. Five of his followers were killed in two degrees of severity. Another was whipped, deprived of his house and goods, and sent away as a serf. About eighteen others, including Ch'oe Pu, were whipped and exiled. Others were dismissed or demoted.[24] Nor was that the last of it: later some of the exiles were killed, and the fathers and brothers of the victims were also punished.[25]

Ch'oe had been banished to Tanch'ŏn. The next purge, which occurred in 1504, started (according to the traditional account) as the King's revenge on those who had condemned his mother, but the victorious party of 1498 added to the victims remnants of their enemy. Forty-eight men were killed or otherwise punished, and Ch'oe was among the killed.[26]

Today it is hard not to feel that punishment so vengeful and relentless exceeded indignation for a dead king. A modern explanation argues that in impeaching the conduct of individuals the defeated party had been attempting to subordinate the power of the sovereign theoretically to Confucian morality and to limit it institutionally by means of the offices of remonstrance. The purge, then, had been an attack on the moralists of the *Sallim* school and on the censoring power.[27] The violence of the attack is the significant quality for us, for it places Ch'oe's Confucianism in a heated political atmosphere and helps to explain its zeal.

Ch'oe's concern with filial obligations, mentioned before, also shows the kind of zeal that embattled Korean Confucianists might have developed, and it leads to the thought that something about Korean conditions may have placed an emphasis on that Confucian principle above others. Ch'oe indicates that his family requires his first loyalty. He frequently laments his failure to reach his father's grave and comfort his mother, and once he worries that by sustaining injuries he has been unfilial. A Chinese is quick to point out that the fault is Heaven's, not Ch'oe's. Ch'oe shows the order of his concern in a prayer. "Let me ... bury my ... father," he says first, "and take care of my ... mother. If, by good fortune, I am also able to bow before the Court ... I shall truly be content to die ..." Early in his travels, a Chinese officer, curious about Ch'oe's despondency, says, "Among those who serve, the state is all, the family is forgotten. You should turn your filial piety into loyalty. Why brood over family

[24] This summary omits many personal names and much detail on grounds of distraction, but a full version of the story may be read in *Changnung chi* (Sŏnnyŏng namhak myŏngja, transl. by Hosoi Hajime, in *Chōsen sōsho,* ed. by Hosoi Hajime, Chōsen Mondai Kenkyūsho, Tokyo, 1936, 3 vols.).

[25] See, for example, the note to that effect in *Yŏnsan'gun ilgi, ch.* 56: 11 *v.*

[26] *Hōtō shika no kentō* by Hosoi Hajime, *Chōsen kenkyū sōsho,* No. 7, Tokyo, 1921, pp. 1-4.

[27] For a development of this argument, see Wagner, "The Recommendation Examination," especially pp. 4-8.

matters?" But for Ch'oe there is no question. "Look for the loyal subject," he says, "at the gate of the filial son. There has never been a man not thoroughly filial to his parents yet loyal to his lord." So clear a statement of the primacy of family loyalty is especially remarkable when it is remembered that Ch'oe is writing his diary specifically for the eyes of his King. Whether such emphasis rose from the nature of Korean society it is impossible to say. Here it is notable as being a steadfast element in a Confucianist who in this seems more doctrinaire than his Chinese peers.

To Ch'oe's concern for moral rectitude, heightened by political partisanship, should be added two distinguishing qualities: his love of Korea and his love of Chinese civilization. That his heart is with Korea and his home is clear in his many lamentations at being away. Careful to be on his best behavior while Chinese eyes are upon him, he feels that he may relax somewhat when in the company of a countryman. He has passed up many cups of wine in China, for example, for in mourning, he says, "We do not drink wine or eat meat, garlic, oniony plants or sweet things for fully three years." When he reaches Manchuria, however, he permits himself to sit with a Korean envoy in a garden in the moonlight and drink some wine in consolation. Meeting men from Liaotung also seems a special pleasure for him, since they come from a land once part of a Korean kingdom and still close to home. At one point in the journey he is even willing to depart from Confucian convention when an opportunity arises to bring home knowledge of a new, useful machine. Orthodox indifference to mechanics swept aside, he insists on learning how to make a water wheel, because it will be, he says, "an inexhaustible benefit to my Koreans for all ages."

He is also Korean in matters of diplomacy, concerned both to enhance his country's reputation in the mind of Chinese officials and to maintain its dignity and security. No doubt he recalls that the Yi dynasty had made allegiance to China a keystone of its foreign policy. After rather stormy early relations, the investiture and seal that the Emperor had withheld for eleven years reached Korea in 1403.[28] From then on, friendly relations were virtually unmarred. The Koreans annually sent tribute at the New Year, on the Emperor's birthday, and on extraordinary occasions. The Chinese eventually revised, though incompletely, the objectionable historical notices mentioned before; often returned Korean castaways;[29] and gave sanction to the accession of Korean kings, appointment of heirs apparent, and royal marriages.

That Ch'oe endorses that relationship as not only politically prudent but also right in a broader sense, according with his personal convictions about the right arrangement of the world, is obvious almost from the beginning of the book. When they are still at sea, he tells his men, "If we manage to land in China, well, China is our homeland." A surprising statement nowadays, but a

[28]*SIK*, p. 30; *CYC, ch.* 1: 9 *v.*

[29]Ch'oe Pu's experience is, of course, one example of this Chinese kindness. His diary refers to others. *SYC, ch.* 1: 14 *v.*, records an instance (in 1494) in which the Court not only returned some castaways but sent interpreters with them to order the King to pardon them for losing their cargo.

clear sign of how close he felt to China. Later he refers to "our *Yung-lo* period," and once to "our Great Ming." He leaves no doubt, even when diplomatic courtesy might be satisfied with milder words, of his awe of the Emperor. When an official asks him whether his King is called Emperor, he says, "In Heaven there are not two suns; how under the same Heaven can there be two Emperors? My King's one purpose is to serve your country devotedly." Perhaps he exaggerates, but there is no reason why, in an account written for a Korean king, his statement should be taken to express other than a Korean conviction. One reason to believe him is that he is convinced that advantage lies in allegiance to China. He tells his group, when they ask him how to explain their good fortune in China, "[Our blessings] have all been brought about by the virtue of our sage Highness in benevolently caring for the people and sincerely serving China." When they receive gifts, he reminds them, "The Emperor's taking care of us and giving us awards are due to the virtue of our King, who fears Heaven and serves China . . ." Ch'oe feels that respect for China is a wise policy, perhaps even one demanded by the Neo-Confucian Way. His loyalty to China and the Emperor is, then, though somewhat magnified by his position, largely genuine.

Nevertheless, certain subjects concerning Korea Ch'oe chooses not to discuss. One is the King's surname and taboo name. Ch'oe refuses to say them, even though he is outside Korea, on the grounds that he is Korean no matter where he may be. Another has to do with Korean security. Twice the Chinese ask Ch'oe how big Korea's military supplies are, presumably meaning stored rations, and both times Ch'oe says that he does not know. He may not, of course, but he has served in military offices and as a capital official would likely have known anyway. The Chinese also ask directly once about the Korean military organization, of which, of course, Ch'oe denies knowledge. Even less direct questions appear to bear too much on military matters to be answered. Ch'oe gives no figures on the Korean population or land tax, both of which interest the Chinese, perhaps because military strength is related to them. More than once he exaggerates the distance to Korea, perhaps for safety, though that may be reading too much into it.

On another subject, relations with countries other than China, Ch'oe offers as little information as possible. He tells the Chinese that Korea has no relations with either Japan or Ryukyu, a statement that, though perhaps not literally false, falls short of being candid. Certainly regarding Japan it was a wise thing to say, considering the Chinese troubles with Japanese, as will be mentioned later.

Korea had not sent embassies to either country for some years prior to 1488. Embassies to Japan had stopped after 1479.[30] Until then, official relations had been very active; for a time the Koreans supplied Japanese embassies with

[30]Seno, *(Kinsei-shi)*, p. 71.

allowances of food while they were in Korea and sea rations for the voyage home.[31] All that, it is true, had stopped, and if embassies were being exchanged at all, they were few and little known, but nevertheless Korea was in touch with Japanese in 1488. Since about 1425 she had permitted Japanese to trade, fish, and dwell in season in three southern ports. In 1443 an agreement had been made on the numbers of Japanese ships to be allowed to call at the ports. When in violation of the agreement Japanese began to settle in the ports permanently — in about 1471, 2,177 Japanese lived there and had fourteen temples — Koreans did not drive them out. At about the time of Ch'oe's accident, messengers from Tsushima visited Seoul rather frequently.[32] Though violence later (1510) occurred, it is certain that in 1488 there were Japanese colonies in the three ports and likely that they had some kind of relations with Korean officials.[33]

The last mission from Ryukyu had come in 1477. From 1409 until then, thirteen embassies of tribute had reached Korea. Ch'oe implies that the two countries maintained no relations because they were far apart, but that does not account for the previous embassies and is not supported by other sources. The real reason for the stopping of the missions is not clear, but the cordiality of the Ryukyuans whom Ch'oe meets in Peking implies that the two countries held no enmity. In common with the Japanese, however, Ryukyu fell short of the Korean standard of good conduct in diplomatic relations with China. Like the Japanese, Ryukyuans had furnished several of their tributary missions to Ming with large quantities of "supplementary goods," that is, goods for trade, and some members of the missions had conducted themselves poorly in Chinese eyes, probably in connection with their taste for commerce. The unseemly injection of commercial interest into what should have been an orderly rite of vassalage impelled the Chinese Emperor in 1475 to restrict the number and size of tributary missions to be received from Ryukyu, much as the missions from Japan had been restricted.[34] If Ch'oe had some idea of the reputation Ryukyuans had established, his reticence to expound on Korean relations with a less satisfactory vassal state becomes understandable.

Although Ch'oe holds the Chinese at arm's length on some subjects, for the most part he sees his journey through China not as a test of his loyalty to Korea but as an opportunity to confirm the Chinese greatness attested in the books he had studied since childhood. Indeed, a sense of intellectual indebtedness to China may partly account for the self-consciousness of his Confucianism, as if he felt compelled to show the people from whom sprang such powerful thought his mastery of it. Meeting the Chinese means more to him, however,

---

[31]Seno, *(Kinsei-shi)*, p. 43.

[32]In *Chōsen-shi* (Chōsen Sōtokufu, Chōsen-shi Henshū-kai, Keijo, 1932-1938, 34 vols.), for example, Tsushima messengers are noted in 1487, 1488, and 1489 *(Chōsen-shi* 4:5:589, 609, 630). An envoy from the Ōuchi family is reported in 1487 *(Ibid.,* p. 589).

[33]See also *TRD,* III: 413.

[34]See Wu Chuang-ta, *Liu-ch'iu yü Chung-kuo*. Shanghai: Cheng-chung shu-chü, 1948, 188 pp.; pp. 73-82.

than passing a test. The cultivation he owes largely to the Chinese has gone to his heart and sometimes prompts him to act with the confidence of familiarity. He behaves, for example, as a member of an international civilization, treating Chinese of lower rank with a certain firmness. This is especially evident on the occasion of his meeting a Chinese *Chin-shih* who takes him home. The *Chin-shih* boasts of his academic rank and shows Ch'oe a glorious banner-gate. Not to be outdone, Ch'oe takes out an examination list he happens to be carrying and points out his own high position, upon which the *Chin-shih* immediately recognizes Ch'oe's superiority. Later, at another place, Ch'oe expresses the feeling of a common society in broader terms. Saying farewell to a hospitable Chinese officer along the way, he thanks him for making clear his attitude that, as Ch'oe puts it, "though my Korea is beyond the sea, its clothing and culture being the same as China's, it cannot be considered a foreign country. That is especially so now, with Great Ming's unification ... All under Heaven are my brothers; how can we discriminate among people because of distance?"

His disposition to think well of Chinese also appears in the care with which he records the acts of kindness, expressions of affection, and pleasant meetings that lighten his journey. Perhaps even his attempt to show that bandits south of the Yangtze, since they do not kill their victims, are decent at heart rises from his favorable cast of mind. In combining sympathy with perception, Ch'oe establishes his credentials as a reporter.

THE DESCRIPTION OF CHINA

The diary shows a great country worked and molded by its people, organized by its government, and supporting life for the most part in stability and order. The South, however, prospers far more than the North. In the Yangtze Valley, Ch'oe finds rich fields, luxuriant fruit trees, and fair scenery. Villages cluster across the countryside. Most remarkable of all, the great cities of the South contain magnificent houses, a multitude of markets, wine shops and music halls, and crowds of ornamented and splendidly dressed people. Large numbers of ships gather at Hang-chou, Su-chou, and the junction of the Grand Canal and the Yangtze, indicating a flourishing waterborne commerce. The great gates and other architectural monuments of the cities defy his attempts to record them all.

The North, on the other hand, conveys a feeling of poverty and desolation. Sand storms begin to discomfort the travellers. The fields are less bountiful, the villages fewer and more squalid. Though the major cities appear to be thriving, they lack the atmosphere of brilliant prosperity of the southern ones. So it is even for Peking, which receives most of its supplies from the South. The farther north Ch'oe goes, the more desolate the land becomes. Liao-tung, although itself a city of some size, stands like a settled island in a sea of silence.

Two other differences between North and South appear. The first, the prevalence of bandits in the North, no doubt arises partly from economic troubles like famine. The fact that outlaws make travel at night too dangerous even for official boats to risk and that in one incident they attack innocent travelers in full view of officials suggests their strength. The second difference, the tenacity of barbarian ways in the North, can be partly accounted for by long periods of foreign rule. Ch'oe deplores the habits of the Pekingese man in the street and has worse to say of the men farther north.

Once in the hands of Chinese officers, the Korean party travels under escort up the Grand Canal and along the routes of the postal system. As a result, the diary informs us about conditions of official travel and communications, especially in reference to the two major parts of the trip, the passage up the Canal and the journey from Peking to the Yalu River.

When reading Ch'oe's remarks about the Canal, it is helpful to bear in mind the fact that in his day, unlike ours, a distinction was always made between the Grand Canal of Ming and previous canals. The inland waterways that have existed between approximately Hang-chou and Peking from the time of the Sui and T'ang are today sometimes all loosely designated the Grand Canal, but at different times the waterways were different; the parts of rivers incorporated in them changing, the connective canals being in various places, and consequently the main lines of the system following different routes in different periods. In Chinese the term for the system depends upon the period, and it would probably be useful to make similarly firm distinctions in English. What is pertinent here, however, is the point referred to by Ch'oe, that the Ming system was a major improvement over all those that had existed before. A Chinese says to Ch'oe, "Formerly there was no river route from the south of the Yangtze to the northern capital," and he puts the first plan for such a passage in Yüan times—the *Chih-cheng* period (1341-1367), though *Chih-yüan* (1264-1294, part of Kubilai's reign) would be better. He is largely correct, in that although the Yüan had done much work on canals, their waterway had been inferior to the Ming on several counts. It had included portages, it had presented overwhelming problems in hydraulics, and it had been incapable of carrying all the grain wanted in the capital. The Yüan government had never been able to give up transporting a large amount of grain by sea and in the end had neglected the canal system. All the previous systems had suffered from some such limitations. It was only with the reign of Ming T'ai Tsung (1403-1424) that, as a memorial stone quoted in the text shows, an unprecedented feat of surveying and engineering made a system adequate for the traffic of the time. Thanks to the accomplishment of the Ming government, as the stone says, "For the first time, the advantages of water transport extend throughout the Empire to the benefit of the people."

From the suburbs of Hang-chou to those of Peking, Ch'oe's party travels in boats, using three at a time, changing them at stops *(p'u),* and receiving food and supplies at stations *(i)* along the way. At one station the party is permitted, despite heavy rain, to stop over only one night, because, it is explained, the supplies of the station are limited. As a rule, however, nothing indicates that any of the bigger stations are so meagerly stocked. The boats move under sail when the wind is favorable and otherwise are rowed, poled, or pulled by men on tow-paths. For most of the way the boats sail through the night or the greater part of it; when they approach the northern end of the Canal, however, they stop at night for fear of bandits. Stations are from sixty to more than one hundred *li* apart, and stops are from ten to thirty *li* apart. Shoals *(ch'ien)* have been made along the edge of the Canal at six to ten *li* intervals to mark the distances.

The Canal is in good repair throughout its length. At some points there are locks to bring boats to different water levels, and at other points ramps or em-bankments over which winches pull the boats for the same purpose. Along at least one section the towpath is paved with stone slabs fastened with iron bolts and cemented with lime. To slow the current where it is too swift, the banks of the waterway have been widened to make a kind of lake or flood; to clear the stream of debris, wedgelike moles have been set in it. Such moles and all dams are built of stone.

The speed with which the party moves up the Canal can be computed in practically any terms, such as, for example, the average hourly speed of the boats while in motion; but here it may be sufficient to note only a rough figure. Ch'oe gives as the distance between Hang-chou and Peking via the Canal ap-proximately 4,340 *li*. The party leaves Hang-chou on the 13th Day of the Second Month and reaches Peking on the 28th Day of the Third Month, mak-ing the passage about forty-five days long at an average speed of ninety-six *li* a day. Corrected for one or two of the biggest delays—from talking with offi-cials on the way, for example—the rate rises to ninety-nine *li* a day, and no doubt further correction would increase it by a few more *li*. That compares favorably with the southward rate of forty to eighty *li* a day of a larger party fifty-two years later described by the Japanese monk Sakugen in his diary.[35] By comparison, a messenger who is sent from Chekiang to speed by land to Peking and report Ch'oe's arrival takes about thirty-four days, which seems surprisingly slow.

From Peking to the Yalu the party and its escort ride horses, donkeys, and carriages and again pass from station to station, each beyond Shan-hai-kuan enclosed by a wall. Under the circumstances, it is necessary to stop and rest every night. The distance between stations is from thirty to sixty *li*. Inside Shan-hai-kuan there are beacon towers every ten *li*, and beyond it earthen mounds with distance markers every five *li*. The farther the party goes beyond the wall the worse the roads become; beyond Liao-tung they are hardly more than trails. The rate of travel, therefore, from Peking to Ŭiju, the Korean fron-tier town on the Yalu, naturally reflects both the nightly stops and the wildness

[35]See Makita Tairyō, *Sakugen nyūmin-ki no kenkyū*. Kyoto: Hōzō-kan, 1955 & 1959, 2 vols.; II: 63. Sakugen trav-elled much the same route as Ch'oe and gives much complementary information.

of the country. Computed as before, simply as total distance divided by total time, the rate is fifty-one *li* a day. Corrected for rather long stops at two towns, it is sixty-nine *li* a day.

Of the many people Ch'oe meets on his long journey, little can be said to show a characteristic body of preoccupations and attitudes of the age. Frequently, educated men whom he happens to meet or who hear of his presence show a courteous interest in him and a desire to comfort him with conversation or favors. His military guards, though sometimes stern in their determination to carry out their assignment, often show sympathy for him in his plight and even friendliness. Only one attitude appears frequently enough and among enough different people to seem to be pervasive. It appears as soon as Ch'oe's bedraggled party flee their boat and make their way to a Chinese village. There it becomes clear that fear of Japanese pirates dominates the thoughts of the villagers and places Ch'oe's life in jeopardy. The first villagers drive him and his party forward with sticks and swords, passing them on from one village to the next, in what is apparently a kind of vigilante organization. Some make beheading gestures, and many even call out a word of Japanese, indicating considerable familiarity with such visitors. The people are, with few exceptions, hostile and even abusive. One group, taking the party for bandits, refuse an officer's request to put them up for the night. Some even seize belongings of the Koreans.

Official suspicions are as deep as the people's; the first officer to sight Ch'oe's boat at sea reports it as being Japanese; to be precise he reports it as fourteen Japanese boats (his judgment apparently swayed by thought of reward). Later other officers question Ch'oe closely and repeatedly, always with the purpose of deciding whether he is Japanese. A sympathetic bystander makes Ch'oe's hair stand on end with the remark that officers usually behead arrested Japanese first and report them later. The official concern over Japanese pirates arrests attention throughout the first book of the diary.

In late Yüan and early Ming times raiders known best as *Wakō,* the Japanese reading of the Chinese *Wo-k'ou,* began to infest the Chinese coast from Liaotung to southern Kuangtung. Ming T'ai Tsung took steps to hold them off, including the building of forty-five forts from Shantung to Chekiang and the establishment of sixteen centers of defense in Fukien,[36] but they attacked sporadically and rapidly, and it was difficult to organize defenses against them. Both the Korean and Chinese governments repeatedly complained about the raids to Japanese authorities. The raids diminished after official relations between Ming and the Ashikaga became well established and grew numerous and large again only late in the dynasty. Neither the annals nor the section on Japan in the official history, the *Ming shih,* records any raids for the twenty-

---

[36]Wang Yi-t'ung, *Official Relations Between China and Japan,* 1368-1549, Harvard-Yenching Institute Studies IX, Harvard University Press, Cambridge, Massachusetts, 1953, 127 pp.; p. 20.

three years prior to 1488.[37] In view of the lack of notices of raiders during the two previous decades, it would appear that either the memory of the old Japanese raiders was still vivid or occasional small, unrecorded raids had continued to be made along the coast. Whatever the facts, fear of the Japanese persisted. The forts, garrisons, and patrol boats noted in the diary represent clearly a concern for defense.

The measure of the concern appears in Ch'oe's long effort to establish himself as worthy of help despite the Chinese presumption that he is dangerous. Chinese troops are slower to intercept the Koreans than might be expected of troops defending against raiders; Ch'oe's party is ashore some twenty to twenty-four hours before Chinese officers meet them, and they apparently are only an advance party; the first heavily armed force comes up about twelve hours after that. Once there, however, the troops act with firmness and discipline, driving the exhausted Koreans to a garrisoned town.

The examinations that Ch'oe and his men undergo there and elsewhere later illustrate the methods of questioning applied to intruders. They include specific questioning of the Koreans on the circumstances of their arriving in China, repeated later and at other places to permit a check on the uniformity of the story. The same questions, moreover, are separately and privately put to more than one member of the group to test for contradictions. The possessions of the men are examined carefully and repeatedly, but they are not of themselves accepted as proof that the men are Koreans, for, it is pointed out, the things might simply have been stolen from Koreans and used as disguise. Perhaps the most convincing evidence the Koreans can produce are Ch'oe's two long, written depositions on the whole incident, his own background, and on Korean geography, history, customs, and institutions. From the detailed and extensive knowledge embodied in those separate statements, which are compared and parts of which can be checked against Chinese records, comes a fair assurance that Ch'oe is both Korean and well-educated and neither Japanese nor a pirate. His willing and learned comments on Korea make clear his pride in his own country. Since, as has been shown, he best expresses his feelings in Confucian terms, the Chinese become well aware of his Confucian convictions. His ability, moreover, to write poetry and to comment with erudition on points of Chinese civilization also help to establish him as trustworthy. A sense of the importance the Chinese attached to such interrogation, incidentally, comes from the similarity of the description in the diary of Sakugen. Despite the fact that the Japanese mission carried full credentials, the Chinese authorities insistently pressed similar questions.[38]

---

[37]See L. C. Delamarre, *Historie de la Dynastie des Ming Composée par l'Empereur Khian-loung; 1e partie, comprenant les dix premiers livres (1368-1505)* (Paris, 1865, 448 pp.), pp. 329-401; and Ryusaku Tsunoda, *Japan in the Chinese Dynastic Histories: Later Han through Ming Dynasties,* Ed. L. Carrington Goodrich, South Pasadena, P. D. and I. Perkins, 1951, 187 pp., maps; pp. 118-120.

[38]See Makita, *Sakugen,* I: 46, II: 38.

The diary also illustrates how the Chinese authorities reached a decision about·people like Ch'oe. He is questioned formally and at length at least five times before he reaches Peking, generally by higher ranking officials each time. No doubt the favorable decisions that they all reach depend on Ch'oe's consistent and reasonable testimony and are subject to review by the next higher office concerned. In that sense, judgment of the case is made slowly and tentatively. The initial decision about Ch'oe, however, the one that probably saves him and the others from immediate execution, rests with an officer specifically charged with defending a section of the coast against the Japanese. He receives the group on their fifth day ashore and immediately after questioning Ch'oe tells him that he will be courteously treated and sent home. If we may take that statement to be an indication of his authority, it would seem to show that officers along the coast were empowered to make quick decisions about strangers, even apparently peaceful ones. That arrangement would be in keeping with the nature of the raids the officers had to oppose.

As an observer of China, Ch'oe has few opportunities to record events of central political importance, but some of his notes speak to patterns of political behavior. Soon after the party goes ashore, for example, two impulses in official action, one to distort the truth for personal glory and the other to distort it for security of position, come into play. In the first, the officer who originally reports sighting the Koreans at sea says that they have fourteen boats, are Japanese, and have already raided the coast. The Chinese who tells Ch'oe about it says that the officer did so in oɪder to make his intended execution of the group seem all the greater achievement. Needless to say, the original false report makes the Koreans' position difficult and, since it is sent on to superior officers, causes the local Chinese defenders to be hoist with their own petard. A censor charges them with negligence for failing to arrest all fourteen boats.

The second impulse asserts itself when Ch'oe notes in the course of a deposition that he has been attacked by bandits and beaten by villagers. A Chinese officer deletes those sections and, when Ch'oe protests, defends the deletion first on grounds of terseness and then with the admission that the Emperor must not think that bandits are rampant and the coastal officers negligent. Later, in a second deposition to higher officials, Ch'oe again mentions the attacks made on his party, and again the officials suppress the information. If such tampering was customary, reports reaching Peking must have given a false picture of conditions on the coast. The diary alone, of course, cannot establish what was customary. Aside from incidents such as those mentioned here, official conduct appears to be regular. Yet one question would be not whether all officials distorted information but how important the distorted information was. Ch'oe's experience suggests that information essential to the security of the coast could be hidden.

To the considerable evidence in history that the "sub-bureaucracy," the clerks, runners, and the like, of Chinese offices sometimes used their position to extort bribes or gifts, the diary adds a few instances. A henchman of the first officer to deal with the Koreans alternately intimidates and cajoles them until at last Ch'oe takes off the garment he is wearing and gives it to him. Later two clerks of the Ministry of Rites seek to be paid for information they have brought. They, too, want the clothes Ch'oe is wearing and leave in anger when offered money instead. That clerks press a castaway for the clothes on his back does not represent typical behavior even in the diary, but Sakugen, too, complains of hard treatment at the hands of low-ranking office-workers.[39]

A few hints of central political conditions also come to Ch'oe's attention. His own case, for example, apparently provokes a discussion of jurisdiction between the Ministry of Rites and the Ministry of War. He hears of the arrest of two high officials on suspicion of collusion. He sees the *bete noire* of the Confucianists, the eunuch, at his worst, shooting for pleasure at passers by. Sharpest, however, is the sense he perceives and records of the dawn of a new day with the accession to the throne of the *Hung-chih* Emperor. He is recalling the eunuchs and poor officials, bringing the Buddhists back into the world of men, and beginning another great reign in the history of China.

THE TRAVEL DIARY AND P'YOHAE-ROK

As should not be surprising from a man of Ch'oe Pu's education, his book is in a well-established genre. Travel journals in China are sometimes traced from a work of Ma Ti-po (fl. A.D. 56) entitled *Feng ch'an-i chi,* the only remaining part of which contains the line, "In *Chien-wu* 32 [A.D. 56] the Emperor made a tour of inspection of the East, leaving the Palace at Loyang on the 28th Day of the First Month and arriving at Lu on the 9th Day of the Second Month..."[40] Probably few would grant that so little established a genre, but the itinerary form, a prose record of the progress of a trip day by day, is at least suggested. Other elements of the form, however, the use of the first person, the recording of dates of arrival at stops along the way and departure from them, and descriptions of mountains and rivers, first appear in a journal of the famous T'ang Confucianist, Li Ao (d. *ca.* 844), a forerunner of the Neo-Confucian movement. Though a mere 842 characters long, his journal, *Lai-nan lu,* an account of a journey made from Loyang to Canton in 809, is the true ancestor of Ch'oe's book. Like Ch'oe, Li Ao sees fit to record not only his itinerary but also such homely topics as catching cold and dreary weather.[41] After Li Ao, other well-known Confucianists, including Ou-yang Hsiu (1007-72), firmly planted the genre in the Confucian literary tradition, and a fuller record of experiences *en route* became the rule. The developed form, judging from a number of diaries of the Sung, Yüan, Ming, and Ch'ing periods,[42]

---

[39]Makita, *Sakugen,* I: 73, II: 46.

[40]Ao Shih-ying, *Chung-kuo wen-hsüeh nien piao,* Peiping, Li-ta shu-chü, 1935, 4 vols; I:1:40.

[41]See E. D. Edwards, *Chinese Prose Literature of the T'ang Period, A.D. 618-906,* London, Arthur Probsthain, 1937, 2 vols.; 1:25, 149, 150; and Kondō Moku, *Shina gakugei dai-ji-i,* Tokyo, Ritsumeikan Shuppan-bu, 1940, 1446 pp.; p. 130.

[42]As noted in *Ssu-k'u ch'üan-shu ts'ung-mu* (Shanghai: Ta-t'ung shu-chü ed.), *ch.* 57, Ch'uan-chi lei l: 1r.

divided the journey up by days and noted geography or topography, human customs, products or goods, cities and settlements, and frequently historical and literary sites. I have found no discussion of the idea behind the travel diary, but the fact that many men of the late traditional or Neo-Confucian period wrote them makes it clear that the form was a respectable one. Since they usually fall under either "geography (*t'i-li*)" or "records (*ch'uan-chi*)" in Chinese classifications, they must have been valued as contributing to knowledge of the earth and human experience. In Confucianist thought, merely satisfying a curiosity about the exotic, which many of the diaries in part of course do, would be a less valid purpose than exemplifying the "principles" underlying earth and the men on it, seen both in the present and monuments of the past. Few Confucianists, no doubt, would be so metaphysical that everything they saw on a journey would illustrate a law of reality, but their motive or, perhaps, justification may have lain partly in the thought of capturing principles or truth. The hope of scholars, referred to below, of broadening their knowledge by reading Ch'oe's diary suggests the Neo-Confucianists' virtue of extending knowledge and investigating things in a quest for unifying or integrating principles. That many famous Buddhist travel diaries have been written shows, of course, the difficulty of ascribing to any one intellectual influence a form of literature that has attracted men of many sorts.

In 1488 Ch'oe presented *P'yohae-rok* to the King, who was pleased and ordered that it be put into the archives. The next information of its history is that appended to the book, a wood-block copy, used for the present translation. It reads as follows:

"Mr. Ch'oe of Kŭmnam, whose taboo name was Pu and style Yŏn-yŏn, was my maternal grandfather. Because of his classical learning and moral rectitude he was appreciated by King Sŏngjong [r. 1470-1494] and chosen to be an attendant. He had been ordered to go to T'amna [Cheju] and was hurrying home to mourn for his father when he was driven adrift by winds. He reached T'ai [-chou] in China. When he had returned and was outside the wall of the capital, His Highness ordered him to compile and submit a diary of the entire trip.[43] [His Highness] looked at it, was pleased by it, and had it stored in the Archives.

"Although the document is no more than three rolls (*kwon*) long, it not only describes succinctly and profusely the ever-changing ocean, mountains, rivers, products, people, and customs all along the way from Ou to Yen [roughly Chekiang to Hopei]; but also gives some indication of [the author's] abilities.

"Many scholars whose desire it is to broaden their knowledge have wished to see it, but for the past eighty years no blocks have been engraved to make

---

[43]Ch'oe's unauthorized departure from Korea may have been illegal, as Professor Ichisada Miyazaki has suggested. His diary would then serve as an exoneration, even though the King, aware of the circumstances, required it only as a formality, before Ch'oe entered the seat of government.

it widely available. I was granted royal permission to return to the Court from outside the pass and wanted very much to find a way to preserve this book. When the editing was finished, all that was difficult was to arrange for a sponsor. It happened that His Learned Excellency O came to govern West of the Pass [i.e., P'yŏng-an], and I begged him to do something about the book. He gladly assented and ordered Yun Hu-haeng, Prefect of Chongju, to assemble some unemployed [engravers] to finish the task. Thus was the publication of the book accomplished.

"This book was incomplete and lost for one hundred years. Now it has been brought into the light after a long darkness, and it will be widely circulated in the world. How fortunate!

"16th Day, Eighth Month, Lung-ch'ing 3 [September 26, 1569].

"Made by the maternal grandson, Yu Hŭi-ch'un, Minister of Government, Headmaster of the National Academy and the King's Editor. Respectfully recorded."

Yu Hŭi-ch'un, the son, as he says, of a daughter of Ch'oe and, as his titles show, an important official in 1569, kept a diary between 1567 and 1577. In it he speaks of preparing *P'yohae-rok* for printing and of receiving three printed copies from Chongju.[44]

The copy that was photographed for this translation is in the Yōmei Bunko in Saga, Kyoto, which houses the collection of the Konoye family. The book may have come into the collection in the time of Konoye Iehiro (1667-1736), a high Court noble and bibliophile.[45]

Although the phrase, "for the past eighty years no blocks have been engraved to make it widely available," can be taken to mean that the edition to which it is appended was the first printing of the book, a common Korean practice leaves room for doubt. At the time, movable metal type was reserved for official use. It frequently happened that a book would first be printed officially with metal type and only later reproduced from wood blocks for unofficial publication. Since Yu Hŭi-ch'un refers specifically to wood blocks and the spreading of what the diary records, his words may also be taken to mean that while the work had previously been printed from metal type for officials, it would reach unofficial readers only in this, its wood-block edition.

A copy of the book printed from metal type does, in fact, exist in Tokyo in the Tōyō Bunko. It is undated and has no colophon. Its pages are of about the same number of lines of characters on each page and the same number of characters to a line, and the style of the characters is similar but not the same. Word for word, the Tōyō Bunko text differs little from that of the Yōmei

---

[44]*Miam ilgi-ch'o* (*Chōsen shiryō sōkan* No. 8) 2: 91, 93, and 97 (15th, 17th and 23rd Days, Eighth Month, 1569) refer to preparation of a colophon and title page; 2: 310 (27th Day, Sixth Month, 1570) notes the arrival of two copies of the book from P'yŏngan; and 2: 346 (22nd Day, Seventh Month, 1570) refers to the arrival of three copies printed in Chŏngju.

[45]See Makita, *Sakugen*, II: 233.

Bunko book, and the differences observed are not such as to establish either edition as the earlier.

A third copy of the book exists in the Kanazawa Bunko, Yokohama. It has a preface written by Yu Hŭi-ch'un and dated 1573. Republication of the book only four years after its first appearance in the Yōmei Bunko edition indicates, as Dr. Kumahara Masao, Librarian of Kanazawa Bunko, has pointed out, a lively demand for it.[46] The Kanazawa Bunko book resembles the Yōmei Bunko one closely, its size, numbers of lines per page and characters per line being the same. The style of its characters is very like that of the Yōmei Bunko book, but there are several small differences. The two books, therefore, were not made from the same blocks. It is not, for that matter, certain how the Kanazawa Bunko book was made, whether from blocks or movable type, but a librarian considered the spacing of the characters too regular and their balance too irregular for a wood-block. There was no time to examine the book thoroughly, but it appeared otherwise extremely close to the Yōmei Bunko copy. Two other copies of the book, both manuscripts of the Tokugawa period, have been reported in Japan. One is in the Kennin-ji, Kyoto, and the other in the Naikaku Bunko, Tokyo.[47] The Harvard-Yenching Institute Library has a copy of Kwon I, but I have not seen it.[48]

A Japanese interest in foreign countries must have prompted the publication in 1769 of an abbreviated translation by Seida Tansō (1721-1785). The book, entitled Tōdo kōtei-ki and also commonly known by its original title (J. Hyōkai-roku), in places paraphrases rather than translates the original. It contains most of the interesting events of the original but omits many details, including many personal names and the texts of documents. To the originally unillustrated text have been added prints of a whale, West Lake, Peking, the monkey god of the Huai River, and other sights, no doubt enhancing the popular appeal of the book. Seida Tansō, a well-known Confucian scholar and official, was an ardent Japanese patriot whom the Korean Ch'oe Pu frequently seemed to rub the wrong way. The notes to the translation, therefore, in addition to clarifying difficult passages, sometimes express Seida's impatience with the posturings of a man born in the wrong country.[49]

The text of the Yōmei Bunko copy has been published by Makita Tairyō in his Sakugen nyūmin-ki no kenkyū, Volume II.

---

[46]In this question of demand for books, Mr. Kim Won-yong, in Hanguk kohwalcha kaeyo (Early Movable Type in Korea), National Museum of Korea Series A Vol. 1, Seoul, 1954, 36 p. + 26 plates + 15 English p.; English p. 6, points out that the slowness of printing from bronze type and the restricted circulation of books meant that the government almost never printed more than one hundred copies of a book.

[47]Makita, Sakugen, II: 233.

[48]A Classified Catalogue of Korean Books in the Harvard-Yenching Institute Library at Harvard University. Cambridge, Massachusetts, 1962, p. 35.

[49]For further notes on Tōdo kōtei-ki, see Makita, Sakugen, II: 234-236. For Seida Tansō, see Hara Zen and Tōjō Kō, Sentetsu sōdan (Tokyo: Shōei-dō shoten, 1899), kōhen ch. 6, p. 155.

NOTES ON THE TRANSLATION

The following pages translate about four-fifths of Ch'oe Pu's book. Most of the passages left out do little more than record the names of places along the way. To bridge such gaps I have inserted in brackets some such statement as, "We set out from A and went as far as B." Anyone who wishes the details may refer to the complete translation in my Columbia University dissertation of 1958.

In the original many characters are incorrectly written. When errors have left the meaning in doubt, they have been noted, as has faulty Chinese. The texts of Chinese official documents and memorial inscriptions, written in a difficult style, have often seemed corrupt and are diffidently translated.

All quotations from *Yü kung* are rendered in Legge's translation (James Legge, *The Chinese Classics,* Vol. III: *The Tribute of Yu*). The page on which each quotation occurs is given immediately following in brackets instead of in a footnote. I have changed the spelling of proper names from Legge's to the modified Wade-Giles version.

The names of Korean offices generally follow those in Edward W. Wagner, "The Recommendation Examination of 1519: Its Place in Early Yi Dynasty History," *Chōsen Gakuhō* 15 (April, 1960), pp. 1-80 or the description of the positions in W. H. Wilkinson, *The Corean Government: Constitutional Changes, July 1894 to October 1895*, Shanghai: The Inspectorate General of Customs, 1897, 192 pp.

Chinese offices and titles generally follow the terms in Charles O. Hucker, "Governmental Organization of the Ming Dynasty," *Harvard Journal of Asiatic Studies* 21 (1958), pp. 1-66. Occasionally a different rendering has seemed to clarify the diary. In such instances, I have provided a transliteration of the Chinese for reference to Professor Hucker's "An Index of Terms and Titles in 'Governmental Organization of the Ming Dynasty,'" *Harvard Journal of Asiatic Studies* 23 (1960-1961), pp. 127-151.

A RECORD OF
DRIFTING ACROSS THE SEA

P'YOHAE-ROK
A RECORD OF DRIFTING ACROSS THE SEA

BOOK I

I, Ch'oe Pu, while in mourning, went adrift from Cheju,[1] landed east of Ou, and passed from south of Yüeh to north of Yen.[2] On the 14th Day of this Sixth Month [July 22, 1488] I reached Ch'ŏngp'a Station[3] and respectfully received a Royal edict for a diary of the journey. I have compiled it and now submit it.

On the 17th Day, Ninth Month, *Ch'êng-hua* 23 [October 3, 1487], as a Commissioner of Registers for the three towns of Cheju,[4] I took leave of the Court. I went to Chŏlla Province and gathered six men—Chŏng Po, an official under the Prefect of Kwangju; Kim Chung, an official of Hwasun District, who had been sent by the Governor on orders; Appointee Yi Chŏng; Son Hyo-ja, a secondary official from Naju; Ch'oe Kŏisan,*[5] an official of Ch'ong-am Station; and Mansan, a family slave—as well as Grooms An Ki and Ch'oe Kun. We returned to Haenam District and waited for the wind. On the morning of the 11th Day, Eleventh Month, we shared a ship with Hŏ Hŭi, the new Prefect of Cheju, and went to Kwanduryang. On the evening of the 12th Day we reached Choch'ŏn-gwan, Cheju, and landed.

30th Day, First Month, Hung-chih 1 [February 12, 1488]. Cloudy.

Between 3 and 5 p.m. my slave Makkŭm* arrived in Cheju from Naju. He brought mourning clothes and told me of my father's death.

1st Day, Intercalary First Month. Rain.

The Prefect came twice, morning and evening, to express his sympathy. A boat of Chija, a priest of Sujŏng Temple, being strong, fast and unmatched by the official boats, [the Prefect] ordered military policemen Ko Ik-kyŏn, O Sun

---

[1]Cheju, some 140 *li* off the southern tip of the Korean peninsula, was called T'amna in earlier times and is also known as Quelpart Island today.

[2]Ou is an archaic name for the land approximately encompassed by Wên-chou-fu, Chekiang, in the Ming dynasty; Yüeh and Yen marked the southern and northern limits of the China of the Warring States period (fifth to third centuries B.C.), so that the phrase amounts to saying, "from southernmost to northernmost China."

[3]A station outside the south gate of the wall of Seoul. See *TY*, Sheet 22.

[4]The three chief towns of Cheju, as shown on *TY*, Sheet 22, are Cheju, Sŏnŭi, and Taejŏng.

[5]Names followed by an asterisk use *i-du* phonetic transcriptions and might on study be shown to be read differently.

and others to take it round to Pyŏlto-p'o, moor it, and make it available for my crossing.

Judge Chŏng Chŏn sent Pyŏn Sok-san, an officer, to offer condolences.
2nd Day. Cloudy.

Early in the morning I went to the Hup'ung-gwan in Pyŏlto-p'o. Ch'oe Kak, the Superintendent of Education of Sŏnŭi District; over twenty students, including Kim Chŏng-nin, of the regional school;[6] Pak Chung-han, a Secretary of the Office of Supplies; and Ch'oe Kun and others walked with me. When we had gone about fifteen *li* Hŏ, the new Prefect, came hurrying up and offered his condolences.

This day the officials who had accompanied me, Chŏng Po, Kim Chung, and others sealed records[7] that they had kept of private venality, of exiles, containment of outbreaks, suppression of secret societies, and people falsely pretending loyalty; seventeen volumes plus one volume of dossiers we had brought from Chŏnju Prefecture to the three towns of Cheju; and various ledgers, house registers, and military registers presented by the officials of the three towns of Cheju; and turned them over to the office in charge of the Prefect's treasury. They received a list of the documents and brought it back.

3rd Day. At sea. This day was cloudy and sometimes rainy. The wind was from the east and slightly favorable. The sea was deep green.

Chŏng Sa-sŏ, Junior Director of Taejŏng District, and No Kyŏng, Superintendent of Education, had heard that there had been a death in my family and came in haste to express their sympathy. More than ten men—Ch'oe Kak, Pak Chung-han, Kim Kye-uk (the Superintendent of Japanese Studies),[8] Ch'oe Chung-jung (an officer), Kim Chung-ni (a Security Officer), and others—and in addition School Masters Kim Chol-lyŏ and Kim Tŭng-nye and over twenty students saw us off at the river mouth. Chol-lyŏ and Tŭng-nye tried to stop me from going, saying, "We old men were born and grew up by the sea, and we know much about the sea lanes. When it is changeable on Mt. Halla,[9] now cloudy, now rainy, the wind is sure to shift, and it will be impossible to sail boats. Not only that, the commentary under 'Travel on First Hearing of a Relative's Death' in the *Chia li* says, 'One travels one hundred *li* by day, but not at all by night. Though grief is great one still avoids injury.'[10] If night travel

[6]Ch'oe describes the school system on page 95.

[7]The description of the records that follows is quite an uncertain translation.

[8]That Koreans had for long given attention to the Japanese language is suggested in the record, kept by the monk Ennin, of a Japanese embassy to China in the ninth century. Ennin's party addressed Chinese through a Korean interpreter. See E. O. Reischauer, tr. and ed., *Ennin's Diary: The Record of a Pilgrimage to China in Search of the Law.* New York: The Ronald Press Company, 1955, p. 5. In the Yi dynasty, a schedule of state examinations governed the organized study of foreign languages. See, for example, Yi Man-gyu (Lee Man Kyoo), *Chosŏn kyoyuk-sa.* Seoul: Uryu Munhwasa, 1947, 2 vols., I: 292 *ff.*

[9]The principal mountain of the island, 20 *li* south of the town of Cheju. See *TGYJ, ch.* 38, p. 5.

[10]The book, more commonly called *Chu-tzu chia li,* was traditionally attributed to Chu Hsi, though it is not now, and explains in concrete terms practical etiquette for everyday home life, marriages, mourning, sacrifices, and other domestic occasions. The line in the edition consulted *(Ch'ung-k'o Chu-tzu chia li,* by Chu Hsi, *Shou-chüan* + 8 *chüan, Tzu Yang shu-yüan,* 1701, *ch.* 5, 7 *v.)* reads, "On first hearing of a relative's death, one changes clothes and then goes." The commentary on it is the same as that quoted here. Coming from the tongue of a school master, it suggests, as the rest of the diary will abundantly show, the Chinese content of Korean education.

is improper, how much more could crossing this great sea be disrespectful!"

Some of those in the room urged me on, some held me back. The sun was high, and I had not decided. Security Officer An Ŭi came and told me, "The east wind is just right. You can go." Then Chung-han, Chung-jung and others also urged me to go. Finally I took my leave and got into the boat.

When we had rowed five *li,* Kwŏn San, Hŏ Sang-ni and other soldiers said to me, "Today first the wind waxes, and then it wanes; the clouds and fog roll in, and then they scatter. We fear that if on a day of such unsteady winds you travel in a heavy sea like this one, you will regret it later. Let us turn back to Pyŏlto-p'o and wait for [a more favorable] wind before starting again. We shall not lose too much time that way."

An Ŭi said, "Heaven's weather is not something people can forecast. How do you know that the clouds will not scatter and that we shall not see fair skies again soon? Moreover, private boats that cross this sea capsize and sink one after another, but the ministers of the Court who have received the King's command (except Yi Sŏm, the former Junior Director of Sŏnŭi District[11]) seldom go adrift or sink. All that is because His Majesty's virtue is extremely great and is known to Heaven. Anyway, with suggestions from everyone, the matter will never be settled. How can we set out only to return and delay?" He shouted a command to set sail.

Shortly after we passed Taehwat'al Island, all the men in the boat thought that if the boat headed for Sinyoryang and cut across the sea upwind, we should land at Ch'uja Island very quickly. Kwŏn San would not listen to them. He grasped the tiller and went with the wind. We passed Ch'udŏk Island and went west. The sea was dark, the wind weak. It began to rain. As we were approaching the harbor of Ch'uja Island, the evening tide was very swift, and the sky was dark. When the overseer gave orders to the troops, all the soldiers at the oars said, "Whose fault is it that we sailed on a day like this?" They nursed rebellion and would not obey and man the oars.

We drifted off to Ch'oran Island, dropped anchor off the west bank, and moored. In the third watch of the night, Sang-ni said, "This island blocks the east wind, but we are open to the waves on three sides; it is not suitable. Now, too, the wind is shifting to the north. We can neither go on nor retreat; it is a bad position to be in. The boat, moreover, is not where we first moored it. It is gradually drawing off into the sea. I am afraid the anchor with which we moored may already have broken. Under the circumstances it is best to raise the anchor, go forward a bit, and make fast to the shore. It will then be possible to wait for the sky to clear and row into Ch'uja."

Then we raised the anchor, and it was, indeed, broken. Rowing, we could not draw near the shore and were driven off by the north wind to an unpro-

---

[11]Yi Sŏm's adventure, of the kind about to befall Ch'oe, had happened recently enough to be fresh in the minds of the men. In the spring of 1483, Yi went adrift with forty-six men and spent ten days in the open sea before reaching the coast of Yang-chou. Fourteen of the men had died. The rest were escorted back to Korea by way of Peking. *Sŏngjong sillok* 14: 8: *keng-wu.*

tected part. It rained on, never stopping, the wind beating upon the water. We rose and fell with the waves and did not know where we were going.

4th Day. Drifting into the Open Ocean. This day there were rain and hail. High winds roiled the sea. Terrible waves swelled into the sky and churned the ocean.

The sails were completely ripped. The masts, being tall, were in danger of breaking and crushing the [superstructure] of the boat. I ordered San Kŭn-bo to take his axe and cut them down. Ko I-hok bound straw mats to the stern of the boat to ward off the waves. At noon, the rain abated somewhat, and a strong east wind rose again. We went heeling and pitching along, and I realized immediately that we had already entered the Western Sea. The helmsman pointed to the northeast. I saw there an island like a pellet of shot on the horizon. He said, "That may be Hŭksan Island." After we went past it, there was no island in any direction. Water and sky met in endless space.

All the men, not knowing what to do, lay down prone in the boat. I commanded An Ŭi to direct the soldiers to do such things as bail out the water and repair the boat. One soldier, Ko Hoe, shouted, "The Cheju sea lanes are very dangerous. Everyone who travels in them waits months for the wind. In the case of the former commissioners, they waited as long as three months at Choch'ŏn-gwan and Sujŏng Temple before they went. This present voyage comes just at the time of unsettled wind and rain. We did not forecast the weather for a single day, and we have come to this extremity. We have brought it all upon ourselves."

All the other soldiers said, "That is so. Even if we exhaust our will and strength bailing water and repairing the ship like this, in the end we still shall die. Rather than use up our strength and die, let us lie easy and wait for death." They all closed their ears and would not obey orders. They would not even get up when whipped.

Song Chin, a great shirker, being beaten grew angry. He said, "A long-lived one, this ship! Since she is going to break up sooner or later, why doesn't she do it quickly?"

Chŏng Po said, "Cheju men appear to be stupid, but inside they are wicked. They are obstinate, rude, rebellious, and cruel, and they take death lightly. That is why they talk like that."

I, too, thought that we were sure to drown. If we received help from Heaven and were fortunate enough not to drown, then surely we should drift indefinitely until the day we died. What else could be? I was also exasperated at the insolence of the troops.

Then I counted over the men in the boat. There were my staff—Chŏng Po, Kim Chung, Yi Chŏng, Son Hyo-ja, Ch'oe Kŏisan, Makkŭm, and Mansan—; and those assigned by the Prefect of Cheju to escort us—Security Officer An Ŭi, Recorder Yi Hyo-ji, Keeper of the Seals Hŏ Sang-ni, Ship Captain Kwŏn San, Helmsman Kim Ko-myŏn, Privates Kim Koe-san, San Kŭn-bo, Kim

Kujilhoe*, Hyŏn San*, Kim Sok-kwi, Ko I-hok, Kim Cho-hoe, Munhoe*, Yi Hyo-t'ae, Kang Yu, Pu Myŏng-dong, Ko Naeŭltong*, Ko Pok, Song Chin, Kim To-jong, Han Mae-san, Chŏng Sil; Escort Troops Kim Sok, Kim Chi-nŭmsan*, Ko Hoe, Kim Song, Ko Po-jong, Yang Tal-hae, Pak Chong-hoe, Kim Tŭk-si, Im San-hae; and public slaves Kwŏn Song, Kang Nae, Yi San, and O San*. Altogether there were forty-three men, including me.

I called An Ui and questioned him: "I am a man in mourning. I am not in official standing. It is extremely awkward to have so many men aboard. How is it that the Cheju men on board come to thirty-five?"

An Ŭi said, "What our Prefect was at great pains to do was to meet the protocol for a commissioner. Sailing a large boat, furthermore, takes the work of many, and when the sea route is long and, as at Wi Island and other places, pirates are active, the escort must all the more be strong."

I said, "It is possible to cross the sea successfully with only a few sailors and navigators, if they are carefully chosen. These men, now, are all lazy and insolent. In numbers they swell the roster, but in fact they are nothing. If the boat should drift and we all die, their presence would only increase the number of wailing [widows and orphans]."

I called out to the troops, "I am hurrying into my first mourning. My feelings permit not even a slight delay. Since someone did urge me to go, as a son can I delay for a moment? It is true that you have been cast adrift on the sea because of me, but circumstances are also responsible.

"Since it is common nature to all men to love life and hate death, how can you not want to live?

"If the boat breaks up or sinks, that will be all. My view is that the boat is now sound and tight. Probably it will not break up easily, and if we do not strike a rocky island, we can repair it and bail out the water. If by luck the wind settles and the waves calm down, we may drift to another country, but we shall save our lives. You, too, have fathers, mothers, wives, children, brothers, and relatives, who hope that you will live and fear that you might die; yet, without considering their feelings or the danger to your own lives; you have refused to work because you think I am to blame. It is the height of stupidity to bring death upon yourselves thus."

Over ten men, including Sang-ni, said, "The troops are a gang of stubborn ignoramuses. That is why they reason in such an absurd fashion. But everyone has his own way of thinking. We shall work with all our strength until we die."

During the night, the wind and rain did not stop. The waves were enormous. They washed into the bow and stern, and as they came in, we bailed them out. In, perhaps, the second watch, terrifying waves swelled up and straddled the mat shelter. The boat half sank. The clothing and baggage were soaked through, and freezing cold pierced us to the bone. Our fate lay in the moment. I took Yi Chŏng's hand and pillowed my head in Chŏng Po's lap. Kim Chung and Hyo-ja were at my left and right sides. Thus sprawled about, we waited to die.

A man nearby was trying to hang himself and was about to die when Yi Chŏng untied him. [The man] proved to be O San. Kŏisan, Makkŭm, and others worked as hard as they could bailing out water. The water seemed not to diminish.

I assumed that if the boat was still sound and we did not bail out the water washing in above and leaking in through cracks, we should sit and wait and sink. If we did bail, it might be possible to survive. I forced myself to get up. I called to Kwŏn Song to kindle a fire by friction, roll up the mats and dry them. I also called to Kŭn-bo, Ko Pok, Ko-myŏn, and others personally to search out the leaking places and plug them. Then I took off my clothes and divided them among Kwŏn San, Ko-myŏn, Kŏisan, Koe-san, and Sang-ni as encouragement. Chŏng Po, Kim Chung, and Hyo-ja also took off their clothes and divided them among the troops. Soldiers such as Kujilhoe, Mun-hoe, To-jong, Mae-san, and Hyŏn San, full of gratitude, exerted their utmost strength to bail all the water out of the boat. They had got it almost all out, and the boat seemed for the most part safe, when almost immediately it again headed into a rocky island. In the confusion, Kwŏn San, sailing the boat, had not realized where he was going. Sang-ni and Kujilhoe seized poles, but they were useless. Fortunately, we were driven off by a heaven-sent wind and avoided crashing.

5th Day. Adrift in the Open Ocean. This day a dense fog obscured everything. Things a foot away could not be made out. Towards evening, rain streamed down heavily, abating somewhat with night.

The frightening waves were like mountains. They would lift the ship up into the blue sky and then drop it as if down an abyss. They billowed and crashed, the noise splitting heaven from earth. We might all be drowned and left to rot at any moment. Wiping away tears, Makkŭm and Kwŏn Song said to me, "Conditions are critical; there is no hope. Please change your clothes and wait for your fate to come."

I did as they said. I pocketed my seal and horse permit against my chest and put on my mourning hat and gown. Anxiously I joined my hands and prayed to Heaven. "In the world I have tried only to be loyal, filial, friendly, and loving. My heart has had no deceit. I have done no wrong, I have killed no one. Far away above us though you are, Heaven, you must be aware of this. Now, again having gone out on my Sovereign's orders, I have been hurrying home to mourn for my father. I do not know for what sin I am to blame. If I have sinned, let punishment come to me alone. Will you, Heaven, presume to be so unmerciful as to let over forty innocent men drown with me? Heaven, if you pity this poor person, reverse the wind and still the waves. Let me return alive to the world, bury my newly dead father, and take care of my aging mother. If, by good fortune, I am also able to bow before the Court, then I shall truly be content to die ten thousand deaths after that."

Before I had finished speaking, Makkŭm suddenly embraced me. He said, "A whole family for their entire life, in pain and pleasure, have relied on me. They have been like ten blind men leaning on one staff. Now it has come to this. I shall not see my family again." Then he beat his breast, stamped his feet, and wept. The secondary officials and those below them also wept. They folded their hands and prayed for Heaven's protection.

6th Day. Adrift in the Open Ocean. This day was cloudy. The wind and waves were a little calmer.

First I directed Kujilhoe and others to repair the ripped mats for a sail, erect the mizzen for a mast, and split off the base of the former mast for an anchor. We went west with the wind.

Looking out over the broad waves, I saw something, the size of which I did not know. The part I saw above the water was like a long shed. It spurted spume into the sky and stirred up waves. Shaking his hand, the helmsman cautioned the men in the boat not to speak. Only after the boat had passed far beyond did he call out, "That was a whale. Big ones swallow boats, and little ones overturn them. It was luck that we did not meet. We live again!"

As night fell, the wind and waves grew strong again. The boat went very fast. An Ŭi said, "I have heard that the sea has a Dragon God who is very greedy. Let us throw away the baggage and things we have as a sacrifice to him."

I would not permit it.

All the men in the boat said, "Men have their bodies first and things later. These are all things apart from the body." They vied with each other searching out clothing, weapons, iron implements, and rations, and threw them into the sea. There was no way for me to stop them.

7th Day. Adrift in the Open Ocean. This day was cloudy. The wind was very bad, and the waves were heavy. The sea was white.

Ch'ae Ku-he, the Junior Director of Sŏnŭi District, had said to me, "The old men of Cheju say that if you climb to the top of Mt. Halla on a clear day and look southwest to the farthest reach of the sea, there seems to be a strip of white sand." Now that I saw this, it was not white sand but this white sea that they saw and spoke of.[12]

I said to Kwŏn San and others, "In the Koryŏ period Cho Tae-won of your Cheju caught favorable winds from Myongwŏl-p'o, kept a direct course, and crossed the ocean through the White Sea in seven days and nights. Now we cannot tell whether our drifting through the sea has been on a direct or erratic

---

[12]Unusually colored water, most likely the discharge of great rivers, has been noted by other early voyagers in the China Sea. Ennin's ship, for example, sailed into whitish water three days out from Kyushu (E. O. Reischauer, *Ennin's Diary. The Record of a Pilgrimage to China in Search of the Law.* The Ronald Press Company, New York, 1955, 454 pp.; p. 4, 5, 114) and Fr. Martín de Rada, writing of 1575, notes it "20 leagues" before reaching Amoy (Boxer, *South China*, p. 244).

course. Since we have been fortunate enough to enter the White Sea, I suspect that the coast of China must be near. If we manage to land in China, well, China is our homeland. Right now, whether we live or die is up to Heaven. Whether the wind is favorable or otherwise is also at the disposition of Heaven. The east wind has not changed now for several days, so I suspect Heaven intends to let us live. Let each of you be diligent in the things that are within the power of men and accept the fate [decided] by Heaven."

With evening, the wind again shifted from east to north. Kwŏn San still held the tiller bearing west. The night was not yet far advanced when violent waves rose wildly. They again broke over the mat awning, striking the men's heads and faces. All the men closed their eyes and could not open them. The captain and helmsman wept bitterly and did not know what to do. I, too, knew that we could not escape death. I ripped a sheet into strips, bound my body several times round, and fastened myself to a cross-beam of the boat, for I wished that after I died my corpse and the boat should not be separated for a long time.

Makkŭm and Kŏisan wept. They both embraced me and said, "We shall even go to death together."

An Ŭi wept loudly and said, "Rather than die from swallowing salt water I will kill myself." He tried to strangle himself with a bow string, but Kim Sok saved him from dying.

I called out to the captain and helmsman, "Is the boat stove?"

They said, "No."

I said, "Is the tiller lost?"

They said, "No."

Then I turned to Kŏisan and said, "The waves are dangerous and matters grave, but actually the boat is sound. It will not easily be lost. If we can keep on bailing to the very end, we may save our lives. You are strong, you go start the bailing."

On receiving my command, Kŏisan wanted bailing to be done, but the bailing buckets were completely smashed. There was no means to carry out the order. An Ŭi split off small drum heads with a knife to make buckets and gave them to Kŏisan. Kŏisan, Yi Hyo-ji, Kwŏn Song, To-jong, and Hyŏn San bailed water with all their might. It seemed to be knee-deep. Hyo-ja, Chŏng Po, Yi Chŏng and Kim Chung either scooped up water themselves or oversaw seven or eight soldiers, including Kujilhoe. Going one after another, they scooped it all out. We had barely managed not to be sunk.

8th Day. Adrift in the Ocean. This day was cloudy. After noon a northwest wind again blew strong. The boat again turned off its course and headed southeast. We travelled through the night.

I said to Kwŏn San, Ko-myŏn, and I-hok, "In holding the tiller and trying to keep the boat steady, you must know where you are going. I have examined maps, and northeast from Hŭksan Island of our country is the coast of our Ch'ungch'ŏng Province and Hwanghae Province. Due north are P'yŏng-an, Liao-tung, and such places. Northwest is the coast of the old Ch'ing-chou and Yen-chou of *Yü kung*.[13] Due west is the area of Hsü-chou and Yang-chou. In Sung times traffic with Koryŏ sailed from Ming-chou, which was the land from the Yangtze River south.[14] Southwest is the old Min territory, the present Fu-chien-lu.[15] South-southwest and then west are the countries of Siam, Champa, and Malacca. Due south are Great and Little Ryukyu.[16] Due south then east is I-ch'i-tao of Nü-jên-kuo.[17] Due east is Tsushima-shu of Japan. We have now drifted with the wind five days and nights, going west. I believe we almost reached Chinese soil, but then, unfortunately, we met this northwest wind and turned back to the southeast. If we do not reach Ryukyu or Nü-jên-kuo, we shall sail out beyond the Sea of Heaven and rise through the Milky Way, and there will be no end. What are we to do then?

"Mark my words. Keep the helm steady."

Kwŏn San and others said, "Even if the sky were clear and we could calculate by the sun, moon, stars, and planets, we still could not know the four directions of the sea. Now there are clouds, fog, and darkness day after day. We cannot even keep track of dawn and dusk, day and night. We only guess at the four directions from changes in the wind. How can we distinguish a right direction?" They huddled together and wept.

9th Day. Adrift in the Ocean. This day floating clouds dotted the sky. The sea was extremely white.

By now, the boat had been pounded by waves for a long time. Three beams, the ridge pole, wind strut, and bow sprit, were shivering and straining to split. Moreover, water was seeping in, and the boat was about to break up. Kŭn-bo, Ko-myŏn, and Sang-ni cut line and bound the boat bow to stern.[18] They shaved wood and caulked it. Then they looked at each other and wept. They said, "It is not that we do not put all our will into repairing the boat, but hunger and thirst have afflicted us for almost ten days. Our eyes see nothing, our hands and feet are paralyzed. We can neither nourish our bodies nor fully

[13]*Yü kung (The Tribute of Yü)* is in Hsia Shu, Book I, *Shu ching*. While it includes information on tribute and revenue paid, it deals in general with the work of Yü in overcoming floods and drawing boundaries. See Legge, III: 93.

[14]Ming-chou was, more exactly, the later Ning-po-fu (*SRCY* p. 619).

[15]Ch'oe Pu reveals a knowledge of historical if not up-to-date geography in using this Sung designation for Fukien Province. Min, 933-945, was one of the Ten Kingdoms of the Five Dynasties period.

[16]*TDC*, pl. 20 and *WPC*, 210: lv., 2r., label Formosa Little Ryukyu and the present Ryukyus simply Ryukyu. Great Ryukyu corresponds to the Ryukyu Islands, united in the *Yung-lo* period (1403-1424) under a single king and tributary to Ming (Wada Sei. *Chūgoku-shi gaisetsu*, Iwanami Zensho 120, Tokyo, 1950, 2 vols.; I: 242).

[17]In a sixteenth-century Korean map of the world, Nü-jen-kuo appears as a state in a continuous ring of land that follows the circular edge of the world. The center is China, and Nü-jen-kuo is in what would today be considered a southeasterly direction from China. See Kim Hyontay, *Folklore and Customs of Korea*, Seoul Korea Information Service, 1957, 137 p.; facing back cover. I-ch'i-tao should be the Japanese Iki-shima, but I have found no evidence connecting it with a Nü-jen-kuo.

[18]Meaning unclear.

exert our strength. Though we repair it, therefore, we still cannot make it sound. What are we to do?"

Suddenly a flock of sea gulls flew by. When the men in the boat saw them, they joyfully said, "We have heard that water birds disport at sea by day and roost in islands at night. We have drifted across a vast ocean. Since, such a great distance out, we have the good luck to sight these birds, islands cannot be far."

I said, "Gulls are not of one kind only. There are some that bob about the islands of rivers and lakes. If they are ocean gulls, the flocks soar with the tides in the vast sea. Usually they only return to their islands when the winds of the Third Month come. Since it is now the First Month, it is just the time when the flocks of gulls are flying in the open ocean." Before I had finished speaking, we saw several pairs of fishing cormorants fly past. I, too, wondered a little whether islands were perhaps near.

At noon we looked south. There were banks of clouds and, obscurely, the shapes of mountains. There was, too, an atmosphere of human settlement. I felt it was a shore of Ryukyu. We were going to go there and moor when in an instant an east wind again rose strongly, and the boat again headed west. With night, the force of the wind was very strong. We scudded along as if flying.

10th Day. Adrift in the Ocean. This day it rained. An east wind, as on the day before. After noon the sea became green again.

Previously when we had left Cheju, the boatmen had unwisely loaded water from land into a tender to be towed after us. After drifting away with the wind, we were separated from it and lost it. There was not one container of fresh water in the boat. We were not able to boil water or cook food and had nothing to eat or drink. We were in a desperate condition. Kwŏn Song told me, "I have noticed that some of the men in the boat brought yellow oranges and refined wine, and they are greedily eating them up. Let us have them collected and taken to the upper storehouse. We can store them and relieve our thirst with them."

I ordered Kŏisan to search through all the baggage in the boat. He got more than fifty yellow oranges and two jugs of wine.

I said to Son Hyo-ja, "When they are together in a boat, men of Hu and Yüeh are like one.[19] That is even more so with us, all men of one country, of the same flesh and bones. If we are to live, let us all live at the same time. If we are to die, let us all die at the same time. These oranges and this wine are all there are. One drop is worth a thousand pieces of gold. You take charge, therefore, and do not waste any, so that they can be used to relieve the thirst of the men in the boat."

---

[19]Men, that is, from the farthest North and South.

Hyo-ja inspected the men and gave those whose lips were parched and mouths cankerous some oranges and wine to eat and drink. He gave them only enough to moisten their tongues.

In a few days both the oranges and wine were consumed. Some of the men chewed dried rice grains fine and caught their urine in their hands to drink. Before long the urine, too, dried up. Their diaphragms dry and burning, unable to utter sounds, they were almost dead.

At that point, rain fell. Some of the boatmen held up the awning flaps and caught the drops, and some used rain hats and cauldrons to gather the drops. Some curved mats ·and got them, and some tied paper strings[20] to the mast and oars and took what dripped down. [By these means] they hoped to get some water and lick it off with their tongues.

An Ŭi said, "If we took the moisture from clothing wet by the rain and drank it, we should really get a good deal. But the boatman's clothes have all been soaked by salt water. Even if we soaked them in the rain for moisture, we could not drink it. That being the case, what can be done?"

I then picked and brought out several pieces of clothing that had been stored. I ordered Kŏisan to let them be soaked with rain and to collect the moisture from them. It came to several jars, I ordered Kim Chung to ration it with a spoon and let [the men] drink. Chung raised the spoon, and the boatmen opened their mouths wide, like fledgling swallows waiting to be fed. Only afterwards were they able for the first time to move their tongues and belch. They felt a little more like living.

11th Day. Adrift in the Ocean. This day was cloudy.

At dawn we came to an island that had sheer stone precipices and was extremely forbidding. The sea was heavy, and the waves dashed up the rocks some ten or twenty feet. The boat was following the waves directly in, threatening a crisis in which we should be broken to bits. Kwŏn San wept loudly and then tried with all his strength to turn the boat. Hyo-ja and Chŏng Po seized the ropes along the edge of the sail and pulled on them or let up according to the direction of the wind and waves. At the time, the current was from the sea to the island, and the wind was from the island to the sea. The boat followed the wind and turned back, and we avoided disaster.

In the evening we came to a large island. It, too, had cliffs and rocks rising steeply. We wanted to moor the boat but could not. I-hok took off his clothes, jumped into the water, and swam ahead, guiding the boat. He climbed the shore of the island and fastened the boat to it. The men, overjoyed, tumbled out recklessly, sought out a stream, took the fresh water in their cupped hands, and drank. Turning from drawing the water, they wanted to prepare food. I said, "In the extremity of hunger the five organs are stuck together. If you suddenly eat to the full, you will surely die. It is better first to drink rice

[20]Meaning unclear.

water and follow it with congee. You should stop when you have had the right amount." The boatmen all boiled congee and sipped it.

Since there was no place to escape the wind on the island, at night we freed the boat and went.

12th Day. An Encounter with Pirates at the Boundary of Ning-po Prefecture. This day was cloudy and sometimes rainy. The sea was again white.

At dusk we came to large islands that lay opened out like a screen. We saw that there were two boats among them. Both carried small boats. They pointed directly at my boat and came toward us.

Chŏng Po and others knelt round me and said, "In all things there are rules and exceptions to the rules. Please take off your mourning clothes and, as an exception, wear your silk gauze cap and round collar and thus display the signs of an official. If you do not, they will make us out to be pirates and humiliate us."

I said, "We have drifted at sea by the will of Heaven. We have repeatedly approached death and regained life by the will of Heaven. We have also arrived at these islands and met these boats by the will of Heaven. Heaven's principles are just. How can I go against Heaven to practice deceit?"

Very quickly, the two boats drew near and met us. In each boat there were about ten men, all of whom wore black, padded trousers and straw boots. Some had towels wrapped round their heads, and some wore bamboo-leaf rain hats and coir-bark raincoats.

They clamored and shouted loudly. It was all in Chinese, and I judged them to be men of China. I ordered Chŏng Po to write [a message] on a piece of paper and send it to them. It said, "I, Ch'oe Pu, a minister of Korea, received the King's order to go to an island in the sea. I was hurrying to mourn for my father, and, crossing the sea, met a wind and drifted here. I do not know what land or district this is."

The men answered, "This is the region of Ning-po Prefecture, Chekiang, China." They also said, "If you want to reach your own country, it would be well for you to go to China [first]."

Chŏng Po pointed to his mouth with his hand. The men brought two buckets of fresh water and gave them to us. They rowed their boats away to the east.

I commanded the boatmen to scull into an island and seek shelter. There was another boat, which also carried a small boat and had about seven or eight soldiers. Their clothes and speech were the same as those of the men we had previously seen. They came to meet my boat and said, "What country are you from?"

I had Chŏng Po answer again as before. Then we asked, "What country and place is this?"

The men pointed to the island and said, "This is Hsia-shan,[21] in Ning-po

---

[21]Hsia-shan is a common name for small places. Since many islands lie off this portion of the coast, the landfall would be hard to identify. It was apparently a good distance north of the point at which the party eventually went ashore.

Prefecture, China. If the wind and water are right, you can return home in two days."

I replied, "We, men from a strange land, have encountered a storm and, despite ten thousand brushes with death, have been fortunate enough to reach the shores of China. We are happy to have reached a place where our lives are saved." Then I asked them what their names were.

A man answered, "I am Lin Ta of China. If you are going to China, I shall accompany you. If you have valuables, you should give them to me."

I answered, "I am an official on a mission, not a merchant. After drifting and bobbing about, furthermore, how could I have valuables?"

I took rice from our rations and gave it to him. The man accepted it and replied, "If you moor your boat to this island you need not fear the northwest wind, but the south wind is not good. Follow me to moor it." He led my boat to an island anchorage. He said, "Here, this is where you should moor."

I did as he said. We went and moored the boat, and there was, true enough, no wind. It was a place ringed by the island, in which boats could find shelter. On the west shore were two thatched huts that looked like houses in which salt fish were prepared. The other men moored their boat below the huts. The men in my boat, at the extremity of prolonged hunger and thirst and having toiled without sleep for a long time, had got food and eaten and had got a place protected from the wind and moored. Then, exhausted, they dropped down in a jumble of limbs in the boat.

In the second watch of the night, the one who had called himself Lin Ta came at the head of his band of over twenty men, some carrying spears, some carrying swords, but without bows and arrows, and holding torches. They came without leave into my boat. The pirate chief wrote [a message] that said, "I am the Buddha Kuan-yin. I see through to your heart. You have gold and silver, and I am going to look for it."

I answered, "Gold and silver are not produced by my country. I have not had any from the first."

The pirate chief said, "If you are an official, how can you not have brought any? I'll take a look."

Now I, Chŏng Po, Yi Chŏng, Kim Chung, and Hyo-ja, because it was uncertain how long a voyage to Cheju and places at sea would take, had sailed with several pieces of clothing for all seasons. This pirate chief, now, shouted to his band to make a thorough search for clothes in my portmanteau and those of my secondary officials and for the boatmen's rations and to load them into his boat. They left behind only such things as the clothes drenched in salt water and all the books and documents.

Among the pirates there was a one-eyed one who behaved especially badly.

Chŏng Po said to me, "When the pirates first came, they showed something like courtesy. When they saw that we were weak, they gradually came to show their true colors. I suggest that we make one strong attack to decide who should die and who should live."

I said, "Our boatmen, after being on the brink of death from hunger and thirst, have lost their courage before the pirates. The pirates, therefore, take advantage of the circumstances and inflict on us their violence. If we fought with them, our men would all die at the pirates' hands. It is better to give up all our baggage and beg for our lives."

The pirate chief also seized the seal and horse permit that I had and put them into his sleeve. Chŏng Po followed after him and asked him to return them but did not get them. I said, "Take away everything in the boat, but the seal and horse permit are symbols of state and of no use to unauthorized persons. You had better return them to me." The pirate chief returned the seal and permit.

Then he went out the door of the shelter and stood lined up with his band on the gunwale of the boat. They argued noisily for some time and then came back into the boat. First, they took off Chŏng Po's clothes, bound him and beat him. Next, they cut the frog of my gown with a sword and stripped me naked. They put my hands behind me, bent my legs, and bound me. They beat my left arm with a stick seven or eight times and said, "If you love life, better bring out the gold and silver."

I shouted, "You can cut my body and break my bones, but where am I to get gold and silver?"

The pirates did not understand what I said. They untied my bonds to let me write what I meant, and I wrote it. The pirate chief was angry. He stared ferociously, his mouth wide open. He pointed at Chŏng Po and shouted, pointed at me and shouted. He pulled me by the hair and again bound me. He raised his sword and aimed it at my throat to cut it, but the sword happened to miss and struck something by my right shoulder, the blade glancing off. The pirate again raised the sword and was about to behead me, when one of the pirates came, took hold of the arm that raised the sword, and restrained it. The pirate band all raised great shouts, but I do not know what was said.

At the time, the boatmen were beside themselves with fright. They scurried about to hide, but there was no place. Only Kim Chung and Kŏisan clasped their hands and begged on their knees that my life be spared.

Then, after torturing me and terrifying the boatmen, the pirate chief led his band off. They cut away the boat's anchor, oars, and all ropes and threw them into the sea. Then with their boat they towed my boat toward the open sea and turned it loose. By the time they boarded their boat and disappeared, it was already late at night.

13th Day. Adrift Again in the Ocean. This day was cloudy. A strong northwest wind rose. We drifted again into the limitless sea.

The padded clothing packed by me and the boatmen had all been lost to the pirates, and the clothing that we were wearing had been soaked in salt water for a long time. The sky, moreover, was constantly clouded, giving us no chance to dry it out, and the time when we should die of exposure was drawing near. All the rations loaded in the boat had been seized by the pirates, and the time when we should die of starvation was drawing near. Because the anchor and oars had been thrown away by the pirates and the makeshift sail ripped by the wind, the boat simply went east or west with the wind, or in and out with the tide. There was nothing for the helmsman to work at, and the time when we should sink was also drawing near.

All the boatmen had stopped-up throats and could not utter sounds. They sat and waited for the time to die. Hyo-ji said to me, "For us, death is part of the job. It is only the death of a commissioner we should lament."

I said, "Why do you consider death part of your job?"

Hyo-ji said, "Our department is far out at sea, more than nine hundred *li*. The waves are much worse than those of other seas. Of the unbroken lines of tribute and merchant boats that sail out, five or six of every ten are driven out to sea and not heard from again, and the men are drowned. Most of the men of the department die thus sooner or later. The graves of men, therefore, within the borders are extremely few. In the villages there are three times more women than men. When as fathers and mothers the people produce a girl, they say, 'This is one who will be good and dutiful to us.' When it is a boy, they all say, 'This thing is not our child, it is food for whales and turtles.' Our lives are as uncertain as the day-fly's. Even if we had continued in our normal way, we should not have expected to die in our own rooms, under our own windows.

"Ministers of the Court, however, going and coming, wait at their convenience for the wind. Their boats and oars are nimble and strong. Those who have died in the wind and waves, therefore, have been few in the past. But now this fate has befallen you, honored Commissioner, and, Heaven not rendering its unseen assistance, you have come to this extremely dangerous pass. That is why we mourn for your fate."

14th Day. Adrift in the Ocean. This day was fair.

Between 3 and 5 p.m. we sailed into an island. In three directions, east, south, and west, nothing met the eye. It was a place sheltered from only the north wind, and we were concerned about not having an anchor. When we had first left Cheju, because the boat was very large and carried nothing in it, we had put in a number of stones to keep it from rolling. Now Sang-ni and others tied four stones together with line for a makeshift anchor, and we moored there.

An Ŭi talked with the soldiers in my hearing: "I know why we have come to the point of drifting off and dying on this trip. Ever since olden times, everyone going to Cheju has first sacrificed at Mudungsan Shrine in Kwangju and Kŭmsŏngsan Shrine in Naju. Everyone sailing from Cheju has first sacrificed at Kwangyang, Sŏgwi, Ch'ŏnwoe, and Ch'och'un shrines.[22] Therefore they

[22]These are all well-known shrines, listed in *TGYJ*, the ones in Cheju in *ch.* 38 and the others under their prefectures.

received the aid of the gods and successfully crossed the ocean.

"The present Commissioner, however, has arrogantly ignored these measures. He came without sacrificing at Mudung and Kŭmsong shrines, and he went without sacrificing at Kwangyang and the other shrines. He is contemptuous of the gods. The gods, in turn, have not pitied us and have sent us to this extremity. Who is at fault?" The soldiers agreed with him and all blamed me.

Kwŏn Song, however, said, "That is not so. Before this, Yi Sŏm of Sŏnŭi fasted three days and sacrificed punctiliously to Kwangyang and the other gods. He, too, went adrift, almost died, and survived. Commissioner Kwŏn Kyŏng-u did not sacrifice at all, yet he came and went swiftly and surely, without the slightest discomfort. Thus, the ease or difficulty of crossing the sea depends on waiting for the wind; it has nothing to do with sacrificing or not sacrificing to the gods."

I also admonished them, saying, "Heaven and Earth are not partial, and the gods and spirits do their work silently. They are strictly impartial in blessing good and damning evil. If a man is wicked and toadies for blessings, can they bless him? If a man is good and neither is deluded by heretical doctrines nor offers blasphemous sacrifices, can they damn him? Can one say that Heaven, Earth, the gods and spirits send down damnations and blessings on men for the sake of flattery, food, and drink? That cannot possibly be.

"Sacrifices, moreover, have fixed ranks. For gentry and commoners to sacrifice to mountains and rivers goes against the code of propriety. A sacrifice opposed to propriety is an evil sacrifice. I have never known of any man who obtained blessings by improper sacrifice.

"You Cheju men are devoted to gods and spirits. You build shrines to gods in all the mountains, marshes, rivers, and swamps. At such temples as Kwangyang you sacrifice respectfully morning and night, leaving nothing undone. That being so, when you cross the ocean you ought not to have mishaps like drifting and sinking. Yet today such-and-such a boat goes adrift, tomorrow such-and-such a boat sinks, and so it goes with one after another. Can these things be taken to mean that these gods are powerful and that sacrifices to them can bring blessings?

"Of the people in this boat, moreover, I alone have not sacrificed. All you soldiers devoutly fasted and sacrificed and then came. If the gods are powerful, how can they deny the devotion of the fasting and sacrificing of you forty-odd men because I alone did not sacrifice? Our boat has gone adrift solely because the baggage was unevenly stowed and because we were not good at forecasting the weather. Is it not foolish to blame me for having neglected the sacrifices?"

An Ŭi and the others seem to consider what I said irrelevant and wrong.

15th Day. Adrift in the Ocean. This day was cloudy. The sea was red and muddy. An east wind had arisen again.

Again we went with the wind and set the helm heading west. Of the men in the boat, some, such as Pak Chong-hoe, Mansan, and Yi San, were sick and not able to work. Ko Po-jang, Yang Tal-hae, Ko Hoe, Kim Cho-hoe, and Im San-hae, from the time we went adrift until the present, had lain down and not risen to work. Though we directed them to bail and do other things, they ignored the commands completely. Chŏng Sil, Pu Myŏng-dong, Kim Tŭk-si, Kang Yu, Song Chin, Kim Sok, Kang Nae, O San, and Ko Naeŭltong had to be called ten times before they would answer once. Some worked only when they could not help it. Among San Kŭn-bo, Kim Koe-san, Ko Pok, Kim Song, Kim Sok-kwi, Yi Hyo-t'ae, and Kim Chin-san*,[23] some worked hard by day and slacked by night, and some worked hard at first and became lazy later. Hŏ Sang-ni, Kwŏn San, Kim Ko-Myŏn, Kim Kujilhoe, Ch'oe Kŏisan, Kim To-jong, Ko I-hok, Munhoe, Hyŏn San, Han Mae-san, Kwŏn Song, and Makkŭm worked hard night and day and made the sailing of the boat their responsibility. Chŏng Po, Kim Chung, Yi Chŏng, Son Hyo-ja, Yi Hyo-ji, and An Ŭi, either personally undertook jobs or oversaw the repairing of the boat in the hope of finishing the work. But after we met the pirates and again were set adrift, they gradually changed from what they had been before, and none of them cared whether he lived.

The ship had been pounded by violent waves now for many days. There were a hundred holes and a thousand strains; no sooner was one stopped than another leaked. So much water came through the cracks that we could not bail fast enough to keep up with it. I said, "With the water leaking like this and, too, the boatmen's loyalty as uncertain as it is, how can I in foolish pride sit and wait for death?" Then with Chŏng Po and five other men I myself bailed the water almost all out. More than ten men, from Sang-ni down, also regained a little of their strength and got up.

At night there was no wind, but it rained. We came to a large island, and though we wanted to approach and moor, we could not, since the evening tide was against us. We rode in the current at sea.

16th Day. Arrival and Mooring at Niu-t'ou-wai-yang. This day was cloudy. The sea was red and black and thoroughly muddy. To the west we saw rows of peaks, range behind range, reaching up to the sky and cradling the sea. They gave an impression of people living there.

When we rode in on the east wind, we saw that on top of the mountains there were many beacon towers in a line along the peaks. We were overjoyed to have reached the shores of China again.

After noon, the wind and waves were exceedingly rough. Rain fell in a

[23]Previously Kim Chinŭmsan.

drizzle, and it was dark. The boat being driven by the wind, in the twinkling of an eye, we drifted between two islands. As we passed by a shore, we saw that there were six boats moored in a row. Chŏng Po and others made a request of me, saying, "Previously, when we reached Hsia-shan, you did not display the signs of an official, and we attracted pirates. We barely escaped dying. Now you should follow the exception to the rule. Put on your cap and sash and show them to those boats."

I said, "How dare you suggest to me a thing harmful to morals?"

Chŏng Po said, "This moment we are close to death. What time is there to observe propriety and morality? For the time being, practice the exceptions so that we can survive; later observe your mourning with propriety. That is not harmful to morals."

I disagreed with him. I said, "To take off mourning clothes and put on festive ones goes against filial piety. To take advantage of men by deceit goes against sincerity. I would rather die than oppose filial piety and sincerity. I must conform to what is right."

An Ŭi came and made a request, saying, "For the time being, let me wear this cap and gown and appear to be an official."

I said. "No. If those boats are of the type in which we met the pirates before, something like that would be all right. If they are loyal boats, they will surely drive us on to a public office to take a deposition. What statement would you make then? If there was the slightest discrepancy, it would give rise to suspicion. It is better to observe the strictest honesty."

Suddenly the six boats rowed up and encircled my boat. There were about eight or nine men in each boat, and their clothing and speech were of the kind of the pirates we had met at Hsia-shan. They wrote and showed us a note that said, "We see you are foreigners. Where do you come from?"

I ordered Chŏng Po likewise to write and answer them. We said, "I am a minister of the Court of Korea. I had undertaken to tour an island in the King's service and was hurrying across the sea into mourning when I was blown here by a wind. I do not know this sea or what country this land belongs to."

The men answered, "This sea is Niu-t'ou-wai-yang. It is now part of the land of Lin-hai County, T'ai-chou Prefecture, China."[24]

Chŏng Po pointed to his mouth. The men brought buckets of water and gave them to us and then pointed to the north, where there were mountains, and said, "Those mountains have springs, where you can draw water and cook a meal to eat. If you have black pepper, give us two or three ounces."[25]

[24]This bay in which Ch'oe Pu arrived may have taken its name from a moderately prominent island, Niu-t'ou Island, off the coast of Lin-hai County, or Niu-t'ou-mên, in the same region. (*Lin-hai-hsien chih,* ed. by Hung Jo-kao, 1683, 15 *ch.*; *ch.* 1, 7*r.*, 10*r.*, 15*r.* It is not clear whether the three references are to the same island.). The beacon towers he noticed were those built in the Ming dynasty in a line from T'ao-chu Chiliad via Niu-t'ou to Chien-t'iao Chiliad. The beacons, five hundred boats, and seven thousand soldiers put at T'ao-chu Chiliad are said to have eliminated raids by pirates (*Ibid., ch.* 2, 4*r.*, *v.*)

[25]The demand for black pepper was characteristic of the times. There was "as great profit in taking spices to China as in taking them to Portugal"; pepper could be sent from Malacca to China at a profit of 300%. See Boxer, *South China*, p. xx.

I answered, "My country does not produce black pepper. I did not start out with any."

The men then rowed their boats off a little, surrounded my boat, and dropped anchor. My boat, too, drew near the shore and moored. I ordered An Ŭi, Kŏisan, and Sang-ni to disembark and climb a mountain. They looked round for human settlement. This was, indeed, a place joined to the mainland.

XXX[26] Though the vast expanse of water through which I had passed on this voyage seemed to be a single sea, the current and color of the water differed according to the place. In the sea of Cheju, the color was deep green and the current violent and swift. Though the wind was slight, wave climbed over wave, boiling and swirling. There was nothing to equal it. It was like that as far as west of Hŭksan Island. When we had gone four days and nights, the color of the sea was white. In two more days and nights it became whiter, and in another day and night it was green again. In two more days and nights it was white again. Three days and nights after that it was red and muddy. One more day and night and it was red and black mixed with mud.

In sailing the boat we simply followed the wind, north, south, east, or west, drifting aimlessly. The colors of the sea that I saw in that time were generally as above, going from white back to green.

Though the force of the wind was strong, the waves were not very high. There were first islands from the time that the sea became white again. The islands were all precipitous, with cavernous valleys and masses of stones. On the tops lay earth, and there was a variety of plants and fragrant grasses, luxuriously green and vigorous. The current was very weak. When we did not meet high winds, we had little trouble with violent waves. If the sea in which I met the pirates and was set adrift again had been as perilous as the Cheju sea, we could never have sighted islands again. *XXX*

XXX In general, the First Month of every year being the middle of winter, violent winds rage, and enormous seas run. That is the season that travellers avoid. With the Second Month, the winds gradually grow calmer. In Cheju it is popularly called the Festival of Lights.[27] But even then it is forbidden to cross the sea. Men in the bays of Kangnam[28] do not sail the sea in the First Month either. After the rainy season of the Fourth Month has passed, the winds suddenly become steady, and ocean junks begin to cross. They are called the junk-driving winds.

[26]*XXX* here and subsequently is the equivalent of a large circle in the original used to set off a passage of general comment.

[27]In a custom now apparently dead, some communities on Cheju used to observe a festival, presumably in homage to a god of the sea, from the 1st to the 15th day of the Second Month, when they would erect twelve long poles ornamented with silk horse-heads. At night, lights were hung on two of the poles, giving the name Festival of Lights. Sang-su Choe, "Korean Annual Custom and Festival," *Korean Quarterly* IV: 1 (Autumn, 1962), p. 137.

[28]This may be a way of referring to the southern Korean coastline, but the final *ch'ao* is an odd ending. Professor Chi-chen Wang wonders whether Chiang-nan and Ch'ao-chou (Kwangtung) are meant.

I drifted to sea in the season of dangerous wind and waves. The sea and sky were darkened by violent storms for days on end. The masts, sails, lines, and oars were either broken or lost. We spent ten days at a time suffering from hunger and thirst, and more than once or twice a day we came close to sinking. But fortunately we were just able to survive and moor on a seashore. That was not only because we collected rain water that had soaked us to wet our parched insides but also because the boat was truly sound and nimble and could withstand the wind and waves. *XXX*

17th Day. Leaving the Boat and Landing. This day it rained.

At dawn the six boats came crowding round. They addressed us: "You are law-abiding men, we see. Come with us; if you have rare things, give us a few."

I answered, "We have drifted a long time. All the things we had have been scattered in the sea. If you show me the way to rescue, the boat and oars by which we sailed are all yours as they are." Then I asked how far we were from the nearest settlement.

One of the men said, "This place is near a public office. If you want to go there, it is no trouble."

Another man said, "If you go ahead one *li* there is a settlement."

Another said, "Even though a settlement is far from here, you must not stop here."

Then I asked whether the public road was far.

One of the men said, "T'ai-chou Prefecture is 180 *li* from here."

Another said, "150 *li*."

Another said, "240 *li*."

There were contradictions among them, and they could not be trusted.

The men, jostling and shoving one after the next, fought to come into my boat. Whatever their eyes fell on, though small, worthless things, they seized. They said to us, "If you do not go with us, we shall be angry."

An Ŭi asked me, "Leave the boat, get into their boat, and go where they go." Yi Chŏng wanted to attack one man and kill him, to drive them away.

I said, "Neither of your plans will do. It seems to me that since what they say is untrue and since they have been robbing us greedily, it is impossible to tell how honest they are. If they are of the type of the previous ones, the Hsia-shan pirates, and we follow An Ŭi's plan and go with them, they will row to a remote island and drown us to cover their tracks. If they are fishing boats or defense boats and we follow Yi Chŏng's plan and attack and kill [a man], they will cover up what they have done and instead will make us out to be foreigners who have come to plunder and kill men. Then there will be an uproar along the coast of China and we shall be falsely accused of being pirates. Our language, moreover, is different, so that it will be hard for us to argue our case. We shall all be executed by the coast guards. By either of your plans, we should bring death upon ourselves. For the time being, it is best to refuse and see what their attitude is."

I said to the men, "We have sailed on the sea for many days. In extremities of hunger, thirst, and suffering, our lives hung by a thread. Please let us make a meal to satisfy our hunger, and after that we shall go with you."

The men replied, "Stay here a little and do not go." They rowed their boats off a bit and about two or three *li* away encircled my boat again and anchored. Because of the rain they all went into the cabins of the boats. No one was looking out.

I said to the men in the boat with me, "I see that the speech and actions of those men are untrustworthy. I see that this mountain joins a way to the mainland: it must lead to a settlement. If we do not make the best of this moment, our lives will lie in their grasp, and eventually we shall be ghosts in the briny deep." I then led the secondary officials off the boat first, and the troops followed in our footsteps.

We fled hiding into the rain and woods. We crossed two ridges that overlooked the sea. There were rocks like those of a walled road. When we had gone six or seven *li*, we reached a village. I said to the secondary officials and the troops, "You share with me this mortal suffering; there is no difference between us. If we defend each other from now on, we can return home safe and sound. If, when you meet troubles you overcome them together, when you get a meal you divide it to eat, when there is sickness you support each other, we can manage without losing a single man."

They all said, "As you command."

I said, "Our country is a country of propriety and morality. Though we are in flight and distressed, we ought still to show a dignified bearing and let the people of this land know that the formality of our country is as it is. Whereever we go, the secondary officials should bow to me, and the troops should bow to the secondary officials. There should be no skipping over ranks. When, moreover, crowds come and look at us in front of villages or in walled towns, we must bow with hands folded and not venture to be too abrupt."

They all said. "As you command."

When we came to the village, the people, young and old, male and female, all marveled at us. The onlookers were like a wall. I and my staff advanced and folded our hands in greeting. They all brought their sleeves together and bowed in answer. Then I informed them about how we had come from Korea.

There were two men whose appearance showed that they were not common. They said to us, "If you are Koreans, why did you enter our country? Write it all out for us, whether you are pirates, or bringers of tribute, or men displaced by a wind. We shall send you back to your country."

I said, "I am a minister of Korea. I received the King's command and went to an island. Hurrying into mourning for my father, I was crossing the sea and met a wind. I was blown adrift and came to a sea coast. I left the boat, went ashore, and, seeking human settlement, came here. I beg you gentlemen to inform the public office of this and save us from impending death." Then I showed them the seal, cap, sash, and documents that I had. When the two men had finished looking at them, they pointed to the Security Officer and secondary officials in front of me, who were prostrated in order of rank. [The two men] said to me, "We have long heard that your country is a land of protocol and morality. This indeed proves what we have heard." Then they summoned house servants and had rice water, tea, and wine brought to us all, including the troops. They let us drink and then pointed to a Buddhist temple in front of the village.

They said, "You may stay in that temple and rest."

I went to the temple, took off my damp clothes, and aired them. Soon the two men had more food prepared, brought, and served to us. They were truly worthy men, but I have forgotten their names and positions.

Suddenly, the two men came and said, "You must get up. We shall send you to a good place."

I asked, "How many *li* away is this good place?"

They lied and said, "It is two *li* more."

I said, "What is the name of the place?"

They said, "Hsi-li-t'ang."

I said, "It is raining hard, and the road is muddy, and, too, it is toward evening. How can we go now?"

They said, "The place where you are going is not far. You must not worry."

I did as they said. As I set out at the head of my staff, some of the people of the village took up staves and swords and some beat gongs and drums. I heard the sound of gongs and drums on the road ahead, [and when we advanced that far] people gathered round like clouds and shouted at us threateningly. They pressed in on our left and right, crowded before and behind us, and drove us on. They passed us on successively, each new village like the previous one. When we had gone more than fifty *li,* the night was already well advanced.

18th Day. An Encounter with Chiliarch Hsü Ch'ing on the Road. This day it rained hard.

By midnight, then, as we were driven on by villagers, the road passed over a high hill, where pines and bamboo grew thickly. We met a man, named Wang I-yüan, who described himself as a recluse scholar. He pitied us for braving the night and the rain and being driven on painfully. He stopped the villagers briefly and asked me what had happened, and I informed him, too, of the circumstances of our being blown adrift by the wind. I-yüan grieved for me; he called for wine and urged it on me. I said, "When we Koreans observe mourning for parents, we do not drink wine or eat meat, garlic, oniony plants, or sweet things for fully three years. I am deeply grateful for your kindness in offering me wine, but I am in mourning now, and I venture to decline."

I-yüan then served me tea and my staff wine. He asked, "Does your country have the Buddha, too?"

I answered, "My country does not revere the Buddhist law, it honors only the Confucian system. All its families make filial piety, fraternal duty, loyalty, and sincerity their concern." I-yüan took my hands and looked at me compassionately, and we parted.

The villagers drove us on, and we came to a large mountain range. My feet were swollen like cocoons, and I could not go forward. The villagers seized my arms, pulled me from in front, pushed me from behind, and over we went. We were passed on for over twenty *li* [and came to another village, where] there was a big bridge. The villagers, who struck us indiscriminately with crooked sticks, were recklessly cruel and plundered greedily. O San was carrying my horse saddle, but a man beat him off, seized it, and took it away. Beaten forward with sticks, we fell down and wept.

We crossed two ranges and were turned over to another village. It was approaching dawn. When I asked what the village with the big bridge had been, a man said, "Hsien-yen Village."

Ever since we had landed, all the onlookers by the road had sawed their arms across their throats, making gestures at us as if to cut off their heads, and we did not know what they meant.

We reached P'u-fêng Village. The rain let up a little. An official came with military officers and asked me, "What is your nationality? How did you come here?"

I said, "I am a Korean. I have placed in the examinations twice and am a minister close to the King of the country. I had been given the state duty of touring an island, but hurrying into mourning, I put out from land, encountered a wind, and drifted here. Through hunger and thirst enough for dying many times, I have barely clung to life. I have been repeatedly driven on by villagers. In this extremity of suffering, I am fortunate enough to meet an official here, making it the moment of my rescue."

The official first served me congee and then solid food. He also ordered my staff to prepare food and eat. When I asked the official's name and position, one Wang Kua said, "He is Hsü Ch'ing, Chiliarch [*Ch'ien-hu*] of Hai-men Garrison [*Wei*].²⁹ He defends T'ang-t'ou Stockade; having heard that Japanese were raiding the coast, he came specifically to take them prisoner. Take care."

I lay down exhausted at the side of the road; my four limbs would not move. Hsü Ch'ing said to me, "The laws of China are strict. You strangers may not stay here long upsetting the law-abiding people." He ordered military officers to drive us on quickly. When we had gone about five *li*, there was a public office, which was T'ang-t'ou Stockade. We passed a long embankment, somewhat over ten *li* long. Rain fell heavily again.

²⁹For the garrison and chiliad (*ch'ien-hu-so*), the fundamental units of the defense system, called the *wei-so* system, see Hucker, pp. 59, 60 and *TRD* VIII: 159-161.

I hobbled along, crippled, moving my legs hardly at all. I fell in the road and said, "My strength is gone, I am going to die. If I had known earlier that it was to be like this, it would have been easier to die at sea." Chŏng Po and those below him wept bitterly for me again. We were urged on by the military officers and could not delay a moment. Yi Chŏng, Hyo-ji, Sang-ni and Hyŏn San, men with sound bodies, took turns carrying me along.

We crossed two ranges, and when we had gone almost thirty *li*, there were many houses, in front of which was a Buddhist temple. Since it was about to get dark and the rain did not stop, Hsü Ch'ing wanted to put us up in the temple. All the villagers felt that could not be permitted. Hsü Ch'ing said to me, "All the people here suspect that you are bandits and, therefore, will not let you be put up. Though it is hard for you to walk, we have no choice but to go on." He ordered the military officers to drive us on.

We crossed a large range and in the second watch of the night came to the bank of a river. Yi Chŏng and the others had also exhausted their strength and could not take care of themselves, nor could they carry me. My whole staff, too, were weary and wasted and could not go on. Hsü Ch'ing himself took my hands and raised me. Both my feet were swollen and lame, and I could not move them a step. Ko I-hok was enraged. He pointed at me and said, "These Chinese! They must be mad! If you are really at the end of your strength, you had better just drop and not get up." I agreed with what he said. I would rather die, I felt, and it was just as well to die here, so I lay down again and did not get up. Most of the rest fell down helter-skelter. Hsü Ch'ing ordered the officers to urge some of us on and strike at others, but they could not make us move.

After some time, another official came with soldiers carrying torches. They were impressive with their armor and helmets, their spears, swords, and shields. Their gongs, drums, and firearms[30] made a tumult. Without warning they surrounded us, drawing their swords and handling their spears in motions as if to practice attacking and cutting. The shock to our eyes and ears terrified us, and we did not know what to do.

The official and Hsü Ch'ing drew their forces up in formation and drove us on. In about three or four *li*, there was a big house, surrounded by a wall like a fortified pass. I asked about it. It was Yü-tu-ch'ang, the present T'ao-chih Chiliad;[31] some said it was P'i-yen Chiliad.[32] Inside the wall was An-hsing Temple. They stopped us at the temple and let us stay there for the night. When I asked who the official was, a priest said, "He is the Chiliarch of T'ao-chu Chiliad. He heard that Japanese were raiding the borders and had weapons brought here and set up. Then, receiving Chiliarch Hsü's report, he led soldiers

---

[30]*WPC* shows no special weapons with this name, so that the term is perhaps simply a general one for arms that use explosives.

[31]Literally T'ao-chih-so. As a suffix in a place name, *so* is an abbreviation of *ch'ien-hu-so*, chiliad.

[32]Yü-tu-ch'ang is an error for Tu-tu-ch'ang, which is the way the name appears later in the text and in *Lin-hai-hsien chih, ch.* 1, 33*r*. The other names do not appear in that source, and the similarity of T'ao-chih-so and T'ao-chu-so, which appears several lines later, suggests that something is wrong with the text.

out to drive you on and bring you here. But he does not know yet whether you are honest or dishonest. Tomorrow you will reach T'ao-chu Chiliad, and he will question you."

19th Day. Arrival at T'ao-chu Chiliad. This day there was heavy rain.

The two Chiliarchs, riding abreast, drove us on, into the face of the rain. I ordered Chŏng Po to say to Hsü Ch'ing, "Hungry and thirsty, we drifted at sea, staring at death and regaining life. Barely staving off our dying gasps, we reached your border, met an official, and, yesterday morning, ate a full meal. We thought we had got to a place of rescue, where now, in continuous rain and muddy roads we stumble and fall in gullies and strike rocks and mud. Our bodies are frozen, our legs have sores, our hearts are anxious, and our strength is exhausted. Last night we did not eat, nor did we eat this morning, yet we are driven on, into the rain. We shall probably die on the way."

Hsü Ch'ing replied, "Yesterday you brought hunger on yourselves by not walking far enough to reach the authorities. Now, if you get there in good order, the authorities themselves will supply you. Hurry, hurry!"

I took a step, failed, and lay down at the side of the road. My whole body had collapsed and would not rally. Hyo-ja, Chŏng Po, Kim Chung, Makkŭm, Mansan, and Kŏisan sat round me and wept bitterly. Just then, a man leading an ox happened to pass by. Chŏng spoke to the Chiliarch: "Please let us take off our clothes and buy this ox to carry our chief."

Hsü Ch'ing said, "How can I, too, help but pity you all for the suffering you are undergoing? But since I am bound by the laws of the country, I cannot take your part."

Yi Chŏng, Hyo-ji, and Sang-ni again took turns carrying me. We crossed one range and in somewhat more than twenty *li* came to a wall, which was T'ao-chu Chiliad of Hai-men Garrison. As we approached the wall, for seven or eight *li* there were troops wearing armor and holding lances. Fire weapons and bold shields filled the roads. When we arrived at the wall, it had a double gate, and the gates had iron knockers. Watch towers were built along the top of the wall, and within it markets and shops were continuous and the people prosperous.

We were led to a public guest house and allowed to stay there. My appearance was emaciated, my hat and gown muddy. The onlookers doubled up with laughter. One Wang Pi wrote a statement to me: "Yesterday it was reported to the authorities that fourteen Japanese boats had violated the border and attacked people. Are you really Japanese?"

I said, "I am not Japanese, I am a Korean gentleman."

There was also a Lu Fu-yung who called himself a scholar. He said to me, "Why, when your carriages have the same axle-width and your books the same writing as those of China, is your speech not the same?"

I answered, "The same wind does not blow over a thousand *li*, the same customs do not obtain over a hundred. If you wonder at the sound of my words, I wonder at the sound of yours. It is a matter of custom. But if we share the nature given by Heaven, my nature, too, is the nature of Yao, Shun, K'ung, and Yen.[33] How can one object to a difference in speech?"

The man applauded and said, "When you go into mourning, do you observe the [rules of] Chu Wen Kung's *Chia li*?"

I answered, "In observing mourning, every one of my countrymen respects the *Chia li*. I should have followed it, but being driven off by winds, I have not yet been able to weep before the coffin. For that I grieve bitterly."

The man then asked, "Do you write poetry?"

I answered, "Poetry is something by which the frivolous moan about the wind and moon and not a thing indulged in by sincere men devoted to the Way. I take as my study the investigation of things, extension of knowledge, and pursuit of truth. I do not pay much attention to poetry, but if someone addresses a poem to me, I am bound to respond with one of my own; that is all."

Another man wrote on my palm: "I see that you are not an evil man. But simply because your speech is not the same, you are really like someone blind and deaf. I truly pity you, and I shall tell you something; remember it. Be very careful of yourself. Do not talk freely to people. From olden times, Japanese bandits have repeatedly raided our borders. The state, therefore, has set up Anti-Japanese Commissioners and Anti-Japanese Commanders[34] to cope with them. If they seize Japanese, they behead them all first and report it later.

"Now the place where you first tied your boat was in the area of Shih-tzu Stockade. The Stockade Commander falsely accused you of being Japanese. He wanted your heads for the reward, and in his first report, therefore, he said, 'Fourteen Japanese boats have violated the border and attacked people.' As he was about to lead soldiers out to take you and behead you, your group left the boat and ran into a village, where many people were. He could not, therefore, perpetrate his scheme. Tomorrow, the Commander will come and question your group. Explain things to him minutely. If there is the slightest discrepancy or error, there is no telling what might happen."

When I asked his name, he said, "I have told you this because I like you. I have risked danger."[35] He turned and left.

When I heard what he said, my hair stood up on end; so I said to Chŏng Po and others, "When the people on the road pointed at us and made gestures as if to cut off their heads, it was because all of them were deluded by this plot."

---

[33]Two of the sage-kings, Confucius, and Yen Hui, a favorite disciple of Confucius.

[34]*Pei-wo tu-chih-hui* and *Pei-wo pa-tsung-kuan*. It is unclear whether the former were regular Regional Military Commissioners (see Hucker, pp. 58, 59) whose titles acquired the prefix "Anti-Japanese" from the special military problems of the region they commanded or a different group of commissioners in charge of sections of the coast. See also Boxer, *South China*, p. 155. The latter defended relatively smaller territories. Chekiang, for example, had six of them—Ting-hai Anti-Japanese Commander, etc.,—ranking seventeenth to twenty-second in the table of officers. See *WPC* 215: 10*v.*, 11*r.*

[35]Or, "And you are in danger." Not clear.

In the evening, seven or eight officials, including the Chiliarch, had a large table put in place and stood round it. They had Chŏng Po brought before them and asked, "Is it true that your group had fourteen boats?"

Chŏng Po replied, "No. We had only one boat."

They motioned Chŏng Po out, had me brought in, and asked, "How many boats did you start out in?"

I said, "Only one."

They said, "Fourteen Japanese boats were sighted from above our coast. They were anchored together at sea yesterday. Because of the Stockade Commander's report, therefore, we have already reported the fact to our superiors. Where did you put the other thirteen boats?"

I said, "When I arrived at the coast, men of your country were sailing there in six boats. We moored together. If you question the men of those six boats, you will know how many boats we had."

They said, "Why have you Japanese come here to raid?"

I said, "I am a Korean. My speech is different from Japanese, my hat and gown are of different style. By those things you can tell us apart."

They said, "Some of the Japanese who are clever at banditry change their clothes and pose as Koreans. How do we know that you are not a Japanese like that?"

I said, "If you observe my conduct and examine my seal, permit, cap, sash, and documents, you can tell the true from the false."

The Chiliarch and others then ordered me to bring my seal and other things and present them as evidence. They asked, "Are you not perhaps Japanese who robbed Koreans and got these things?"

I said, "If you doubt me in the slightest, order me sent to Peking. A word with a Korean interpreter, and the truth will be apparent."

They asked, "What is your name? What are your department and county? What is your official position? On what business did you come to our border? Explain the facts in writing and dare not lie. We shall report this to our superiors."

I said, "My name is Ch'oe Pu. I live in the capital of Naju, Chŏlla Province, Korea. I placed twice on the examination lists, and I have served notably at Court for some years. In the Ninth Month of last year I received the King's command to go to Cheju and other islands, but on the 3rd Day of this Intercalary First Month I was setting out to mourn for my father. Returning home in confusion, I met a wind and was blown to sea, and I happened to come here."

They said, "What was your father's name? What was his position? Where did he die?"

I said, "My father's name was T'aek. He passed the *Chinsa* examination[36] but in order to care for his parents did not take an appointment. He had laid

---

[36]The Korean *Chinsa,* unlike his Chinese confrere, was not qualified for a position in government, which depended on other examinations. The *Chinsa* degree marked principally academic advancement.

aside his mourning clothes scarcely four years when he, too, died in Naju."

When the deposition was finished, they lodged me in the guest house annex and gave me and my staff food.

The people of our country go on official and private business to and from Cheju, and those who meet winds and get lost are beyond counting. Those who finally return home alive are barely one or two in a hundred; is it likely that all of them drown at sea? Those who drift to the island barbarian countries like Siam and Champa have no further hope of returning. Even if they drift to the borders of China, they are still wrongly accused by the people on the coast of being Japanese pirates. If their ears are cut off for the reward, who can tell the truth? How could people like us, if we had not landed beforehand by ourselves or did not have such signs as seals and permits, have escaped disaster?

Let our state follow the system of the Chinese Court and issue to all officials number tablets and pewter tablets with their names and positions thereon in seal characters to identify them. When any official, great or small, is sent anywhere, tallies and halberds should be provided to honor the King's command. Let even people living by the sea, though they cross the sea in private trade, be issued number tablets, inscribed such-and-such country, such-and-such department and district, such-and-such name, such-and-such appearance, and such-and-such date, to identify them. A consul should also be put at Cheju, and all commissioned ministers and magistrates of the three cities should always, coming or going, carry [their tablets] with them to provide for what may happen. If all that is done, then and only then will everyone be able to avoid tragedy.

20th Day. At T'ao-chu Chiliad. This day was alternately cloudy and fair.

I asked the name of the Chiliarch of T'ao-chu Chiliad; it was Ch'ên Hua. Ch'ên Hua came with an official to see me. He pointed to my bamboo hat and said, "What kind of hat is that?"

I said, "This is a mourning hat. It is a national custom for everyone to dwell in a hut by the grave for three years. If, unfortunately, one should be cast adrift like me or must travel far, in order to maintain the mood of grief, one dare not look up at the sun and sky. That is why we have these deep hats."

At meal time, Hsü Ch'ing led me to his table. A man seated there wrote with his chopstick on the table, "Do you eat pork?"

I said, "The people of my country observe mourning for three years and do not eat fish, meat, preserved meat, oniony plants, or garlic." The man took separate plates, loaded them with vegetable courses, and served them to me.

Hsü Ch'ing then saw that my clothing was not yet dry. He said to me, "It is sunny today; you might take off your clothes and dry them."

I answered, "All my clothes are damp. If I take these off, there is nothing I can wear. I cannot dry them."

Hsü Ch'ing led me to a sunny place and seated me so that I might dry out.

An official came and asked, "Is the King of your country called Emperor?"

I answered, "In Heaven there are not two suns; how under the same Heaven can there be two Emperors? My King's one purpose is to serve your country devotedly."

Then he asked, "Do all the officials of your country really wear rhinoceros [horn] girdles?"

I said, "The first and second ranks wear gold, the third and fourth silver, the fifth and sixth and all those below black horn, but there are no rhinoceros [horn] girdles.[37]

He asked, "Are there gold and silver in your country?"

I said, "Gold and silver are not products of my country."[38]

He said, "But then, how are there gold and silver girdles?"

I said, "They all come in trade from your country. That is why they are prized." When I asked the official who he was, he took out a public document and showed it to me. It [showed that] the Commander had previously dispatched this official with a permit, sending him on to T'ao-chu Chiliad posthaste. He was to place us under guard, question us, and bring us back without fail. This, then, was that Hsieh Min.

Another man came and said, "I am from Ting-hai Garrison, Ning-po Prefecture. I was sent here by the Regional Military Commission [*Tu-chih-hui shih-ssu*] of that place."

I then asked, "Is there a Hsia-shan in Ning-po Prefecture?"

He said, "There is."

I told him about our previous arrival and mooring at Hsia-shan, meeting pirates, and being set adrift again. The man said, "I shall take this paper and inform the Prefect so that he will make inquiries."

I asked his name, which was Wang Hai.

Other outsiders came in crowds and eagerly took paper and brush and asked questions. I could not keep up with them in my answers. An official secretly wrote and showed me a note that said, "The people here are a bad lot. Do not talk with them."

21st Day. At T'ao-chu Chiliad. This day was fair.

People came in crowds to look at me.

Wang Hai pointed to a portrait on the wall and said, "Do you know that picture?"

I said, "I am not acquainted with it."

---

[37]With one exception, the statutory description of Korean officials' formal dress in *KT* (p. 232-235) confirms Ch'oe Pu's list. The exception is for officials of Rank 1, who are said to wear the very rhinoceros horn girdles that Ch'oe Pu denies. Was it in order to remain the good vassal that he did so?

[38]Ch'oe answers diplomatically. In fact, silver and gold deposits existed in Korea, as was known in China. See, for example, *SIK,* p. 32. The Korean government had asked that gold and silver not be required in tribute, a request to which the Chinese Emperor acceded in 1429. Apparently to strengthen the Korean position against the Ming desire for the metals, moreover, the government at one time closed all deposits. See Seno, *(Kinsei-shi),* pp. 40, 41, and Kim Yongdok, in *Korea, Its Land, People and Culture of All Ages* (Seoul: Hakwon-sa, 1960, 718 pp.), p. 46.

Hai said, "It is Chung K'uei, a *Chin-shih* of the T'ang Dynasty."

I said, "Never in his life did Chung K'uei rise to *Chin-shih*. How can you call him a *Chin-shih*?" Wang Hai and the others laughed uproariously.[39]

Then a white-haired old man came, and I asked him, "How many *li* from here are the T'ien-t'ai and Yen-tang mountains?"[40]

The old man answered, "Mt. T'ien-t'ai is north of T'ien-t'ai County, two days' journey from here. Mt. Yen-tang is one day's journey south of Mt. Tien-t'ai.

I then asked, "What is the guardian mountain of this town?"

He said, "Mt. Stone Pillar." He led me outside the gate and pointed out Mt. Stone Pillar, which was, indeed, a mountain of stone cliffs, at the peak of which there was a great stone shaped like a pillar.

I said, "How many *li* is it from here to Peking?"

The old man said, "Over 5,800 *li*."

I asked how many *li* it was to the Yangtze River.

The old man said, "Over two thousand *li* to the north."

I mentioned Yang-chou Prefecture, at which Yi Sŏm had landed, and asked, "How many *li* is it from here?"

The old man said, "After you cross to the north of the Yangtze River, you are in Yang-chou."

I asked how many *li* it was to Nanking.

The old man said, "Over two thousand *li* to the northwest. But all these are only estimates; I should not presume to know."

A great official came, heralds before him and throngs behind, troops impressively drawn up in display. He sat in the Huang-hua-kuan, and I asked about him. He was Liu Tse, Anti-Japanese Commander for Sung-men and Other Places.[41] He called us before him and said, "Since you crossed the border illegally, you ought to be judged by military law, but because I think that some of the circumstances in the case may warrant sympathy, I have not, for the time being, put you to death. State truthfully whether or not you encroached on China, so that we can act accordingly."

I stated, "My name is Ch'oe Pu, and I live in the capital of Naju, Chŏlla Province, Korea. I placed twice on the examination lists and was a minister close to the King. On the 17th Day, Ninth Month of last year, I received the King's command to be a Commissioner for Cheju and other places. Cheju is

[39]Chung K'uei played several roles in Chinese lore, one story making him a patron spirit over aspirants in the state examinations. He had been famous for his literary skill and had passed the metropolitan examinations in first place. He was, however, very ugly, and when he appeared before the emperor to receive the rose of gold that by custom came to the highest candidate, the emperor would not give his confirmation to a man with such a face. In despair Chung threw himself into the sea, only to be rescued and sent to Heaven. See E. T. C. Werner, *Myths and Legends of China*, New York: Brentano's, 1922, p. 106. The laughter of the Chinese shows the pleasure they have taken in Ch'oe's quick recognition of their prank.

[40]In inquiring about Mt. T'ien-t'ai, the great seat of earlier Chinese Buddhism and Yen-tang, famous for its spectacular scenery, Ch'oe again displays elements of his broad knowledge of China.

[41]*Pa-tsung Sung-men teng-ch'u pei-wo chih-hui.* One of six local commanders charged with defense against Japanese, listed twenty-second in the provincial military table. See *WPC* 215: 11r.

in the South Sea and is over one thousand *li* from Naju by sea. On the 12th Day, Eleventh Month of the same year I crossed the sea. I was correcting entries on registers and the work was not completed when I heard, on the 30th Day of this First Month, that my father had died. On the 3rd Day, Intercalary First Month, not waiting for a favorable wind, I set out in confusion to cross the sea. We were driven off course by the wind and in the terrible, mountainous waves, would first almost sink and then almost capsize. We hungered for food, thirsted for water, and almost died. On the 12th Day of this month we arrived at an island, the name of which I do not know, and moored there. Fishing boats came and asked, 'What country are you from?' We answered that we were Koreans and [told] how we came to have gone adrift.

"Then we asked, 'What country's territory is this?'

"The men answered, 'It is Hsia-shan, Ning-po Prefecture, China.'

"That night pirate boats and over twenty men came. They scared us with their swords and wanted to cut off our heads. They seized our clothing, rations, and baggage and then cut away our oars and anchor and left, and we drifted again in the open ocean.

"On the 17th Day we came again to land and moored on a shore the name of which I do not know. Again there were fishing boats, six in a row, and I was afraid that they were of the type of the pirates we had met previously. We left the boat, went ashore, and crossed two ranges. In about six or seven *li* there was a settlement, from which we were passed along successively, reaching Hsien-yen Village at night. The villagers fought to beat us with crooked sticks and rob us. They turned us over to a place where we met an official, and he drove us on to this town."

He then asked, "What was the year in which you placed on the examination list? What offices have you held? In what departments and districts do the men who accompany you live? What articles are in your baggage? How many boats did you have originally?"

I said, "I passed the *Chinsa* examination in third place in 1477, and 1482 I was the first man in the second category of the Civil Service Examination. I have been Writer and Doctor of Learning in the Printing Office, Auditor in the Military Supplies Commission, Archivist in the National Academy, Supervisor in the Office of the Inspector-General, and Assistant Writer and Writer in the Office of Special Counselors. In 1486 I was first man in the second category of the Civil Service Second Examination. I was Junior Fifth Counselor in the Office of Special Counselors, and Lieutenant and Assistant Captain of the Yongyang Garrison.

"Of the men with me, there are four secondary officials—Chŏng Po, an official under the Prefect of Kwangju; Kim Chung, an official of Hwasun District; Son Hyo-ja, an official under the Prefect of Naju; and Yi Hyo-ji, an official under the Prefect of Cheju. There is one companion, Yi Chŏng, from the capital. There is one Security Officer, An Ŭi, from Cheju; one Station Master,

Ch'oe Kŏisan, from Ch'ongam Station, Naju; and two slaves, Makkŭm and another. There are four Cheju public slaves, Kwŏn Song and others; nine loyal escort troops, Kim Sok and others; and twenty marine privates, Hŏ Sang-ni and others. They are all from Cheju.

"We sailed in only one large boat. Masts, sails, and oars were lost when we met the wind, and anchor and oars were lost when we met the pirates.

"As to the things we have, there are one seal, one horse permit, silk gauze hats, horn girdles, pertinent documents, an examination list for my Second Examination, books, one bow, one knife, and the clothes worn by the individual men. There is nothing else."

The Commander checked over the seal and other things. He asked, "How far away is your country? How many prefectures and departments are there? About how great are the military supplies? What things produced in your country do you prize? Which of the books you read do you revere? Your clothing, ceremonies, and music follow the styles of what dynasty? Answer in writing, one by one, as a basis for verification."

I said, "My country is some several thousand *li* away. It has eight provinces, in which the prefectures, departments, counties, and districts total more than three hundred. Our products are talented men, the five grains, horses, oxen, fowls and dogs. The things read and revered are the Four Books and Five Classics. All our clothing, ceremonies, and music honor the Chinese styles. As to military supplies, being a Confucian minister, I have had no experience with them and do not know the figures exactly."

He asked, "Does your country have relations with Japan, Ryukyu and Koryŏ?"[42]

I said, "Japan and Ryukyu are in the great sea to the southeast. They are far away, and we do not communicate with them.[43] Koryŏ has become our present Chosŏn."

He asked, "Does your country, too, pay tribute to our Court?"

I said, "Every year at such times as the Imperial Birthday and the New Year, we most respectfully pay tribute."

He asked, "What regulations does your country have? Do you have your own reign-titles?"

I said, "In our reign-titles and regulations we follow Ming completely."

When the Commander had ended his questioning, he said, "Your state has paid tribute for years; you have acted as a good subject state. Since there is nothing to indicate seditious intent, you shall be treated courteously. Be at

---

[42]Conceivably Liu Tse had an unclear picture of recent history on the Korean peninsula. A map in *WPC* (*ch.* 210, 1v., 2r.), showing Silla between Chosŏn and Japan, indicates that great confusion was possible. Korean communities in China or even ambiguity in names may have obscured conditions. Compare, for example, Fr. Martín de Rada's report of hearing that the nations represented by wards of their own in Peking in the sixteenth century included "Chausin" [Chosŏn] and "Cauli" [Kao-li; Koryŏ]. Boxer, *South China*, p. 303. Or again, Liu may have been setting a trap.

[43]Relations of a sort between Korea and Japanese existed, as the Introduction points out.

ease, each of you, and do not worry; we shall send you to the capital and let you go home. Hurry with your baggage. I will permit no delay." He served us tea and cakes.

I wrote a poem of thanks and bowed. The Commander said, "You need not bow," but I did not understand what he said and ventured to continue bowing. The Commander rose, too, and returned the courtesy.

22nd Day. At T'ao-chu Chiliad. This day was cloudy.

The Commander had me brought before him again. He took the statement of the previous day and scratched off the parts about meeting the bandits at Hsia-shan and being driven and beaten at Hsien-yen and the wordy passages and ordered me to rewrite the sheet. Hsieh Min was standing by the table and said to me, "This document will be presented to the authorities and passed to the Emperor, so the text must be terse. That is why our chief erased the wordy parts, made them more concise, and asked you to rewrite them. You ought not to have misgivings."

I would not write it. I said, "A deposition ought to be honest. Even if it is wordy, what is wrong with that? The part erased, moreover, was the matter of meeting the bandits, yet he has added a line saying, 'The soldiers' clothes were all intact . . .' He has suppressed the truth about my meeting the bandits; what does he mean by that?"

Hsieh Min wrote something secretly and showed it to me. It said, "The present Emperor has recently ascended the throne, and the laws and ordinances are strict. If he were to see what you wrote previously, His Majesty would infer that bandits are rampant and would punish the border commanders. That would be no small matter. As far as you are concerned, you should concentrate on returning home alive instead of making trouble."

I listened to what he said and, thinking it was so, took up the brush and rewrote the statement as revised. Hsieh Min said to me, "You were Auditor in the Military Supplies Commission; why do you say that you do not know the amount of military stores?"

I said, "Before I had been in the Military Supplies Commission a full month, I was transferred. That is why I do not know the exact figures."

He asked, "When you were sailing at sea, how many days was it that you did not eat?"

I said, "From the 3rd Day to the 11th Day."

He said, "But how did you keep from starving to death?"

I said, "For a while we chewed dried rice grains and drank urine. When the urine was gone, we waited for it to rain. We soaked our clothes and drank the moisture from them and prolonged our lives a hair's length. It was just fortunate that we did not die."

He asked, "How old are you?"

I said, "Thirty-five."

He asked, "How many days have you been away from home?"

I said, "There have been six full moons."

He said, "Do you think of home?"

I said, "My father is dead, and my dear mother has already deviated from the custom of our country in weeping for him at home.[44] Now, in addition, she has been led to believe that I have been drowned, so she must be grieving all the more. When I, having now reached a foreign country alive, think of these things, there is not a day that I do not weep bitterly."

He said, "Among those who serve, the state is all, the family forgotten. You drifted here in the King's service; you should turn your filial piety into loyalty. Why brood over family matters?"

I said, "Look for the loyal subject at the gate of the filial son. Never was a man not thoroughly filial to his parents yet loyal to his lord. How can I help but think of my dead father and dear mother, especially when it is already too late to care for one and death from age approaches the other?"

He asked, "What are your King's surname and taboo name?"

I said, "The son in mourning cannot bear to mention the names of his father and mother; he would as soon, therefore, hear of the scandals of others as hear the names of his father and mother. How much less can a subject speak loosely to anyone the taboo name of the ruler of his country?"

He said, "It does no harm when you are beyond the borders."

I said, "Am I not a Korean subject? As one who serves, can I, by crossing the border, turn my back on my country and change my actions and words? I am not like that."

Hsieh Min gave the statement of questions and my answers to the Commander, who alternately read and nodded his head. He turned to me and said, "Tomorrow I shall commission an official to start out with you. Write out, item by item, and bring a list of the baggage that accompanies you, so as to avoid losing it on the road ahead." I withdrew to my quarters.

One Wang K'uang, Hsü Ch'ing's henchman, was there. He had been first intimidating and then beguiling us with insatiable appetite, but in my baggage there was nothing for me to satisfy him with. Now he came again and said, "You must repay my chief's favors." I took off the padded, figured lining I was wearing and gave it to him for Ch'ing's son Lung.

XXX. T'ai-chou is the land of the old Tung-ou-kuo.[45] It was east of Min and south of Yüeh. But such places as Niu-t'ou-wai-yang are in Lin-hai County. In the extreme southeast region of T'ai-chou, then, the wind is warm. It rains most of the time, and it is seldom sunny. It is, in fact, a jungle-like, malarial region.

---

[44]Ch'oe refers to the custom according to which he himself should be the chief mourner at home. See, for example, Yu Chongyol, in *Korea: Its Land, People and Culture*, pp. 620-622.

[45]Tung-ou-kuo was a Han dynasty fief corresponding to Yung-chia-hsien, Chekiang (*SRCY* 471).

I arrived in the First Month, but the weather was the same as that of the Third or Fourth Month. The barley and wheat were about to come to head, bamboo shoots were at their height, and peaches and apricots were in full bloom. The mountains were high, the rivers large, and woods and preserves formed screens and shades. The people were thriving and the houses splendid. *XXX*

23rd Day. Setting out from T'ao-chu Chiliad. This day was cloudy.

The Commander again had me and my staff brought before him and ordered me to call out the names [of the men] and check their number. He commissioned Chiliarch Chai Yung and over twenty military officers to escort us to the Regional Commander [*Tsung-ping kuan*]. I and the subordinate officials rode in sedan-chairs. Yang Tal-hae, a crafty one, pleading illness and leaning on a stick, appeared to be unable to walk, and the Commander allowed him a sedan-chair, too. In all, eight people rode in sedan-chairs.

Chai Yung, Hsü Ch'ing, and Wang K'uang crossed with us over Shan-ch'ang and Wu-t'ou ranges. Between them were three large rivers, and below Wu-t'ou Range was Chien Stream. Hsü Ch'ing took us to a house at the edge of the stream and had food cooked and served to us.

Even though it was night we went on, across T'ang-t'ou-p'u Ridge and other places. We came to a Buddhist temple by the road and lodged there. The village gate in front of it was that of Hsien-yen Village, and the road there from T'so-chu Chiliad was that along which I had previously been driven. That night, Hsü Ch'ing and Chai Yung questioned the head of the village, arrested the fellow who had stolen the horse saddle, reported him to the officials, and returned the saddle to me. We did not get any of the rain hats, net wraps, or other things that had been stolen from the soldiers.

XXX Generally, bandits kill and plunder, and there is no limit to their violence. Now, though some of the Chiang-nan people, driven perhaps by motives of gain, rob and steal, the robbers of Hsia-shan did not kill us, and they even left some things behind. The men of Hsien-yen did not hide what they had stolen and in the end returned the saddle they had taken. From this we can see that their nature is mild and their hearts not wicked. *XXX*

24th Day. Arrival at Chien-t'iao Chiliad. This day was fair.

At dawn we passed Pierced Cliff Village. West of the village was a mountain, and on it were stone cliffs. Its peak was lofty and arched and had a great hole that looked like an arched gate. The village got its name from that. We crossed T'ien Range. At the peak, priests had built a Buddhist temple across the road, and travelers passed through the temple. Though on level ground we sometimes rode in the sedan-chairs, we frequently got out of the sedan-chairs and walked where the ranges were steep and the road difficult. When we came to that temple, we were limping along by whatever means we could. The priests of the temple pitied us, boiled tea and served us, and we stayed a little while.

Going on, we reached a bay in which were warships, all armed and patrolling up and down, looking as if they were in a sea battle. I crossed over in a tender to Chien-t'iao Chiliad. The wall overlooked the shore. The Chiliarch of the place, Li Ang, of powerful physique and handsome appearance, wore armor and carried weapons. He led us through a gate of the wall. The gates were all doubled-walled. The sounds of drums, horns, and fire weapons shook the sea and the hills. All the sournas and other large and small horns curved up in a hook at the ends and faced back toward the blowers' foreheads. The people and houses in the town were even more prosperous than those of T'ao-chu Chiliad.

Li Ang led me to a guest house. He and Chai Yung, Hsü Ch'ing, Wang K'uang, Wang Hai, and a Chuang and Yin from the place — I have forgotten their given names; they were both fat old officials — stood at the left and right of a table. They asked me how I had come to sail adrift, which I briefly outlined to them. Li Ang asked that we go up to the main hall and perform the ceremony between host and guest. Ang went up by the west stairs, I by the east, and we bowed twice to each other. Afterwards, Ang served me tea and fruit and my staff wine and meat. He showed a marked spirit of true hospitality.

The old official named Yin took Chŏng Po and others to his own house. After giving them food and drink, he introduced his wife, concubines, sons and daughters, and they extended greetings. The man's heart was as pure and full as that.

A man brought an abbreviated examination list for 1486 and showed it to me. He said, "This is the notice of my placing in the examinations." He pointed to the two characters "Chang" and "Fu" on the notice and said, "There is my name."[46] Then he asked, "In your country, do they honor those who place on the lists, too?"

I said, "Yes."

He said, "Under our system, all provincial scholars who place on the lists are given public stipends. Banners are displayed at their gates, and on their name cards is written the rank *'Chin-shih* of Such-and-such Place in Such-and-such Section.'" He took me to his house, and in front of the house in the street was, indeed, a gate of two stories and three doors, built of stone pillars carved with dragons. Its glitter and brightness were dazzling. At the top was written large the sign. "House of Chang Fu, Examination of 1486." The reason Chang Fu had shown me this was to boast.

I, too, boasted extravagantly: "I placed on the list twice. I receive two hundred *shih* of rice annually,[47] and my banner gate has three stories. You are

---

[46]Chang Fu is listed as a *Chü-jên* (passed in the provincial examinations) of 1486. *T'ai-chou-fu chih*, 1722 ed., *ch.* 8.

[47]As an Assistant Captain of the Yongyang Garrison, the last post Ch'oe mentioned in his earlier deposition, he held Rank 5b, which provided an annual statutory stipend of 28 *shih* of rice, 15 *shih* of other grains, and smaller

not my equal."

Chang Fu said, "How do I know that?"

I said, "My banner gate is far away, and I cannot bring it here, but I have a short list of the Civil Service Second Examination here." I opened it and showed it to him.

When Chang Fu saw my name and position in the list, he knelt and said, "I am not at all your equal."

25th Day. Arrival at Yüeh-ch'i Police Station [Hsün-chien ssu]. This day was cloudy, with dust blowing.

Li Ang, Hsü Ch'ing, Wang K'uang, Chuang, and Yin escorted me to the sea. Ang took my hands and said, "There was one chance in a thousand years that you and I, from places far apart, would ever meet. Parted we shall not see each other again."

I got into the boat and took my leave with these words: "When I came, General [*Chiang-chün*], you lined the wall and filled the gates with thousands of arms and shields. Masses of pennants fluttered. Gongs and drums rumbled. You displayed your might to a stranger, General.

"When I lodged at the inn, you went up to the main hall and performed the ceremony faultlessly. You served us food in great abundance. The sincerity in your heart was apparent; at a glance, it was as if we were old friends. You treated a stranger generously, General.

"As I leave, you walk out west of the city, escorting me a long way to a nook of the sea. You help me into the boat and say good-bye to me. You accompany a stranger kindly, General.

"I am a stranger, we have not been acquainted a day. Yet you have shown me your might, treated me generously, and taken leave of me kindly. Certainly that shows your feelings that though my Korea is beyond the sea, its clothing and culture being the same as China's, it cannot be considered a foreign country. That is especially so now, with Great Ming's unification and Hu and Yüeh under one roof. All under Heaven are my brothers; how can we discriminate among people because of distance? That is particularly true of my country, which respectfully serves the Celestial Court and pays tribute without fail. The Emperor, for his part, treats us punctiliously and tends us benevolently. The feeling of security he imparts is perfect.

"But I am a Korean minister. You, too, General, are the Emperor's minister outside the gates, and you embody the Emperor's love of the humble. Is it not also loyal service to treat a stranger to this extent? The magnanimity of your

amounts of oil, cloth, and money. In addition, he probably received income from "stipend lands" that went with offices, but his full statutory income must not even have approached 200 *shih*. See *KT* 169-184. A Chinese official of the same rank nominally received 168 *shih*. See *TMHT, ch.* 29, 4*r*. Seida Tansō, the Japanese Confucian translator of the diary, finds Ch'oe's boasting distasteful, not because it concerns personal wealth but because petty sums are involved. If the poor Korean, he says, were told about the richness of Japanese daimyo, he could not believe it. It would be like "telling a summer bug about ice." *Tōdō kōtei-ki, ch.* 2, First Month, 25th Day. Seida's own stipend was about 25 *shih*. See Hara Zen and Tōjō Kō, *Sentetsu sōdan, kōhen*, p. 155.

feelings in this period I have felt deeply. Though I have not had a day's free time to talk at leisure with you, General, and the two officials Chuang and Yin, to reveal what is in my heart, I shall always remember you, as long as I live and no matter how far away I am."

Then I took leave of Hsü Ch'ing, saying to him, "You, General, and your Wang K'uang met me at the village of P'u-fêng, filled me in the last stage of my hunger and thirst, and put life into me when I should long before have died. Over many *li* of dangerous ground, to Tu-tu-ch'ang,[48] to T'ao-chu Chiliad, and to this town, for seven or eight days you have helped and protected me. The extent of your kindness is immeasurable. Once we have parted, it is unlikely that we shall meet again, and I am sadder for that."

I then bade them leave and, riding in the same boat as Chai Yung, went across a sea. Yung said to me, "When one sails out into this sea, Mt. T'ien-t'ai is visible in the west, but it happens to be cloudy and foggy everywhere now, and we shall not get to see it."

In the evening we arrived at Yüeh-ch'i Police Station, Ning-hai County. The town was at the top of a mountain, and troops, all wearing armor, lined the shore. Yung and his staff got out of the boat and went into the town, leaving us on the shore. I do not know what they did.

26th Day. Passing Ning-hai County. This day it rained.

On the shore opposite the police station was Yüeh-ch'i Stop [*P'u*]. We left the boat in front of the stop and went by land. We walked along the bank of the stream, the mouth of which, where it entered the sea, was very wide. I do not know the source from which it came. We crossed Hsi-yang Range and Hsü-chia Mountain and came to Shih-ao Stop. The people at the stop served us many cups of tea. We went on and reached Pai-ch'iao Range. Over twenty soldiers had come there carrying sedan-chairs to greet us. Eight of us riding again, we passed Chin-shih-fang and came to Pai-ch'iao Station [*I*] of Ning-hai County. The station was in the county seat, and the County Magistrate, T'ang, served us food. We ate enough to be full and then got into the sedan-chairs and went on, braving the rain. We passed T'ung-shan Stop, Mei-lin Stop, Chiang-[chi?] Range, Kang-k'ung Stop, and Hai-k'ou Stop. In the interval there were three big rivers and two big bridges, the names of which I have forgotten. In the second watch of the night we came to Hsi-tien Station and put up there. The station was guarded like a defense point by armed men.

27th Day. At Hsi-tien Station. This day there were high wind and heavy rain. The stream was a flooding torrent. We had no alternative to staying at Hsi-tien Station.

28th Day. Arrival at Lien-shan Station. This day it rained hard.

Chai Yung said to me, "The laws of China are strict; if there is the slightest

---

[48]The correct form for what was previously written Yü-tu-ch'ang.

delay, it will bring punishment upon us. It is raining hard now, but we cannot stay longer."

Neither Chai Yung's military officers nor my own staff were willing to go. They said, "The rain today is extremely heavy, and the water is overflowing the gorge. We cannot go."

Chai Yung said, "The waters of the gorge are in flood, but they will recede. The supplies of this station, moreover, are limited. Yesterday's [unscheduled] stay has already strained its resources." With that he went with us into the rain, [past Shan-hsü Stop, Shang-t'ien Stop, and beyond].

We stopped at Lien-shan Station in Feng-hua County. The county seat was two *li* east of the station, and the County Magistrate was named Tu An.[49] The Station Master saw that the rain had soaked through our clothing and that the cold had raised goose flesh on our bodies. He then had stumps kindled in a hollow in front of the main hall, and I and my staff sat in a ring close to the coals to warm ourselves. A man came from outside and, surly and malicious, kicked and trampled on the stump fire. We were frightened and ran for cover.

Both Chai Yung and the Station Master were humiliated by him. Chai Yung said to me, "This man, having been told by someone that you were bandits, did not want the station officials to give you supplies. I explained to him that you are a well-read gentleman, but he was still enraged. You may write a deposition saying that he took away your clothes, packages, and so forth, and present it to the County Magistrate."

I said, "I certainly want the man's wickedness to be punished, but to accuse him falsely of seizing what has not been seized and to bring the man down for something of which he is not guilty, is highly contrary to justice. You, now, have come to protect us; it would not be unreasonable for you to handle the man by accusing him of assault." Chai Yung then wrote a deposition and sent it to the county officials.

29th Day. Passing Ning-po Prefecture [Fu]. This day it rained.

Chai Yung and we rode in sedan-chairs and crossed a large river. On the bank of the river was an extremely beautiful Buddhist temple, in front of which were five small pagodas and two big ones. Then we passed [from Hsü-pai-kuan to the Pei-tu River].

From Niu-t'ou-wai-yang northwest to Lien-shan Station, mountain peaks rose everywhere in clusters and ranges, some crossing others. Rushing streams and steep cliffs were scattered through them thickly. When we reached that river, flat, open lands and broad fields were apparent at a glance. We saw the distant mountains only as eyebrows. On the north shore of the river an embankment had been built, which was a place up over which boats were pulled. North of the embankment a levee had been built to canalize the river. Tenders

---

[49]Tu An was the Vice Magistrate sometime in the 1480's. A "sub-official" *(li-yüan)*, he probably lacked the academic standing to have been promoted to Magistrate. See *Feng-hua-hsien chih* (1908 ed.), *ch.* 16; 27*r*.

were moored to the bank in a row.

Chai Yung led us into the boats, and we passed thirteen stone bridges and went more than twenty *li*. On the east levee of the river, village gates were everywhere. To the southwest we saw the Ssu-ming Mountains, adjoined to Mt. T'ien-t'ai in the southwest and to the K'uai-chi, Ch'in-wang, and other mountains in the northeast. It was where Ho Chih-chang had been when he was young.[50]

We rowed up to the wall of Ning-po Prefecture. The wall was built across the stream, and all the gates of it were double and of two stories. Outside the gates was a second wall, and the moat, too, was double. All the gates of the wall were arched and had iron doors that would admit a single boat. We rowed inside the wall and came to Shang-shu Bridge. Beyond the bridge the width of the river was about five hundred feet. We passed Hui-cheng Bridge and She-chi-t'an. Altogether we passed more than ten big bridges in the town. I cannot record adequately the wonderfully beautiful sights. We rowed out the north gate, which was the same as the south gate. I do not know the circumference of the wall, but the prefectural capital, Ning-po Garrison, the seat of Yin County, and Ssu-ming Station were inside it.

We reached and passed Ta-te Bridge, which had three arches. It was raining extremely hard, and we moored for the night in the river.

1st Day, Second Month. Passing Tz'u-ch'i County. This day it rained.

We passed [two places] and came to the Shrine of General Shih of the Sung Dynasty.[51] The shrine was as big as a public office and had a gate with banners. From the wall of the prefecture to that place was over ten *li*. In that distance, on both banks of the river, markets and warships were gathered like clouds. After we had passed there, pines, bamboos, and citrus and orange trees lined the banks in groves.

[We went on to Ch'e-chiu Station.]

2nd Day. Passing Yü-yao County. This day was cloudy.

We started early, the boats going upstream to the northwest. The rivers and mountains were big, the fields broad, and the settlements thick. The scenes of beauty were innumerable. [We went from Wu-ling Shrine by way of Yü-yao County to the Shang-yü River.]

3rd Day. Passing Shan-yü County. This day was fair.

We went upstream past two big bridges. On the south side of the river, an

---

[50]The famous T'ang poet (d. 659) lived for a time at Moon Lake, southwest of Ning-po. *Ning-po-fu chih* (1846 ed.), *ch.* 10; 8r., v.

[51]Shih Shou-hsin (926-984) was one of the greatest lieutenants of the founder of the Sung dynasty, but the story of the shrine concerned an event more than a century after his death. In the *Chien-yen* period (1127-1130), Emperor Kao Tsung was touring the region when men of the Chin state, Sung's northern enemy, attacked the party. During the battle, a dense fog suddenly turned day into night. Divine soldiers appeared across the field, at their head a great banner inscribed, "General Shih." Immediately the Chin men turned and fled, to be caught and defeated later. The Emperor escaped by sea. *Ning-po-fu chih, Ch.* 10; 11r. The story, if Ch'oe heard it, may have appealed too little to his rational disposition to merit recording.

official came riding in a sedan-chair. He was the Magistrate of Shan-yü County and he came from the county seat, which was two or three *li* from the bank of the river.

We then passed [more bridges, stops, and a gate and] came to Ts'ao-ê Station, where the Station Master was Hsü Shen. An embankment was north of the station. We left the boats, passed the embankment, walked to the Ts'ao-ê River, and went straight across it. On the opposite bank was another embankment, which faced the Liang-hu Police Station north to south. Again we left the boats and walked past the embankment, coming to Tung-kuan Station, two *li* to the west. We got into boats again and [proceeded past several stops]. In the fourth watch of the night we reached the bank of a river, the name of which I do not know, and moored for the night.

4th Day. Arrival at Shao-hsing Prefecture. This day was fair.

We poled into the Chien River and went upstream. The river came as a branch from Lake Ching, meandering round and through towns. At sunrise we reached Shao-hsing Prefecture. From south of the wall we went up the Ching River, first east and then north, passed Ch'ang-an Stop, and rowed inside the wall. The wall had an arched gate just at the mouth of the river. [The gate] was quadruple, and in each [section] an iron door was hung, through which we passed. There were Kuang-hsiang Bridge, four other big bridges, Ching-k'uei Gate, Lien-kuei Gate, Yu-sheng-kuan, and a hydrographic marker.

When we had gone about ten *li*, there was a public office, and Chai Yung led us on to the bank. The profusion of gates and crowds of people were three times as great as those of Ning-po Prefecture. Supreme Anti-Japanese Commander and Concurrent Assistant Military Commissioner Huang Tsung, Chekiang Surveillance Vice Commissioner for the Maritime Circuit Wu Wen-yüan, and Right Assistant Administration Commissioner Ch'en T'an, sat in a row along the north wall of the Ch'eng-ch'ing Hall.[52] Arms, armor, and bamboo

---

[52]Provincial government in the Ming dynasty had come under three separate offices that divided responsibility roughly according to administrative, surveillance, and military spheres and were called respectively the Provincial Administration Office, Provincial Surveillance Office, and Regional Military Commission. Together, they were often called the Three Authorities or Three Offices *(San-ssu)*, as Ch'oe will address his questioners. The heads of the three offices were supposed to decide major questions in conference, but their failure or inability to do so led frequently to the appointment of extraordinary officials to take special charge of some provincial matters or to coordinate the work of the three offices. Later, broadly empowered officials, in effect governors or even viceroys with authority over several provinces, became established as leaders of regional administrations. See Hucker, pp. 39-42; *TRD* VIII: 152, 153.

Here, however, the three men about to question Ch'oe represent the Three Offices, showing that at mid-dynasty Chekiang government proceeded on some matters, the present one concerning coastal security, by conference. Huang Tsung, as *Tsung-tu pei-wo shu tu-chih-hui ch'ien-shih,* is of third rank in the Regional Military Commission but specially charged with the defense of the whole province against Japanese and the fifth-ranking officer in the provincial military table. See *WPC* 215: 10r. Wu Wen-yüan, as *Hsün-shih hai-tao Che-chiang an-ch'a ssu fu-shih,* is in the second rank in the Provincial Surveillance Office, but since it is his principal duty to supervise and administer naval units in the Chekiang sea, his position also stands in the provincial military table, ranking sixth. See *TRD* VIII: 152, 153 and *WPC* 215: 10r. Nevertheless, Wu, a *Chin-shih* of 1466, belongs primarily in the civil bureaucracy and will later become Surveillance Commissioner of Honan. See *FSJW* 72: 30v.; *LTFC* 11: 10r. Ch'en T'an, as *Pu-cheng ssu fen-shou yu-ts'an-i,* represents the Provincial Administration Office and administers one of the Circuits *(Tao)* into which the province is divided. See Hucker, pp. 43, 44. Wu Wen-yuan and Ch'en T'an are on the rosters in *Che-chiang t'ung-chih* (1884 ed., 280 *ch.*) 118: 19r., 25v.

whips were massed like a forest in front of them. They had a table placed and summoned me to it; I stood facing west. They asked me my name, where I lived, what my position was, the circumstances of my being blown adrift, whether it was true that we had not pillaged, and whether we had implements with us. I answered with the answers I had given the Commander, but I added that we had met bandits at Hsia-shan and been beaten at Hsien-yen. To the [list of] baggage we had I also added one horse saddle.

The three high officials then handed down the Commander's report and showed it to me. They said, "Why are there discrepancies in certain details?"

I said, "It is only that in the beginning, when the Commander questioned me, I answered only with the circumstances of our sailing adrift and arriving here. Today, when you Three Authorities question me again, I inform you in detail about our meeting bandits and other things."

The three high officials said to me gravely, "The statements differ; truly you have done wrong. You must copy your previous statement so that there is exact agreement." I copied it. They then said to me, "Later, when you reach Their Excellencies the Grand Defending Overseer and Three Resplendent Authorities[53] of Hang-chou and the Ministries of War and Rites at Peking, you will be questioned again on the circumstances. Then use this again to answer them. It will never do if there is the slightest discrepancy." They then said, "At first we took you to be Japanese ships plundering, and we were going to arrest and execute you. If you are a Korean, write and bring to us [a statement of] the historical periods of your country, its changes of rule, the capital cities, the geography, the people, the customs, sacrifices, rules for mourning, population, military system, land tax, and styles of dress. We shall compare it with the Histories and note what is and is not so."

I said, "On the changes of rule and capital cities, at first Tan-gun and T'ang Yao rose side by side. The country was named Chosŏn, and the capital was P'yŏngyang. The succession continued for over one thousand years. Wu-wang of Chou enfeoffed Kija (Chi Tzu) in Chosŏn. He made P'yŏngyang the capital and instructed the people in eight articles. The observance by the people now of customs based on ritual (li) and righteousness (i) began from that. When Wei Man of Yen fled, he entered Chosŏn and turned out Kija's descendant Kijun. Kijun fled to Ma-han and made his capital there. About this time, [the country may have been called] Kukwan, I-pu, Sagun, or Sam-han. It was a remote era, and the details are not clear.[54] With the time of Hsüan-ti of Western Han

---

[53]*Chen-shou t'ai-chien hsiu-i san-ssu.* Overseer *T'ai-chien* was a title given to ranking eunuchs. The appointment of an Overseer as Grand Defender at Hang-chou, capital of the provincial administration, illustrates one extraordinary use the Emperor was making of his eunuchs, who may have numbered 10,000 at the time. See Hucker, pp. 10, 11, 24, 25. The term Three Authorities does not usually bear the prefix "Resplendent," literally "Embroidered-gowned," in Ming documents. Precedents for the prefix exist in, for example, the Han dynasty title Resplendent Censor (*Hsiu-i yü-shih*), which may have been echoed occasionally in later titles.

[54]For reviews of modern scholarship on early Korea and comments on the traditional account, which Ch'oe summarizes here, see Gregory Henderson, "Korea through the Fall of the Lolang Colony," *Koreana Quarterly* I: 1 (Autumn, 1959), pp. 147-168; and George McAfee McCune, *Notes on the History of Korea: Early Korea, Research*

[r. 73-49 B.C.], the Pak family of Silla first established a state. The Ko family of Koguryŏ and the Puyŏ family of Paekche rose one after another. They divided into three the land of the old Chosŏn. Silla occupied the southeast area and made Kyongju its capital. Koguryŏ occupied the northwest area and made Liao-tung and P'yŏngyang its capitals; it shifted boundaries several times, but I have forgotten the places. Paekche occupied the central and southwest areas and made Chiksan, Kwangju, Hamyang, Kongju, and Puyŏ [successively] its capitals. In the reign of Kao Tsung of T'ang [r. 650-683], King Wen-wu [r. 661-681] of Silla and T'ang soldiers destroyed Koguryŏ and then Paekche and united the three countries.[55] Later, Chinwŏn rebelled and occupied Chŏnju, and Kungye rebelled and occupied Ch'ŏlwŏn. The Wang family of Koryŏ had great merit and were full of virtue, and the people of the country gave them their allegiance. Kungye fled, Chinwŏn gave himself up, and the King of Silla sealed his treasury and storehouses, made a register of his counties and districts, and surrendered. The three states were again united,[56] and Kaesong was made the capital. The line of succession continued almost five hundred years. The present change is to our Chosŏn, with Hamyang[57] the capital. That is how it has been now for almost one hundred years.

"As to geography, the Changbaek Mountains are in the northeast. They are also called the Paedu Mountains and extend more than one thousand *li,* for over two hundred of which they rise to great heights. On one of the peaks is a deep lake, more than eighty *li* round. Its water flows east as the Tuman River, south as the Yalu River, northeast as the Sokp'yŏng River, and northwest as the Song-hwa River (Sungari River). Downstream the Sungari is the Kondong River. The Myohang Mountains are in the north; the Kŭmgang Mountains, with over twelve thousand peaks, in the east; the Chiri Mountains in the south; and the Kŭwol Mountains in the west. The above four ranges have extremely high peaks and many spectacular sights. Mt. Samgak is the guardian mountain of the national capital. The Taedong River, Sa River, Imjin, Tohan River, Naktong River, Nŭngjin, Tou-ch'ih-chin,[58] and Yongsan-jin are the largest of the rivers.

"As to the personages, from Silla there have been Kim Yu-sin, Kim Yang, Ch'oe Ch'i-wŏn, and Sŏl Ch'ong; from Paekche Kyehaek; from Koguryŏ Ŭlchi Mun-dŏk; from Koryŏ Ch'oe Chung, Kang Kam-ch'an, Cho Chung, Kim

---

Monographs on Korea I: 1, Korean Research Associates, Hamilton, New York (?), 1952.

I have changed Wan-han, as it is in the text, to Ku-hwan, a possible designation of nine tribes referred to in early accounts. The I-pu may have been Lo-lang and Hsüan-t'u (*c.* 82 B.C.–A.D. 204), reduced from the Sagun (Lo-lang, Hsüan-t'u, Lin-t'un, and Chen-fan) established by the Han occupiers (*c.* 108–82 B.C.). The Sam-han may have existed in the first half-millenium B.C.

[55]Silla: ?57 B.C.–A.D. 935. Koguryŏ: ?37 B.C.–A.D. 668. Paekche: ?18 B.C.–A.D. 660. He neglects to mention a community called Karak, Imna, Mimana or other names (?A.D. 43-562), in the southern part of the peninsula. Whether it was independent or a Japanese enclave is disputed.

[56]Koryŏ: 918-1392.

[57]A Chinese name for Seoul.

[58]Faulty text? No such river identified.

Ch'wi-ryŏ, Wu T'ak, and Chŏng Mong-ju; and from our Chosŏn too many to list.[59]

"As to customs, we esteem the codes of etiquette *(li)* and righteousness *(i)*, we understand the Five Relationships, and we respect Confucian methods. Every year in spring and fall we observe the Feast for the Care of the Old, the Regional Archery Ceremony, and the Regional Wine Ceremony.[60]

"As to sacrifices, there are altars of the soil and grain, ancestral temples, the Rite to Confucius, and the mountains and rivers.

"The penal code follows the *Great Ming Code*.[61] The rules of mourning follow Chu Hsi's *Chia li*. In our dress we follow Chinese styles.

"As to the population, military system, and land taxes, I, being a Confucian minister, do not know the details."

Next they asked, "What do you mean by your statement about correcting entries on registers?"

I said, "Cheju is in the great sea, and the sea lanes are extremely dangerous

[59]Ch'oe's list suggests his idea of what was best in Koreans of the past. Presumably he commends the same qualities to the Chinese and his own King. Among the men he has chosen, the outstanding characteristics are Confucian scholarship and statecraft and military genius. Kim Yu-sin (b. 595) distinguished himself as a warrior against Koguryŏ and Paekche and led the Silla army that allied with T'ang forces to attack Paekche. Kim Yang (d. 857), a statesman, was a power behind the Silla throne in the ninth century. Ch'oe Ch'i-wŏn (858-951) went to China in his boyhood, passed the *Chin-shih* examinations, and served in T'ang government before returning home to hold high offices and establish a reputation as one of the earliest great Confucianists. Well before that, Sŏl Ch'ong (fl. 680) had been known for his Confucian scholarship and the development of the *i-du* method of inflecting Korean in Chinese characters.

That Silla was close to T'ang through cultural inspiration if not always through politics may establish it as more civilized in Ch'oe's eyes than the two other contemporary Korean states and as richer in great names. The other states of the period, Paekche and Koguryŏ, though they impress him not especially through their scholars, remind him of great warriors. The one Paekche great in the list, Kyehaek, led Paekche forces against T'ang and Silla in 660; Koguryŏ's great, Ŭlchi Mun-dŏk, was the genius behind the victories over the Sui armies early in the seventh century.

From the history of Koryŏ, a state associated above all with Buddhism, Ch'oe selects men famous as Confucianists or warriors. Ch'oe Chung (984-1068), writer, minister, and teacher, is sometimes called the Confucius of Korea. Kang Kam-ch'an (d. c. 1024) was a scholar, official, and defender against the Khitan. Cho Chung (d. 1220) was both statesman and general. Kim Ch'wi-ryŏ (alive 1218) was a great general, and Wu T'ak (1266-1342) was an early exponent of Neo-Confucianism.

Last on the list comes Chŏng Mong-ju (1320-1392), whose spirit inspired the *Sallim hakp'a*, Ch'oe's own school. To include his name asserts not only reverence for an intellectual master but also, in the light of the literati purges that began toward the end of Ch'oe's life, a political position. Chŏng was the most famous opponent, on grounds of principle, of the revolt of Yi Sŏng-gye, founder of Chosŏn, himself a great general conspicuously absent from the list. Followers of Chŏng figuring among the victims of the later purges, Ch'oe must have known that his list had come to the borders of controversy and had better be closed at the founding of Chosŏn.

For Kim Yu-sin see Hyeon Sang-yun, "A History of Thought in Korea," Part I, *The Journal of Asiatic Studies* III: 2 (December, 1960), pp. 279, 280; Clarence Norwood Weems, ed., *Hulbert's History of Korea*, New York; Hillary House, 1962, 2 vols., I: ED 96-99, 105-108; *CJM* 1017-1019. For Kim Yang see *CJM* 1022. For Ch'oe Ch'i-wŏn see Hyeon, "History," p. 286; Weems I: 124; *CJM* 1391. For Sŏl Ch'ong see Hyeon, "History," pp. 285, 286; *CJM* 1791, 1792. For Kyehaek see *CJM* 1544. For Ŭlchi Mun-dŏk see *CJM* 1. For Ch'oe Chung see Hyeon, "History," (Part II: *The Journal of Asiatic Studies* IV: 1) pp. 342, 343; *CJM* 1361, 1362. For Kang Kam-ch'an see *CJM* 1168, 1169. For Cho Chung see *CJM* 1610, 1611. For Kim Ch'wi-ryŏ see *CJM* 1035, 1036. For Wu T'ak see *CJM* 1293. For Chŏng Mong-ju see Hyeon, "History," Part II, pp. 343, 344; *CJM* 1751, 1752.

[60]Authority for the three ceremonies rests in the Chinese classics *Li chi (Yüeh-ling* 71), *I li (Hsiang she li)*, and *I li (Hsiang yin-chiu li)* respectively. Korean regional officials conducted the rites as examples to encourage virtuous conduct, treating the aged, respectful sons, loyal subjects and the like among the people to ceremonial drinking, eating, and entertainment. The Feast for the Care of the Old was also held annually at the Court for government workers eighty years or more old. Their wives attended a separate banquet in the inner apartments. See *KT*, pp. 265, 266 and Lee Man Kyoo (Yi Man-gyu), *Chosun Kyoyook Sa (Chosŏn kyoyuk-sa)*, Seoul: Uryu Munhwasa, 1947, pp. 243, 244, 246.

[61]Confirmed by *KT*, p. 469.

and long. All criminals flee there to escape. It has long been a refuge for out-laws in flight, so we go and investigate."

They asked, "How many *li* is it from China to Cheju?"

I exaggerated the length of the sea route and said, "I do not know exactly, but generally a boat that meets favorable winds in the great sea can go one thousand *li* a day. We, now, sailed at sea a total, combining days and nights, of twenty-nine full days. We were driven by high winds and raced along as if we were flying, coming down to the Chinese coast. The distance, then, from China to Cheju must be roughly several tens of thousands of *li*."[62]

They asked, "About how far is your country from our Court?"

I said, "I have heard that it is more than 3,900 *li* from the capital of our country to the Imperial capital, going across the Yalu River and through the town of Liao-tung."

The Regional Commander and the other two high officials[63] served me tea and fruit and wrote a list of things to be presented to me. The list [read],

"Honoraria for the Escorted Minister Ch'oe
One plate of pork
Two ducks
Four chickens
Two fish
One beaker of wine
One plate of rice
One plate of walnuts
One plate of vegetables
One plate of bamboo shoots
One plate of wheat noodles
One plate of jujubes
One plate of bean-curd."

They gave food and drink and other things to the secondary officials and the soldiers according to their rank.

I wrote a poem of thanks and bowed twice. The three statesmen also rose and returned the courtesy with respect. They said to me, "We see from your poem of thanks that you are familiar with the geography of this region. How did you acquire such knowledge? It must have been explained to you by natives."

I said, "No one is close to me here, and my language is not understood. Who would talk with me? I have studied maps of China, and now I have simply drawn on my memory."

When the interview ended, I and three or four officials were standing, hands folded, at the table. Outside, one of Chai Yung's military officers was beating

---

[62] As the crow flies, 1200 *li* from Cheju to Niu-t'ou-wai-yang seems truer.

[63] *Tsung-ping kuan san shih-hsiang*. Literally, "the three deputies of the Regional Commander." The Regional Commander, a title for an officer commanding a large region, would refer in this sense to the Grand Defending Overseer. See Hucker, p. 62. The title in its next two occurrences refers, however, as Ch'oe says near the beginning of Book II, to Assistant Commissioner Huang Tsung, whose special assignment against Japanese apparently makes him a Regional Commander. The phrase should be *Tsung-ping kuan teng san shih-hsiang,* as it appears at the beginning of Book II.

and hurting Kim To-jong, a member of my staff. I wrote [an account of the incident] and showed it to the officials. One official hurried to report it to the Regional Commander, who had the attacker seized and punished by flogging. He also had Chai Yung flogged for not having been able to keep order.

We withdrew and again went along the lake. We rowed out through the wall, passed Ying-en Bridge, arrived in front of P'eng-lai Station, and stopped for the night. In the evening the Prefect, named Chou, and the Magistrates of the two counties K'uai-chi and Shan-yin sent abundant amounts of food and drink.

BOOK II

5th Day. Arrival at Hsi-hsing Station. This day was fair.

At dawn the three high officials, the Regional Commander and the others, arrived together in sedan-chairs at P'eng-lai Station. They had me and my staff, bringing our baggage, brought before them again and had everything laid out and examined carefully, one by one. Of the things I had, one seal, one horse permit, one saddle, and a number of documents went into one large and one small box. The clothes, rain hat cords, and bronze bowls went into one small leather bag. My hats were together in a small box. Chŏng Po, Kim Chung, Son Hyo-ja, Yi Chŏng, An Ŭi, Yi Hyo-ji, Ch'oe Kŏisan, and the two slaves had nothing, [their things] being wrapped with the soldiers'. Some of the soldiers had bundles, some bags, and some nothing. When the check was over, they said to me, "You may proceed. When Their Excellencies the Grand Defending Overseer and Three Resplendent Authorities of Hang-chou question you again, make distinct answers, one by one. Let there be no confusion or contradictions." They served us tea and fruit, and I took my leave. Regional Commander was a term used in reference to the Assistant Commissioner.

Shao-hsing Prefecture was the old capital of the kings of Yüeh. In Ch'in [221 B.C.-207 B.C.] and Han [202 B.C.-A.D. 220] it was K'uai-chi-chün and was in the lower reaches of Che-tung.[1] The prefectural capital, the seats of K'uai-chi County and Shan-yin County, the headquarters of Shao-hsing Garrison and Mt. Wo-lung are within the wall. Mt. K'uai-chi is over ten *li* east of the wall. East, south, and west, other high mountains, such as Ch'in-wang, rise in many lofty ranges, covered with rocks and cliffs and vying in grace. The north borders the sea and lies level, without hills. Lan-t'ing, on top of Lou-kung-pu in front of T'ien-chang Temple, was the place where Wang Hsi-chih held a purification ceremony.[2] Lake Ho-chia is more than ten *li* southwest of the wall. The site of Ho Chih-chang's Thousand Autumns Hermitage [*Ch'ien-ch'iu kuan*] is there.[3] Yen Stream is in Sheng County, south of the

---

[1] The part of Chekiang Province southeast of the Che River was called Che-tung.

[2] The famous calligrapher, A.D. 321-379, took part in a purifying or exorcising rite of a kind usually held on the shore of a body of water on the 3rd Day of the Third Month. He commemorated it in his *Lan-t'ing Preface*. See *TRD* I: 329.

[3] When the poet-official was eighty-six he fell sick and asked the Emperor for permission to go home and live as a Taoist recluse. The emperor not only agreed but also provided him a dwelling, among other things, naming it Thousand Autumns. See *T'ang shih chi-shih*, Chi Yu-kung, comp., *(Ssu-pu ts'ung-k'an*, 1st series), *ch.* 17: 1v.

Ch'in-wang Mountains. It is over one hundred *li* away from the prefecture and was the stream on which Tzu-yu sought out Tai K'uei.[4]

The river system has four main streams. One rises in Mt. T'ien-t'ai, T'ai-chou, flows west to Hsin-ch'ang County, continues west to north of Sheng County, passes through K'uai-chi and Shang-yü, and enters the sea. That is the Tung-hsiao River. One rises northwest of Shan-yin, passes east of Hsiao-shan County, enters Shan-yin again, reaches K'uai-chi, and enters the sea. That is the Hsi-hsiao River. One rises east of Shang-yü County, passes through Yü-yao County, goes east through Tz'u-ch'i County to Ting-hai, and enters the sea. That is the Yü-yao River and is the river along which I passed. One rises in Tung-yang, Chin-hua. The P'u River and I-wu flow together and reach Chu-chi County. [The river] passes through Shan-yin to Hsiao-shan and into the Che River. That is the Chu-chi River. Throughout the region, the springs and branch streams that rise and disappear and the dikes and dams that are joined one to another are endless, like a labyrinth of veins and arteries.

I went up the Chien River to the west, [passing from Yün-t'ien Stop to Hsi-hsing Station]. The sky was growing light. The name of the river was Hsi-hsing.

6th Day. Arrival at Hang-chou. This day was cloudy.

Northwest of Hsi-hsiang Station was a broad, level plain, which was the Ch'ien-t'ang River. In flood tides it is a lake, but when the tide ebbs, it is land. On the 18th Day of every Eighth Month there is a big tide with great waves, and the people of Hang-chou watch the bore.[5]

We left the boats in front of the station, went ashore, got into carriages, and went on. In about ten *li* we came to the Che River. We got into boats again and crossed.

The river twists and turns, and the mountains on the side also have the effect of deflecting its waves; that is why it is called Che-chiang, Twisting River . . . The width of the river is about eight or nine *li*. In length, it extends from Fu-chien-lu in the southwest and enters the sea in the northeast. The wall built by Hua Hsin to hold off the tide extends from T'uan-yü-tsui to Fan Village, approximately thirty *li*, and then goes to Fu-yang County, making a total of over sixty *li*. Of stone construction, it is still as good as new. For that reason, the

---

[4]Tzu-yu (Wang Hui-chih, son of the calligrapher Wang Hsi-chih; d. 388), who lived in seclusion, once went in the snow to visit his friend Tai K'uei, or Tai Ta-k'uei, but on reaching the door turned round and went home, explaining that he had started out full of spirits and had come back when they were exhausted. *BD* 2184. Ch'oe's notice of such Taoist stories suggests his interest in more than simply the Confucian history of China.

[5]One of the two greatest tidal bores of the world. The 18th Day of every Eighth Month may tie the event too precisely to the old calendar, but the full moon of the Eighth Month had been known as the time of the greatest bore from the second century B.C. See A. C. Moule, "The Bore on the Ch'ien-t'ang River in China," *T'oung Pao* XXII: 3 (1923), pp. 135-188; and Joseph Needham, *Science and Civilisation in China* (Cambridge: University Press, 1954-, Vols. I-IV[1]) III: 485.

river is also called the Coin Wall (Ch'ien-t'ang) River.[6]

I came to that wall, landed again, and continued on foot. In the west we saw Liu-ho Pagoda, overlooking the river bank. We went past Yen-sheng Temple and Che-chiang Station and came to the south gate of the wall of Hang-chou. The wall was double, the gate multiple, and the gate had a tower of three stories. We went inside the wall, passed Wen-k'uei Gate, Ling-shun-kung, Su-hsien Gate, Ch'eng-ch'ing Gate, Nan-ch'a-yüan, Yu-sheng Hall, T'u-ti Shrine, and Chih-sung-fang Stop, and came to Wu-lin Station. It was approximately ten *li* from the gate of the wall to that station.

Chai Yung had accompanied us for a great distance, over one thousand *li*, in which, except a one-day stop because of rain, we had not delayed and had sometimes travelled at night. Nevertheless, the Grand Defending Overseer, Chang Ch'ing,[7] charged Yung with being dilatory and had him flogged.

In the evening, Yang Hsui-lu, the Station Master, came with food and paid his respects.

7th Day. At Hang-chou. This day was cloudy.

At dawn the Overseer sent an official to question me. He said, "Chŏng In-ji, Sin Suk-chu, Sŏng Sam-mun, Kim Wan-ji, Cho He, Yi Sa-ch'ŏl, Yi Pyŏn, and Yi Kyŏn are all Koreans. What are their positions? Write a report for each of them and bring it here to let me know."

I answered, "Chŏng In-ji, Sin Suk-chu, and Yi Sa-ch'ŏl have reached First Rank. Sŏng Sam-mun has reached Third Rank. Yi Pyŏn, Kim Wan-ji, Cho He, and Yi Kyŏn became *Chinsa* after me, and I do not know their positions or ranks."[8]

One Ku Pi, a fellow who managed things in the station, came and said to us, "Everything you eat is given by the Court. When we calculate our disbursements, we wait a year for the ledgers to reach the Ministry. The Station Master here is a barbarian from Kuei-chou who is as utterly incapable of managing things as a child. He does not know how to provide for all contingencies in his reports to the superiors and brings it about that you do not get enough to eat."

[6]For Hua Hsin, who is supposed to have built the wall in the first century of the Christian era, see Moule, "The Bore," p. 173. The name of the river came not from the wall, as Ch'oe states, but from the region, which was known as Ch'ien-t'ang — the second character originally having been written like the name of the dynasty — before the wall was built. See, for example, Ssu-ma Ch'ien, *Shih chi, Ch'in Shih Huang pen-chi,* 37th year. The view Ch'oe expresses was, however, common among Chinese.

[7]The only other information about Chang Ch'ing to come to my attention supports Ch'oe's impression of his malevolence. When Chang was impeached by a censor, Ch'ang Heng, who is mentioned later in this book, Chang framed charges against the censor, who was demoted. See *CKJM* 1355, 1356; *LCLK Ch'eng-hua* 14, 36v.

[8]I have not searched Chinese records for notices of these men, but some are famous enough to have come to the Overseer's attention through diplomatic reports. Chŏng In-ji (d. 1478), for instance, and Sŏng Sam-mun (1418-?1456) had passed the Civil Service Second Examination, the former in 1427 and the latter in 1447. See *CJM* 1766, 404. Sin Suk-chu (1417-1475), was famous for making thirteen trips to China to consult a Hanlin scholar for advice in the development of *han'gŭl. CJM* 149, 150. No explanation of Ch'oe's failure to mention that these men have died comes to mind. His failure to mention anywhere the recently-invented Korean alphabet (promulgated in 1446), on the other hand, might be expected. His silence would be in keeping with the modest value put upon the system by many Korean literati, but even if he felt otherwise, discretion might urge him not to remind the Chinese that a better script for Korean than theirs had been devised.

Then he said, "The people who come here and look at you are all idlers. Do not talk with them. It is a waste of energy."

In the evening, His Excellency Cheng [Chi],[9] the Surveillance Vice Commissioner for Schools, and another eminent person came to the station. They summoned me before them and asked, "What is the system of scholastic degrees in your country?"

I said "There are the *Chinsa* Examination, *Saeng-wŏn* Examination, Civil Service and Military Service Examinations, and Civil and Military Service Second Examinations."[10]

They asked, "What are those examinations like?"

I said, "Every third year, the most accomplished of the Confucian pupils are brought together and examined in three sessions. The first session comprises two papers in explication, interpretation, or essay [forms on the classics]; the middle session comprises two papers in rhyme-prose [*fu*], memorial [*piao*], or narrative [*chi*] forms; and the last session comprises a problem-essay [*tui-ts'ê*]. From this a certain number of men are selected, and in the spring of the next year they are brought together and examined in three sessions. The first session is recital from memory from the Four Books and Five Classics and expounding on them. Those versed in the Four Books and three of the Classics are passed. The middle session comprises two papers in rhyme-prose, memorial, and narrative forms; and the last session comprises a problem-essay. Thirty-three men are passed. Then the thirty-three are brought together and tested by a problem-essay. The standings are determined and called the Order of Graduates, and permission is given to publish the list. Royal presents of vermilion plaques are made and umbrellas given to the graduates, who parade

[9]Cheng Chi, a *Chin-shih* of 1460, had been appointed to his position in the Chekiang Surveillance Office in 1487. His duties there and his assignment two years after Ch'oe met him to be President of the National University suggest a reputation for academic competence. He was eventually to become Nanking Minister of Revenue. See *CKJM* 1563; *KCLC* 34: 24r.

[10]Ch'oe's first wish is to establish the fact that honor in Korean life follows academic achievement, as in China. The examinations he has named comprised a system quite different from the Chinese in some ways but similar in the kinds of intellectual competence prized. The whole system was too complicated to be described here, but its intellectual substance can be suggested. The *Chinsa* and *Saeng-wŏn* examinations were given to students of regional and capital schools and comprised principally interpretations of the classics and prose composition for the *Saeng-wŏn* and exercises in poetical forms for the *Chinsa*. Students who passed them were not entitled to official employment, though they may sometimes have been employed; their achievement led rather to enhanced social and academic prestige and the opportunity for further study in the central colleges.

The examinations that led to more tangible results were the Civil Service Examinations. It is the principal sequence of these that Ch'oe describes, in a way that differs from descriptions in modern studies only in a few details, in his next statement. His decision to emphasize the Civil Service Examinations is both natural and fortunate, since of all parts of the Korean system they most resembled the Chinese *Chin-shih* examinations in substance and effect.

The Military Service Examinations, like their Chinese counterparts, held little prestige in the eyes of civil officials. The Civil Service Second Examination, on the other hand, signified great achievement. It was held once in ten years for a limited number of officials of Rank 3b or lower. Successful candidates were eligible for appointment to Rank 3a and higher. In addition to the examinations named, extraordinary and specialized examinations in, for example, foreign languages, medicine, Yin-Yang, law, and the arts were conducted; but these would be no more central to Ch'oe's questioners than they were to him.

For the examination system in some detail, see Lee Man Kyoo, *Chosun Kyoyook Sa,* I: 292 *ff.; KT,* pp. 156, 209-16; *KSG,* pp. 164-66. For an indication of the variety of the examinations, see also Choo Young-Ha, *The Education in the Yi Dynasty,* Seoul: The Soodo Women's Teachers College, 1961, English Chapter IV. I am also indebted to Professor Takahashi Tōru of Tenri University and Mr. Key P. Yang of the Library of Congress for helpful conversations.

in the streets for three days. After that, the King gives for them a Banquet of Honor, a Banquet on the Honor to Parents, and a Banquet on the Honor to Ancestors; and they are allowed to enter upon their public careers."

They asked, "What are your literary styles?"

I said, "The memorials follow the polished style of Sung and Yüan, the narratives and essays follow T'ang and Sung. Interpretations are required of passages from the Five Classics, and explications are required of passages from the Four Books. In everything we follow Chinese forms. The problem-essays follow that of *Wen hsüan*."[11]

They asked, "What classics have you mastered?"

I said, "Though I have not studied the Four Books and Five Classics thoroughly, I have browsed in them here and there."

They said, "Name the Classics and the Books in order."

I said, "*The Mean, Great Learning, Analects,* and *Mencius* are the Four Books. The *Book of Changes, Book of Odes, Book of History, Spring and Autumn Annals,* and *Book of Rites* are the Five Classics."

They asked, "What is the significance of the character *i* [change]?"

I said, "In terms of form, the character *i* combines the characters *jih* [sun] and *yüeh* [moon]. In terms of meaning, it has the meaning of 'exchange' and 'substitute'."

They asked, "In what were the diagrams of the *Book of Changes* lodged?"

I said, "The Yellow River put forth the plan, and the Lo River put forth the book. The sages took them as models."

They said, "Without the plan and the book, would it have been impossible to write the *Book of Changes?*"

I said, "All the things of the world have numbers. Though one sees only a rabbit seller, one can deduce the diagrams in the *Book of Changes*."[12]

The two personages stared hard at each other and said to me, "You are truly a well-read gentleman. The people here have not understood that at all."

I have forgotten the given name of His Excellency Cheng. His *hao* was Tung-yüan-tzu and his studio name Fu-chai.

8th Day. At Hang-chou. This day was cloudy.

Ku Pi came and said to me, "I hear now that a man has been commissioned to hurry night and day to Peking to submit a memorial about you. He will not come back until he has a reply. It is about five thousand *li* from here to Peking

[11]*Wen hsüan,* compiled *c.* 530 by Hsiao T'ung, is a selection in sixty *chüan* of choice examples of various forms of writing. Here Ch'oe must refer to the short piece classified *tui-wen* in *Chüan* 45. See *Liu ch'en chu wen hsüan, SPTK,* 1st series.

[12]Ch'oe, after a conventionally modest statement about his knowledge of the classics, demonstrates scholarly familiarity with one of them, the *Book of Changes.* His explanation of the structure of the character *i* was the one generally cited in old dictionaries from the *Shou-wên chieh-tzu* (*c.* A.D. 100) forward; his definition of the character gives the first two meanings found in even modern dictionaries. To explain the source of the diagrams, he quotes from the "Great Treatise" appendix, *I ching, Hsi tz'u* A: 11. On the manifestation of the principles of the diagrams, he appears to quote a commentator, though I have not discovered the source.

on the waterway; you must stay here for many days."

I said, "In coming here with a different language, I am really like one blind and deaf. I hope that you will tell me things that you have seen and heard like this and pity me as a stranger."

Ku Pi said, "The laws of the country are extremely strict, and the punishments decreed are very severe. A new regulation imposes banishment for divulging information to barbarians. Do not show others any of what I have written; it is only for you to know." He bowed and left.

Two officials came and said, "The Supreme Commanding[13] Overseer wants to see the things examined by the Regional Commander—your bow and sword." They took them and left.

A man came and said, "In the Ching-t'ai reign [1450-1456] Supervising Secretary [*Chi-shih-chung kuan*] Chang Ning[14] of our country was made an envoy to your country and wrote 'On Leaving Golden Pavilion' and *Huang hua chi.*[15] Do you know about them?"

I answered, "Supervising Secretary Chang wrote *Huang hua chi* when he came to our country. In it, these lines, entitled 'The Han River Tower,' were much praised:

"'Light plays on the boat with the haw-finch bow,
As I look into the distance—do I see the end of the world?—
I am air-borne; the earth floats under me.'"

The man's face took on a happy expression, and he said, "Supervising Secretary Chang has retired from office and is at home. His house is in Hai-yen County, Chia-hsing Prefecture, one hundred *li* from here. When His Excellency Chang came here to Hang-chou and heard that an educated gentleman from Korea had drifted here from across the sea, he wanted to ask about Korea and waited several days, but he went back a day before you arrived."

I asked the man's name. It was Wang Chieh, and he was a nephew of the Supervising Secretary.

A man who called himself Ch'en Liang came and said, "I went to your country and back with His Excellency Chang Ning [styled] Ching-chih."

I said, "How high did His Excellency Chang rise? Why is he at home and not in office?"

Ch'en said, "He rose in office to Chief Supervising Secretary and later was appointed Censor-in-Chief [*Tu-yü-shih*], but because he had no children he did not take the position. At the age of forty-two he returned home to restore his health."

---

[13] *Tu-tsung,* an inversion of *Tsung-tu,* described in Hucker, pp. 41, 42, but perhaps used here in a complimentary sense, since the title applied most consistently to the Overseer is Grand Defender (*Chen-shou*).

[14] For Chang Ning, *Chin-shih* of 1454, see *MS* 180.

[15] *Huang hua chi* is a conventional title for collections of verse of Chinese envoys abroad and the responses of their hosts. *Huang hua* is an abbreviation of *Huang huang che hua* (*Shih ching, Hsiao ya*), designating an ode on the despatch of an envoy. The figure was applied not only to embassy poetry but also to buildings connected with the despatch of missions. Ch'oe's earlier interview with Liu Tse, for example, took place in the Huang-hua-kuan, which may have had a diplomatic history.

9th Day. At Hang-chou. This day was fair.

The officials who had come the day before and taken the bow and sword came again and said, "Old Grand Defender has kept your bow and sword to look at."

I said, "As you command."

Ku Pi came again and said, "A dispatch came from the naval officers setting forth that you were cruising about with fourteen boats, scourging the sea. Now the Regional Inspector[16] says that if there were fourteen boats, why were they not seized in the first place and brought in? For that he has brought charges against them. The Grand Defender and the Three Authorities discussed the matter without reaching agreement, but since your deposition explained things clearly, they have adjudged that you are not Japanese. They have made their findings and have commissioned Commander [*Chih-hui*] Yang Wang to escort you to the capital, from which you will be sent home.

"There was nothing else. You will be here another three or four days. You may put your mind at ease."

Next, His Excellency the Provincial Administration Commissioner Hsü Kuei and Surveillance Vice Commissioner Wei Fu[17] sat together in the guest house of the station and had us brought to them. They said, "We are sending you back to your country; you may be easy in your mind that you will go home all right."

I wrote a poem to thank them and went back from the house.

Li Chieh, a man from Peking, came and saw that my clothes were tattered and my appearance filthy and said to me, "The people here set store by appearances. That is why all who see you laugh in amazement; they take it that all Koreans are like that. You might wash yourself in a sunny place."

I ordered each of my staff to wash his clothes. Then I sat with Chŏng Po and others in a circle in the sun and bathed away the dirt. Li Chieh came and pointed to the places where my skin had peeled off and my toe-nails fallen out and said, "That is proof that in your sufferings there was no mercy for your body."

I said, "While I was at sea, I vomited several handfuls of blood. There was no saliva in my mouth for three days. Now I realize that my skin, pierced by salt water, has been peeling off and that my feet have been hurt from tramping over difficult ground. I have heard that not daring to injure any part of one's body is the beginning of filial piety. With my body hurt like this, I am certainly not a filial son."

Chieh said, "There is no harm in that. It is not that you have deliberately hurt yourself, Heaven has hurt you. What does it matter, therefore, that you have been hurt? You need not feel badly about it."

[16]*Hsün-an yü-shih.* A censor assigned to a year's tour of a province. See Hucker, pp. 50, 51.

[17]Both men are listed under their offices in *Che-chiang t'ung-chih* 118 (Commercial Press edition of 1934, II: 2091, 2130); for both, however, the given names are written differently.

Li Chieh's friend, whose name I have lost, had a copy of a handbook [*hsiao-hsüeh*] in his sleeve and had Li Chieh present it to me. He wanted a poem. I said, "Accepting someone's gift without merit damages integrity. I make bold to decline it."

Li Chieh said, "This man wants a poem to remember you by."

I said, "I cannot write poems well; I cannot even handle a brush well. I do not want to exchange something not good for something good from him." The man returned the book to his sleeve and left.

Li Chieh said to me, "When the exchange accorded with the Way and the meeting accorded with etiquette, even Confucius accepted something.[18] Why were you so firm in refusing him?"

I said, "That man did not want to give away a book, his mind was on getting a poem. Thus the exchange would not have accorded with the Way, and the meeting would not have accorded with etiquette. Once I accepted, it would have been receiving payment for a poem I had sold. That is why I refused him." Li Chieh agreed and left.

In the evening, Li Chieh, his friend Chin T'ai, and two other men came and served me and my staff food.

10th Day. At Hang-chou. This day was fair.

Ku Pi came and said, "Since you are leaving for the capital, you must know the road ahead. From Su-chou, Hang-chou, Fukien, Kwangtung, and other places in our country, sea-going smugglers go to Champa and Islamic countries and buy red sandalwood, black pepper, and foreign perfumes. The boats go endlessly, and for ten that leave five return. The passage is extremely difficult.

"For going to the capital by water, only the river route is quite good. That is why when Ryukyu, Japan, Siam, and Malacca send tribute [the embassies] all go by way of the Fukien Administrative Region [*Pu-cheng ssu*][19] They land their boats, come to this prefecture, pass Chia-hsing, and reach Su-chou. All the silks and treasures of the Empire come from Su-chou. From Su-chou they pass Ch'ang-chou and reach Chen-chiang Prefecture, where they cross the Yangtze River. The river is more than one thousand *li* from this prefecture. It is violent and fierce and can be crossed only when there are no wind and waves. They cross that river and reach the capital directly. The river route is about a forty-day journey.

----

[18]From *Mencius, Wan chang* B: 4.

[19]Though many embassies went through Fukien, not all of them landed there. Earlier, Ming had established three Maritime Commerce Commissions *(Shih-po t'i-chü ssu)* at Ch'üan-chou in Fukien, Ming-chou (Ning-po) in Chekiang and Kuang-chou (Canton) in Kwangtung. Ryukyu tribute and trade missions were to enter at Ch'üan-chou but from the *Ch'eng-hua* period had been permitted to land at Fu-chou, which was more convenient. Japanese missions were directed to Ning-po, where Sakugen's party landed half a century after Ch'oe's visit. Southeast Asian countries like Siam and Malacca were to use Canton, but it is conceivable that by Ch'oe's time they had been permitted to land farther north. See *Hsu Wen-hsien t'ung-k'ao* (in *Shih t'ung*, Shanghai: Commercial Press, 1936), *ch.* 60 (p. 3350); Hucker, p. 46; Makita II: 42; Wu Chuang-ta, *Liu-ch'iu*, p. 73.

"You people are fortunate to have spring weather. If it were summer, with its heat, humidity, and sicknesses, how could you go? In the three administrative regions of Shantung, Shansi, and Shensi, moreover, there has been drought for several years.[20] Men are eating human flesh, and the people are losing their homes. After you have crossed the Yangtze River and gone more than one thousand *li*, you will be in Shantung. It will be well for you all to be very careful."

Then he gave me some bamboo shoots and said, "That is a vegetable dish, so you can eat it. Are there bamboo shoots in your country, too?"

I said, "The southern part of my country has bamboo shoots. They sprout in the Fifth Month."

Ku Pi said, "Here they sprout from winter to spring, and they are at their height in the First Month. Big ones weigh more than thirteen pounds. The climate here is different from that of your country."

11th Day. At Hang-chou. This day was cloudy.

Yang Hsiu-lu and Ku Pi came to see me. Ku Pi said, "On Pa-p'an Range in the mountains west of Hang-chou is an old monastery named Koryŏ Temple. In front of the temple are two stone tablets that commemorate the old ruins.[21] They are fifteen *li* from here. In the Sung period an envoy from Koryŏ came with tribute and built [the temple]. That your countrymen build temples even beyond their own borders must mean that they revere the Buddha."

I said, "But that was built by a man from Koryŏ. Our Chosŏn, now, has exposed heresies and respects the Confucian Way. The people consider as their duties only filial piety in the home and courtesy outside it, loyalty to their lords, and sincerity with their friends. Anyone who shaves his head is banished."

Ku Pi said, "All people who do not serve the Buddha sacrifice to gods. That being so, does your country serve gods and spirits?

I said, "All my countrymen build shrines and sacrifice to their ancestors. They serve the gods and spirits they ought to serve and do not respect unorthodox sacrifices."

Presently Yang Hsiu-lu left, and Ku Pi showed me an official document. It was a document in which Hang-chou Prefecture notified each prefecture and county on the road ahead that they were sending us on by stations. The text said,

---

[20]The *Ming shih* notes no prolonged drought in those regions in the two or three years before 1488. Since the diary again mentions drought later, however, it would seem to have been a fact. See Delamarre, *Histoire,* p. 332, 349, 356, 385.

[21]Had Ch'oe not deplored Buddhists, he might have given more attention to this famous temple. It had been known in the eleventh century as Hui-yin Temple, a center of Avatamsaka studies under the master Ching-yüan. In 1085 Uich'ŏn (1055-1101), a prince of the ruling house of Koryŏ and a noted Buddhist scholar, went to study there. He formed such close ties with the master and the school that years after he had returned home he sent (1101) a large donation to the temple, which thereafter became known as Koryŏ Temple. See Paul Demiéville, "Les Versions chinoises du Milindapañha," *Bulletin de l'École Française d'Extrême-Orient* XXIV: 199-207.

"Hang-chou Prefecture on a matter of maritime intelligence:

"We have received a copy of orders from the Provincial Administration Office of Chekiang and Other Places. We have received the joint judgment on the above matter of Chang Ch'ing, Overseer of the Imperial Grand Defending Directorate of Chekiang [*Ch'in-ch'ai chen* [*shou*] *Che-chiang Ssu-she-chien t'ai-chien*] and Ch'ang Heng, Regional Investigating Censor for Chekiang [*Hsün-an Che-chiang chien-ch'a yü-shih*].[22] According to a report from Huang Tsung, Supreme Anti-Japanese Commander for Chekiang and Concurrent Assistant Military Commissioner, and Wu Wen-yüan, Chekiang Surveillance Vice Commissioner for the Maritime Circuit, and reports of respective conditions in Ting-hai, Ch'ang-kuo, and other garrisons, and in T'ai-chou Prefecture and other garrison ports:

"On the 17th Day, Intercalary First Month, *Hung-chih* 1, a ship was clearly seen to sail into Shih-tzu Stockade from Niu-t'ou-wai-yang, T'ao-chu Chiliad, Hai-men Garrison. Accordingly, the matter was held to be an important one of seagoing ships, and we ordered maritime and local defending and touring offices of the Supreme Command, coast guards and naval officers in their commands, and warships under control of the Ministry to reconnoiter and take firm precautions.

"Continuing, according to the report of Concurrent Assistant Military Commissioner Huang Tsung, etc., and the reports of the T'ao-chu Chiliarch:

"Liu Ch'un, Centurion [*Po-hu*] of the said Chiliad, and others led banner troops out to Division 20 in front of Lin-hai County and with the local militia of the area arrested the men, seized the boat, and drove [the men] to the Chiliad. When they were questioned, their speech was difficult to understand. Their names and backgrounds, as they wrote them, were copied into a statement, reported, and have come to hand. We met with Ch'ang Heng, Regional Investigating Censor for Chekiang, and discussed the matter. We saw that the contents of the statement began with an interrogation of the barbarian Ch'oe Pu. Although, according to his statement, he was a Korean who had gone to Cheju and other islands and been driven off by violent winds, arriving at the border of the country of the Son of Heaven, we feared that barbarians are often deceitful, and it is hard to judge what is true and what false. That was the more so in this case, since there was no report on the contents of the boat — whether they had been inspected, what implements there were, and what items of baggage there were. It was appropriate that all that be examined.

"According, then, to the report of Huang Tsung, Supreme Anti-Japanese Commander and Concurrent Assistant Military Commissioner; Wu Wen-yüan, Surveillance Vice Commissioner for the Maritime Circuit; Ch'en T'an, Right Assistant Administration Commissioner; and Yang Chün, Regional

---

[22]See Hucker, p. 49. For Ch'ang Heng, *Chin-shih* of 1478, see *CKJM* 1355, 1356, *LCLK Ch'eng-hua* 14: 36v.

Surveillance Vice Commissioner;[23] and the report of Liu Tse, the said Anti-
Japanese Commissioner for Sung-men and Other Garrisons and Chiliads and
Vice Commander [*T'ung-chih*]:

"The forty-three barbarians were brought together and investigated by
having each man write his name and so forth. A second and third time they
were all questioned, and there were no discrepancies. Accordingly, the seal,
horse permit, records, documents, hats, bundles of clothing, and other things
were taken and each checked carefully. Receipts were given to Ch'oe Pu and
the others. The seized boat was also towed outside Ko-shang-wu and a statement of its details prepared. The men, a sword, and a bow were sent off together to this office.

"We have met with [representatives of] the Three Authorities of Chekiang,
Ts'ui Yin, Assistant Military Commissioner for Documents [*Chang-yin tu-
chih-hui ch'ien-shih*]; Hsü Kuei, Left Provincial Administration Commissioner; and Wei Fu, Surveillance Vice Commissioner; and held another
investigation. Since the facts and theories concerning the barbarians and their
boat, aside from the encounter with the wind, are consistent and in harmony,
we put aside that one fact and ordered that the notes of the proceedings in the
matter of the men be turned over to this office. In accordance with the facts
and principles involved in the case, in respect to Ch'oe Pu and the others,
this office grants its endorsement and commissions Commander Yang Wang
to take charge of escorting them to the capital. Let the stations and transfer
stations under this office give to the dispatched official food and boats and to
the escorting troops and Ch'oe Pu and his company rations, red boats, and
laborers. It is fitting that all offices on the road ahead should comply. Let
the sword and bow that have been sent out be turned over to the Public Treasury to be stored. When we have received a report from the Treasury that it
has taken them in, we shall order direct individual and group memorials
requesting the arrangements to be allowed. First, let copies of the handling
of the case be prepared and, as acknowledgement, individually reported here."

12th Day. At Hang-chou. This day was fair.

I said to Chŏng Po and others, "Ku Pi has treated us sincerely. He has told
us all he has heard and seen, hiding nothing, so that we have not been led into
error. He has been very kind, and I want to give him a token of our esteem,
but I have nothing in my baggage. All I have is this gown, which I am going
to take off and give to him."

Chŏng Po and others said, "You took off a gown previously and gave it to
Chiliarch Hsü. If you take off another today and give it to His Honor Ku Pi,
you will have only one gown to wear. When that wears out on the long journey,
who will replace it?"

[23]*Fen-hsün fu-shih.* An official in charge of one of the general circuits into which the province was divided by the
Provincial Surveillance Office. See Hucker, p. 54. Yang Chün, who may have been present but not named at Ch'oe's
earlier interview, was a *Chin-shih* of 1466. For his career, see *FSJW* 57: 41r., v.; *KCLC* 145: 7v.

I said, "There were men in olden times who had one gown for thirty years; yet I have been traveling abroad for less than one year. The days are becoming warmer now, and one piece of clothing is enough. In any case, even snakes and fishes are grateful for kindness and want to repay it; how much more so with men?" I took off the gown to give it to Ku Pi, but he waved his hands and refused it. I said, "Between friends, no gift, not even a horse and carriage, need be refused. How much less [need one refuse] this short gown? Han T'ui-chih of old left a gown as a parting present to Ta-tien, so there is a precedent for leaving a garment with a friend at parting."[24]

Ku Pi said, "I really want to refuse, but I am afraid of offending you." He took it and left.

XXX   The Chekiang Administrative Region extends to the sea in the southeast and the border of Fukien in the south. It has charge of eleven prefectures and departments and controls seventy-six counties. In it, Hang-chou is preeminent, having been the Wu-Yüeh [908-932] of the Five Dynasties period [907-960] and the Lin-an Prefecture to which Sung Kao Tsung [r. 1127-1162] moved his capital when he crossed to the South. The prefectural capital, the seats of Jen-ho and Ch'ien-t'ang counties, the Grand Defender's Headquarters, Regional Military Commission, Provincial Administration Office, Salt Distribution Commission [*Yen-yün ssu*], Provincial Surveillance Office, Salt Law Supervisory Commission [*Yen-fa ch'a-yüan*], Central Surveillance Office [*Chung ch'a-yüan*], Prefectural School, Jen-ho School, Ch'ien-t'ang School, and Wu-lin Station are all within its wall.

Also within the wall is Mt. Wu, a most pleasing sight.[25] On it are ten shrines, Wu Tzu-hsü Shrine,[26] Three Maos Hermitage,[27] Four Sages Shrine, and others. There are also nine wells. Three Lakes and Mt. Wu Great Well are at the top with Kuo-p'o, Upper Eight Eyes, Lower Eight Eyes, Middle Eight Eyes, West Monastery, and other wells following. [The water of] West Lake wells is also led through small conduits into the town. The guardian mountain of the prefecture is Mt. Wu-lin.[28]

[24]Han Yü, styled T'ui-chih (768-824), while he was in banishment in Kwangtung met and much admired the Buddhist monk Ta-tien. See Fung Yu-lan, "The Rise of Neo-Confucianism and Its Borrowings from Buddhism and Taoism," tr. Derk Bodde, *HJAS* VII: 2, pp. 96, 97.

[25]Hang-chou was so rich in beautiful and historical sites that Ch'oe's comments will touch only a few of them. To note fully the qualities and events associated with even those places he names, however, would burden the text unprofitably. Much of the character of the city two centuries before Ch'oe arrived there emerges from Jacques Gernet, *Daily Life in China on the Eve of the Mongol Invasion 1250-1276,* tr. H. M. Wright, New York: The Macmillan Company, 1962. Ch'oe's description can be neither full nor contemporary, since he spent little time in the city, was not free to move about, and learned what he reports from his escort. The places he names are of standard fame, of the kind that guide books and gazetteers note, and I have limited myself on the whole to mentioning sources where the main features are briefly summarized. For Mt. Wu see *Che-chiang t'ung-chih, ch.* 9 (p. 371).

[26]For this famous adviser to the king of Wu, 5th-6th century B.C., see, for example, *BD* 265, 892, 893.

[27]For the Mao brothers, who became Taoist recluses in the Han dynasty, see *CKJM* 716, Mao Ying.

[28]For notes on Mt. Wu Well and Mt. Wu-lin see *Che-chiang t'ung-chih, ch.* 9 (pp. 372-374). For the famous Six Wells that supplied West Lake water to the town see *Che-chiang t'ung-chih, ch.* 52 (pp. 1102 *ff.*); Lin Yutang, *The Gay Genius: The Life and Times of Su Tungpo,* New York: The John Day Company, 1947, pp. 306-308; Gernet, *Daily Life,* p. 45.

West Lake is two *li* west of the wall and is ten *li* north to south and east to west. The mountains and rivers [there] are very beautiful. It is a pleasure resort where singing and music are heard on every side. The Bamboo Pavilion in the Kuang-hua Monastery was built by Po Lo-t'ien [Po Chü-i]. It is the one in Po Lo-t'ien's poem, "Sleeping the Night in a Bamboo Pavilion."[29] The tomb of Yo [Fei],[30] Prince of E, is at Ch'i-hsia Range Pass. Cold Spring Pavilion is in front of Ling-yin Temple and below Fei-lai Ridge. This spring is the Ling-yin Stream from which, according to ancient records, Hsü Yu used to drink.[31] Piao-chung Hermitage is south of Mt. Lung and has a stone with a memorial composed by Tung-p'o [Su Shih]. Feng-huang Range is west of Fang-mu-ma-ch'ang. It is the place where Tung-p'o visited Pien-ts'ai.[32] Nan-p'ing Mountain is behind Hsing-chiao Temple. There remain on the crumbling cliff only the Diagram of the Family, written in square style by Ssu-ma Wen Kung [Ssu-ma Kuang], and the two words "lute terrace", written by Mi Yüan-chang. Tung-p'o's poem, "I Remember the Nan-p'ing Goldfish" [refers to] that place.[33] Su-kung Dike is across from Hsing-chiao Temple and was built by Tung-p'o when he governed Hang-chou. It is over ten *li* long and has six bridges on it.[34] Ching-te Hermitage is below Bridge No. 1 of Su-kung Dike. When Yüan Shao asked in a memorial to build a shrine, he selected thirty-nine people — famous men of Ch'ien-t'ang from Hsü Yu to Chang Chiu-ch'eng and five virtuous women—, compiled their biographies, and established the shrine.[35] Feng-lo Tower is on the bank of West Lake outside Yung-chin Gate, a west gate of the wall. Aquamarine [*huan-pi*] Garden is north of it, and Yü-lien Hall is at Yung-chin Gate. Inside the north gate of the wall there is also Yung-chin Lake. Jade Vat Garden is outside Ch'ien-t'ang Gate. Tung-p'o's poem, "The Rhododendrons of Nan-i Hall" [refers to] that place. West of the gate there is Hsien-te Tower. Cloudy Gorge Garden is north of Chao-ch'ing Temple; flowers and willows grow profusely, and among them are women's graves. Stone Box Bridge is at Water Mill Head. When Po Lo-t'ien,

---

[29]For the Bamboo Pavilion see *Che-chiang t'ung-chih ch.* 40 (p. 913). For Po Chü-i (772-846) in Hang-chou, which he governed from 822 to 824, see Arthur Waley, *The Life and Times of Po Chü-i,* London: George Allen and Unwin, 1949, pp. 147-157. Po's poem on the pavilion is in *Ch'uan T'ang shih,* ed. Ts'ao Yin, Peking: Chung-hua shu-chü, 1960, VII: 4956.

[30]For Yo Fei (1103-1141), the Sung general, see *CKJM* 564.

[31]For Cold Spring Pavilion see *Che-chiang t'ung-chih, ch.* 40 (p. 904). For Hsü Yu, a rustic philosopher who is said to have hurried off to wash out his ears after hearing Yao offer him employment, see *BD* 797; *TRD* II: 268.

[32]For Su Shih in Hang-chou, where he was Deputy Magistrate from 1071 to 1074 and Commander and Governor of West Chekiang from 1089 to 1091, see Lin Yutang, *The Gay Genius,* pp. 141-172, 301-316. Pien-ts'ai was one of the monks whose company Su enjoyed when he was Deputy Magistrate. See Lin, p. 159.

[33]For Nan-p'ing Mountain and the inscriptions see *Che-chiang t'ung-chih, ch.* 9 (p. 374). Ssu-ma Kuang (1019-1086) was the Sung statesman and historian; Mi Yüan-chang (Mi Fu, 1051-1107) the Yüan painter. For Tung-p'o's poem see *Su Tung-p'o chi, Kuo-hsüeh chi-pen ts'ung-shu* ed., Shanghai, Commercial Press, 1958, 3 vols.; *ch.* 18 (I: 4/83); and A. C. Moule, "A Version of the Book of Vermilion Fish," *T'oung Pao* XXXIX: 1-3, pp. 1-82.

[34]For Su-kung Dike see *Che-chiang t'ung-chih, ch.* 52 (p. 1104); Lin, *The Gay Genius,* pp. 308-309.

[35]For Yüan Shao, a *Chin-shih* of the *Ch'un-hsi* period (1174-1189) and a noted official, see *CKJM* 850. For his shrine see *Che-chiang t'ung-chih, ch.* 33 (p. 791). Chang Chiu-ch'eng was a *Chin-shih* of 1132 and official of Southern Sung. See *TRD* VI: 127.

in his "Record on Stone Concerning [Ch'ien-t'ang] Lake," says, "Another name for Ch'ien-t'ang is Upper Lake; to the north there is a stone box," [he refers to] it. Both Fair Garden is west of Te-sheng Hall. Two words were selected from Tung-p'o's poem, "Lightly powdered or heavily painted, both are fair," and the Emperor wrote the name-plaque for the Hall.[36] Tuan Bridge is west of Both Fair Garden. "On Tuan Bridge, slanting sunlight; / On the bank, [rich men's] hats," [refers to] it.[37] West Stone Head is west of Stone Box Bridge and is a place at which Ch'in Shih Huang [r. 221-210 B.C.], sailing the sea on a tour of the east, moored his boats. Mt. Ku is on West Lake Mt. Ku Road. East of Mt. Hsi there are the old foundations of Lin Ho-ching's secluded hut and his grave.[38] Three Worthies Shrine is below Bridge No. 3 of Su-kung Dike and is a shrine for Po Wen Kung [Po Chü-i], Lin Ho-ching, and Su Wen-chung Kung [Su Shih]. All the above historical sites Ku Pi told me about.

Hang-chou is a major urban center of the southeast. Houses stand in solid rows, and the gowns of the crowds seem like screens. The markets pile up gold and silver; the people amass beautiful clothes and ornaments. Foreign ships stand as thick as the teeth of a comb, and in the streets wine shops and music halls front directly each on another. There are flowers that do not fade through the four seasons and the scenery of everlasting spring all the year round. It truly seems a different world, as people say. *XXX*

13th Day. Setting out from Hang-chou. This day was cloudy.

Commander Yang Wang escorting us, we set out from Wu-lin Station. When we had gone more than twenty *li*, we came to the north gate of the wall.[39] It had three stories and multiple walls, and even the outer gate had two stories. Its name-plate said, "Gate of Wu-lin." Within the wall we passed fourteen gates of more than one story, more than ten big bridges, three shrines, and two stops. Riding a donkey and going fast, I did not record the names of some of

[36]For the gardens in this section, see *Che-chiang t'ung-chih, ch.* 39 (pp. 891, 892). "The Rhododendrons of Nan-i Hall" and "Drinking on the Lake, First Fair and Later Rainy," lines of which supplied words for the plaque at Te-sheng Hall, may be found in *Su Tung-p'o chi, ch.* 18 and 4 (I: 4/92 and I: 2/55) respectively. The line from the "Record on Stone Concerning [Ch'ien-t'ang] Lake" is in *Po-shih chang-ch'ing chi, ch.* 59, *SPTK,* 1st series.

[37]Presumably this is a poem by Po Chü-i or Su Tung-p'o, but I have not discovered the source. It is becoming clear that Ch'oe associates some of the places he passes with famous poems. This is the major point for our purposes, since it suggests the place of Chinese poetry in Ch'oe's learning. In the following pages I have identified as many of the poems alluded to or quoted as possible after searching for them a reasonably long time. Beyond doing that, I have not thought it directly profitable to track down the more elusive allusions. Readers who wish to look further may save time knowing that I have consulted the following works for all allusions to poetry: *P'ei wen yün fu; Dai Kan-Wa jiten,* by Morohashi Tetsuji, Tokyo, 1955-60, 12 vols.; *Monzen sakuin,* comp. Shiba Rokurō, *Tōdai kenkyū no shiori* Special No. 1-3, Kyoto: Jimbun kagaku kenkyūsho, 1957-59; *Kan-shi taikan,* ed. Saku Misao, Tokyo, 1936-39, 5 vols.

[38]For Lin Ho-ching, or Lin Pu, poet of the Northern Sung, see *TRD* VIII: 506, 507.

[39]On page 134, Ch'oe reached Wu-lin Station after going ten *li* within the south gate of Hang-chou. That the north gate is twenty *li* beyond the station indicates that the city stretched some thirty *li* (about ten miles) north to south; not up to Marco Polo's famous figure, "a hundred miles round," but still impressive. For a map of the city as it was in the 13th century see A. C. Moule, *Quinsai with Other Notes on Marco Polo,* Cambridge, University Press, 1957, facing p. 1.

the places; I was able to record only those of Shui-t'ing-kung-kuan, Chieh-yüan Gate, Chen-chiao Temple, Teng-ying-chou, Yün-feng Gate, Kuan-kuang Gate, Chin-shih-fang, Kung-yüan, Heng-ch'ü Gate, Ch'ien-sheng Shrine, and Yen-kung Shrine. Outside the multiple wall was Mt. Wu Station, in front of which was also Mt. Wu Stop. There were also three big bridges and four gates, the names of all of which I have forgotten. From outside the gates for more than ten *li*, markets stretched continuously, just as they did inside the wall.

We went on and came to T'ien-fei-kung. In front of the shrine was the Te-sheng-pa River. Pleasure boats, tied together in uncountable numbers, were along the banks of the river. Yang Wang, his younger brother Yang Sheng, Chiliarch of Sung-men Garrison Fu Jung, Ch'en Hsüan of Ch'ien-t'ang, and seven or eight of their staff, including Li K'uan, Hsia Pin, T'ang Ching, and Tu Yü, shared one boat. I, my secondary officials, and Li Chieh and Chin T'ai of Peking, shared another boat; and my company, Hŏ Sang-ni and the others, shared a third boat. We passed P'u-chi Bridge, a bridge of three arches. Above it was Hua-kuang Temple and Chiang-chang Bridge, which had four arches, and above that was Chiang-chang Stop. We arrived in front of Hsiang-chi Temple and stayed there a little while. At the temple were a quartermaster and an accountant, and it was a place that Tung-p'o used to visit. In the interval between it and Te-sheng Embankment, merchant boats from Chekiang and places south—Wen-chou, Ch'u-chou, T'ai-chou, Yen-chou, Shao-hsing, Ning-po, and other places—gather, their masts crowded thickly as in a forest.

At night we passed T'ung-shih Bridge and two other bridges. Because the river was wide, all the bridges had five arches and were extremely big.

14th Day. Passing Ch'ung-te County. This day was cloudy.
[We went up the Hsieh-ts'un River to the Hung-li River.] At T'ang-hsi Market, a public office above the river, an official, Han Shen, said to me, "Does your mother know that you have reached here?"

I said, "The sea and sky are boundless; the wild geese are high, the fish are deep.[40] My mother must think that I am buried in a fish's belly. No one has been as unfilial as I, no one has so broken his mother's heart. Now, if, through great kindness from your country, I return alive to my native place, then the joy of reunion between mother and son will be greater than that of Duke Chuang of Cheng and his mother when they emerged from the tunnel."[41]

[Then we passed from K'ua-t'ang Bridge to Tsao-lin Station and beyond.] We travelled through the night.

15th Day. Passing Chia-hsing Prefecture. This day was fair.
[We went from Three Pagodas Bay to Hsi-shui Station.] Stone pillars had been erected in front of the station, making an arcade into the river over five

[40]Symbols of correspondence; no letters have been exchanged.
[41]From a story in *Tso chuan*, Yin-kung 1/4.

hundred feet long. We tied the boats to the foot of the arcade. Ho Jung, the
Station Master, addressed three quatrains of a poem to us, and I, in turn,
answered them. Ho Jung also presented to us fish and meat delicacies, dried
chicken, eight-band fish, and other things. He said, "Senior Secretary [*Lang-
chung*] Ch'i Shun[42] and Messenger [*Hsing-jen*] Chang Chin of our Court
went on an embassy to Korea and wrote *Huang hua chi*. The people of the
country wrote verses in response to it, Sŏ Kŏ-jŏng[43] being foremost among
them. His poem had the lines, 'If the glorious Emperor asks about the Three
Han,/Their rites, music, and clothes are the same as those of China.' My meeting you now is truly a rare occasion, and you have even condescended to give
me a poem in response. Respectfully I offer you some poor gifts to eke out
your provisions in the boat. If you will receive them, I shall be extremely fortunate."

I said, "Senior Secretary Ch'i's literary accomplishments and virtue are
much admired. What is his position now? And what post is Messenger
Chang filling?"

Jung said, "Senior Secretary Ch'i was demoted to Prefect of Shih-ch'ien
Prefecture, Kuei-chou. He is dead now. Messenger Chang was charged with
wrongdoing and is now banished to the Imperial Bodyguard." Then he
asked me, "What position does Sŏ Kŏ-jŏng now hold?"

I said, "He is Fourth State Councillor."

Ho Jung said, "Sŏ Kŏ-jŏng, by virtue of his writing, is one of Korea's
distinguished men."

From Hsi-shui Station we passed one big bridge and came to Chia-hsing
Prefecture, which was the old Hsi-li-ch'eng, the place where Yüeh defeated
Wu.[44] Inside the wall were the prefectural capital and the seats of Hsiu-shui
and Chia-hsing counties. The river cradled the wall, going from southeast
south, west, and then north. The houses were handsome and the scenery
splendid, the equals of Ning-po Prefecture. From south of the wall, I passed
Shan-ch'ing Lock and came to the native village of Lu Chih, a Minister of
T'ang. The village was west of the wall, and there was a banner gate on the
bank of the river.

We passed [five places]. At night we braved the rain and went with the
wind till dawn, coming to P'ing-wang Station, where we stopped.

16th Day. Passing Wu-chiang County and arriving at Su-chou Prefecture.
This day was cloudy.

The boats were towed up the P'ing-wang River, past [bridges, lakes, and

---

[42]Ch'i Shun, a *Chin-shih* of 1460, went as envoy to Korea in 1475. See *FSJW* 110: 36v., 37r.

[43]Sŏ Kŏ-jŏng (1420-1492) passed the Civil Service Examination in 1444 and rose to a high position in the State
Council. See *CJM* 1311.

[44]In 473 B.C.

[43]For Lu Chih (754-805) see, for example, *BD* 1406. For his village see *Che-chiang t'ung-chih, ch.* 41 (p. 935).

other landmarks], and came to Chiu-li Stone Dike. The embankment bounded Lake T'ai. Lake T'ai is the lake of which it is said in *Yü kung*, "And it became possible to still the marsh of Chen" [Legge, III:110], and is called in the *Chou* (Chih-fang, Yang-chou-sou), "Chü-ch'ü." Some call it Five Lakes; it is so named because it is over five hundred *li* long.[46] It is a place that Fan Li[47] used to visit. In the lake are two mountains, Tung-t'ing East Mountain and Tung-t'ing West Mountain. They are also called Pao Mountain. From them, one can see for a thousand *li*. Their lofty cliffs rise up in ranges, ornaments on the vast expanse of water. Northeast of the lake, Ling-yen Mountain looks down on it. Another name for it is Yen-shih Mountain. It is the Yen-shih on which Wu built Kuan-wa.[48] The mountain is ten *li* from Ku-su Mountain. Mountains lie in ranges, cradling Lake T'ai. In the north there is also a single mountain vaguely visible in the distance. It is Mt. Heng.

We came to Lake T'ai Embankment, which was built of stone and straddled the lake north to south for over fifty *li*. It was Ch'ui-hung Bridge,[49] with at least four hundred arches, one slender one after another. In size it was like such bridges as Mu-chuang and Wan-ch'ing. Going north along Lake T'ai Embankment, we passed Lung-wang Shrine, Lake T'ai Shrine, and Chu-sheng Gate, in front of which was a great pagoda of fourteen stories. All the stories had rooms, and it looked like a ladder rising into the sky.

We passed Chu-chieh Gate and came to Sung-ling Station. We stopped the boats a little while and then went on, past [six gates, a school and a bridge]. Lake T'ai Embankment passed along village gates in front of the station and extended to Wu-chiang County. Along that part, too, was a large stone bridge, with more than seventy arches altogether. Both the station and the county were in Lake T'ai. The houses were beautiful, with stone plinths and well walls laid below and stone columns erected above. The lake water wound in and about them, and masts and sails stood grouped in the villages. It is there of which it has been said, "On all sides fishermen's houses wind round the county wall."

[We went from San-li Bridge to Pao-tai Bridge, another great bridge] of fifty-five arches, a crossroads of boat and wheel traffic spanning Lake Tan-t'ai like a sash spread across the rich scenery of the lake and mountains. It had been rebuilt by Tsou Ying-po.[50]

In the third watch of the night, we followed alongside the Su-chou Wall, east, south, and then west, and arrived in front of Ku-su Station. From Pao-

[46]Lake T'ai was often called Five Lakes, but the reason for the name is uncertain. See the references to the term in *Su-chou-fu chih* (T'ung-chih chung-hsiu ed., 81 *ts'e*), *ch.* 8, 1r., 1v.

[47]For Fan Li, minister of Yüeh in the fifth century B.C., see *BD* 540.

[48]Kuan-wa was a palace said to have housed beautiful women for the kings of Wu. It became a favorite topic for later poets. For citations from several literary sources see *Su-chou-fu chih, ch.* 35, 2v.., 5r.

[49]For Ch'ui-hung Bridge, popularly called Long Bridge, see *Su-chou-fu chih, ch.* 34, 16r. *seq.* Ch'oe may have included other bridges along the embankment in speaking of four hundred arches, since this source mentions eighty-five.

[50]For Tsou Ying-po, an official of the Sung dynasty in the thirteenth century, see *CKJM* 1343.

tai Bridge to that station, shops and markets one after another lined both river banks, and merchant junks were crowded together. It was well called an urban center of the southeast.

17th Day. Moored in Front of Ku-su Station. This day was fair.

Su-chou is the place to which Ho-lü [r. 514-496 B.C.], King of old Wu, sent Wu Tzu-hsü to enclose it with a wall and make it the capital.[51] The circumference of the wall is equal to that of Hang-chou, and the prefectural capital and the seats of Wu County and Ch'ang-chou County are within it. At Hsü Gate in the wall was formerly a Ku-su Tower, which is now done away with for a station. Trees have been planted in the water, forming great pillars, and a stone levee has been built on three sides. Huang-hua Tower stands in front, and Chao-yang Tower is built in the back. I asked Fu Jung about it: "If this station is on the ruins of Ku-su Tower, is this the place where the tower was built by the old King of Wu?"

Fu Jung said, "No. What was called Ku-su Tower in olden times was on Ku-su Mountain. King Ho-lü of Wu put up the tower because of the mountain. Fu Ch'ai [r. 495-473 B.C.] enlarged it. The ruins still exist.[52] In the *Shao-hsing* period [1131-1162], another tower was built here and named Ku-su to keep the tradition. Now it has been done away with for a station. A tower was also built inside the wall and given a signboard with the name Ku-su."

To the east was a transfer station and also Shan-hai Market.

But the waters of Lake T'ai, flowing into the Grand Canal between stone levees, go east and west along the wall and come out at the station. Because Wu Tzu-hsü lived there, it is also called Hsü Lake. It is about five hundred feet wide. In the north it curves round markets and junctions, winding and sparkling among railings, light dancing from it.

Of the mountains west of the wall, the peak T'ien-p'ing is called the guardian mountain of the prefecture. The outstanding mountains of the prefecture are Ling-yen, Wu-wu, Yang-t'ien, and Ch'in-t'ai, one after another. It happens that the station looks out on them, making for an extremely beautiful view.

At noon, two eminent persons, Regional Inspecting Censors [*An-ch'a yü-shih*] named Wang and Sung, came into the Station and received me in the Li-pin-kuan. They asked, "What is your official rank?"

I answered, "Fifth Rank."

They said, "Can you write poetry?"

I said, "The gentlemen of my country consider studying the Classics and probing to principles to be their concern and moaning about the wind and moon to be cheap; I, therefore, have not studied poetry."

[51]For brief notes on Wu Tzu-hsü or Wu Yüan, adviser to King Ho-lü of Wu and his successor Fu Ch'ai, 5th-6th centuries B.C., see *BD* 265, 892, 893.

[52]For historical and literary references to Ku-su Tower, another magnificent resort of the kings of Wu, see *Su-chou-fu chih, ch.* 35, 5v.-9v.

They asked, "Chi Tzu having been enfeoffed in Korea, are there now descendants of his? And are his shrine, grave, and rites still kept up?"

I answered, "Chi Tzu's successor, Kijun, was expelled by Wei Man. He fled to Ma-han, set up a capital, and later was destroyed by Paekche. There are now no descendants. Chi Tzu's shrine is in P'yŏngyang, and every year in spring and fall, the state ritually burns incense and sacrifices animals and money."

They asked, "What great technique did your country have, to have been able to repel the Sui and T'ang armies?"

I said, "The ministers, who planned well, and the generals, who were bold, knew the right way to wage war. All the soldiers cherished their leaders and died for them. That way, Koguryŏ, though a remote little country, was capable of twice repelling the armies of China. Now that Silla, Paekche, and Koguryŏ have been combined into one country, its resources are many, its land big, its wealth great, and its soldiers strong. Its loyal and wise gentlemen are too many to be counted."

When the two eminent persons had finished their questioning, they ordered a deputy secretary to present to us one plate of rice, one plate of bean-curd, and one plate of wheat noodles. I wrote a poem and thanked them.

Then an official named Cheng wanted me to match the rhymes of "*Yüeh hsüan shih,*" and I did so. He presented to me six bushels of rice, one duck, one plate of fish and meat delicacies, and one plate of walnuts.

One Liu, a house servant of Overseer Lo, was fifteen or sixteen years old and elegant of speech. He came from inside the wall and presented food to [me] and my staff. Li Chieh and Chin T'ai also bought food and came and presented it.

In the third watch of the night we rowed the boats north in the moonlight, past Ch'ang Gate. Outside Ch'ang Gate, T'ung-po Pavilion overlooked the lake. Its old name had been Koryŏ Pavilion, and it had been built in the *Yüan-feng* period of Sung [1078-1085] to receive tribute-bearers from Koryŏ. In front of the pavilion, adjoining roofs and rows of masts were as thick as the teeth of a comb.

We rowed to Chieh-kuan Pavilion and stopped. To the west, the pavilion looked out on a great pagoda, which was Han-shan Ch'an Temple, the one commemorated in the line, "Outside the Ku-su wall is Han-shan Temple."[53] I asked the name of the place, and [someone] said, "Feng Bridge." I asked the name of the river, and [someone] said, "She-tu River."

XXX In olden times, Su-chou was called Wu-k'uai. It borders the sea in the east, commands three large rivers and five lakes, and has a thousand *li* of rich fields. Learned men and gentry abound there; and all the treasures of the land and sea, such as thin silks, gauzes, gold, silver, jewels, crafts, arts, and rich and great merchants, are there. It has been accepted in China from

[53]From the T'ang poet Chang Chi (*Chin-shih* of 753). See *Ch'üan T'ang shih, ch.* 242 (IV: 2721).

olden times that the land south of the Yangtze River is the beautiful and good land and that within that land Su-chou and Hang-chou are the first departments, especially Su-chou. Yüeh Bridge is inside the wall and separates Wu and Chang-chou counties. Market quarters are scattered like stars. Many rivers and lakes flow through [the region], refreshing and purifying it. The people live luxuriously. There are solid rows of towers and stands, and in such places as the space between Ch'ang-men and Ma-t'ou [the wharves?], merchantmen and junks from Honan, Hopei, and Fukien gather like clouds. The lakes and mountains are fresh and stimulating, the scenic splendors innumerable.

But we came to Ku-su Station at night. The following day we did not have the pleasure of looking about either, but, traveling again at night, went along and past the wall. I have not been able, therefore, to record in detail any of the seven dams, eight gates, sixty quarters, or 390 bridges spoken of by Po Lo-t'ien,[54] or old things now ruined, new things now added, unusually beautiful scenery, or marvelous remains. *XXX*

18th Day. Arrival at Hsi-shan Station. This day was fair.

When it was light, an official named Wu Mo, who was in the same boat as Yang Wang, sent me a letter that said, "I hear, sir, that you are a gentleman of rank and conduct and want to make your acquaintance. My colleague Yang is also in this boat, and we wish to invite you to come and see us. Do not refuse us."

I went, led by Ch'en Hsüan. When I and Chŏng Po reached their boat, Wu and Yang had put their chairs round a table. They folded their hands in greeting, and we sat down together. They served us tea and things to eat and were very courteous to us.

From Feng Bridge we [reached Ch'ao Barrier]. When boats passing north and south reached there, they were anchored in a cove and inspected before proceeding. An Overseer named Lo was there. Formerly he had been in charge of weaving and dyeing in Chekiang, and now he had left Su-chou and was going toward Peking. He had come there ahead of us and moored.

Three censors who were there came aboard the boats to send us on our way with wine and food. They invited me before them and received me courteously, saying, "You are a good man from a country of propriety and morality. Our important people all respect you." Then they asked, "In the *T'ien-shun* and *Ch'eng-hua* periods [1457-1487], there were overseers who received Imperial orders to go to your country. Can you give their names in order?"

I answered, "In the *T'ien-shun* period I was not yet out of my swaddling clothes, and I knew nothing of affairs of state. In the *Ch'eng-hua* period, Over-

---

[54]Po mentions the dams, gates, and quarters in the poem "Banquet on the Ninth . . ." and the bridges in "Going Out Quietly on the Third of the First Month," which may be found in *Ch'uan T'ang shih* (Chung-hua shu-chü ed., 1960, 12 vols.), *ch.* 444 and 447 (VII: 4968, 4969 and VII: 5026) respectively.

seer Cheng T'ung, Overseer Chiang Yü, and Overseer Chin Hsing came successively as envoys."

They wrote something and showed it to me. It said, "Overseers Cheng, Chiang, and Chin have all become ancient. Only Overseer Chin is in Peking."[55]

I said, "I do not understand the two words, 'become ancient.' "

They answered, "The Chinese speak of dying as becoming ancient, meaning that they have already joined the ancients." Then they asked, "What do you say in your country?"

I said, "We call them 'things old (*wu-ku*).' "

They asked, "What does 'things old' mean?"

I said, " 'Things (*wu*)' means 'acts'; 'old (*ku*)' means 'not to have.' The expression means not again to have power to act."[56]

They asked, "What classics does your country esteem?"

I replied, "All the Confucian scholars master the Four Books and Five Classics. They do not study other disciplines."

They said, "Does your country also have schools?"

I answered, "The national capital has the National Academy and also the Peers' School, Central College, Eastern College, Western College, and Southern College. All the departments, prefectures, counties, and districts have regional schools and local academies. All families have branch academies."[57]

They asked, "What sages of old do you revere?"

I said, "We revere Confucius."

They asked, "How many years do mourning rites last in your country?"

I said, "They follow entirely Chu Wen Kung's *Chia li*. Both the unhemmed garment and hemmed garment are for three years. The coarsely-woven

---

[55]The extra Chin is confusing, but it is not clear where the mistake is.

[56]Contrary to what might be inferred from this conversation, *wu-ku* had a long history in Chinese and was not peculiarly Korean. The censors may have asked for an explanation of the term out of curiosity about Ch'oe's own understanding of it.

[57]For the Korean school system see, for example, Lee Man Kyoo, *Chosen Kyoyook Sa*, I: 139-404; Choo Young-Ha, *The Education in the Yi Dynasty,* esp. chs. 2 and 3; KC, II: 271, 272.

The Korean system differed little enough from that of Ming to seem familiar to the Chinese. Aside from four of the colleges in the capital, each element of the Korean system resembled something Chinese in form. In practice, however, there may have been significant differences. The sources speak as if the capital colleges and the regional schools held classes regularly and actively. In this they would differ from the Ming state schools, some of which served mainly formal purposes, keeping rolls of students who really studied away from school and conducting periodical ceremonies and examinations.

In the Korean system, in brief, the National Academy was the highest state school. It was much smaller than its Ming counterpart, enrolling nominally 200 men from among students of the Four Colleges, holders of *Saeng-wŏn* or *Chinsa* degrees, and men nominated by the king or through special political privilege. The Peers' School trained young men of the royal and noble families. The Four Colleges—Central, Eastern, Western, and Southern, trained about 100 students each at a time in a curriculum leading toward admission to the National Academy or success in examinations. The programs of the colleges were generally directed by the National Academy. The regional schools were maintained by prefectural and lower political centers, enrolling students 16 years old or younger in numbers from 90 to 30, depending upon the standing of the political office. What Ch'oe calls local academies were probably private schools of the kind called *sŏ-dang* established by a community interested in elementary education for its boys. The branch academies may have been of the same class but supported by well-to-do families for their own children.

garment and those below are respectively for shorter periods."[58]

They said, "What are the sections of the Code of Rites of your country and of the Code of Punishments?"

I said, "In Rites there are Sacrifices, Laments, Military Rites, Visits, and Celebrations. In Punishments there are Beheading, Strangling, Banishment, Penal Servitude, and Flogging. They follow entirely the system of the *Great Ming Code*."

They said, "What calendar and reign-title does your country use?"

I said, "We follow the Great Ming calendar and reign-title."

They said, "What is the reign-title this year?"

I said, "It is the first year of *Hung-chih*."

They said, "It has not been so long; how do you know it?"

I said, "When the Great Light (*Ta Ming*) first came out of the sea, all nations were brightened. Especially when my country is of the same house as China and pays tribute without fail, how could I not know it?"

They said, "Are the caps and gowns of your country the same as those of China?"

I said, "In all court and official dress, long gowns and round collars, we follow fully Chinese dress. Only the figured linings and folds are slightly different."

They then ordered me to summon the secondary officials and those below them and have them perform the ceremony as between host and guests. The Overseer and the three eminent persons looked on, talking and laughing. Then they presented to us twenty bushels of rice, one plate of pork, one plate of fish and meat delicacies, one plate of herbs and fruits, and five containers of wine. We thanked them and left.

We then got into the boats and went [from P'u-yüan Bridge to Hsi-shan Station].

19th Day. Arrival at Ch'ang-chou Prefecture. This day was fair.

At dawn the County Magistrate of Wu-hsi County—I have forgotten his name—came and presented food to us. From the station we [continued on through Wu-hsi County and Ch'ang-chou Prefecture to Niu-pen Great Embankment].

20th Day. Passing Lü-ch'eng Station and Arriving at Chen-chiang Prefecture. This day was fair; after noon it was cloudy.

[We went from Chang-tien Stop to Chen-chiang Prefecture.]

---

[58]Ch'oe refers to kinds of mourning attire prescribed according to the degree of relationship between the mourner and the dead. The "coarsely-woven garment" (*ta-kung*), for example, was to be worn for nine months to mourn relatives at a certain remove, such as male paternal first cousins, etc.

21st Day. Arrival at the Yangtze River. This day was cloudy.

From Nan-shui Pass we went [as far as T'ung Ferry]. The water there was shallow, and it was necessary to wait for the tide to come in to be able to pass into the Yangtze River. Making ready to cross the river, therefore, we got into boats again and waited for the tide. Li Chieh and Chin T'ai took leave of me, saying, "We have been honored to come to your notice on the road. Today we part, you going to Yang-chou and we to I-chen. Late in the spring we shall go to Peking again. We shall seek out the Central Post Hotel [Hui-t'ung-kuan] and come to see you."

Chen-chiang Prefecture was Jun-chou Walled City [*ch'eng*]. When Sun Ch'üan moved to Tan-t'u and built T'ieh-weng Walled City, he called it the Capital City [Ching-ch'eng]. The prefectural capital and the seat of Tan-t'u County are inside the wall. East of the wall is the site of T'ieh-weng, but its wall is not there.[59] Hsiang-wu Pavilion is southwest of the wall. Pei-ku Mountain is in the northwest; it was named by Wu Ti of Liang [r. 502-549]. Tai-kung Mountain is in the southwest; there, Wu Ti of Sung [r. 420-422] visited. Both Kan-lu Temple and To-ching Tower are northeast of the wall. Mt. Chiao and Mt. Yin, on both of which large Buddhist temples are built, are north of the wall. Mt. Chin is in the Yangtze, opposite Mt. Yin, and Lung-yen Temple is on top of it. That is the place that Chen Tsung of Sung [r. 998-1022] visited and dreamed in. The northeast corner of the prefectural wall overlooks the bank of the river, which is the Yangtze, commonly called the Son of the Ocean.[60]

The river is more than twenty *li* wide. It rises in the Min Mountains,[61] joins the Han River, reaches the prefecture by way of Nanking, and enters the sea. This is the river of which *Yü kung* says, "From Mount Min he [Yü] surveyed the Chiang" [Legge, III: 137]. In the east it passes through Wu-k'uai, in the west it adjoins the Han and Mien, in the north it extends to the Huai and Ssu, and in the south it reaches Min and Che. Its region is truly one of great urban centers in all directions.

22nd Day. Arrival at Kuang-ling Station. This day was fair.

From Shui-fu-shen Shrine we pushed off the boats and came to the Yangtze River. For five or six *li* along the edge of the river, endless lines of people were moving boats across the country. We hoisted the sails and went into the river. Below Mt. Chin, porpoises played in the waves like galloping war horses. We [went from Hsi-chin Ferry to the Shih-li River].

Yang Wang sent Fu Jung to say to me, "A Dame Han of your country came

---

[59]Chen-chiang was called Jun-chou in T'ang times and Tan-t'u in the Three Kingdoms period, when Sun Ch'üan (182-252) proclaimed himself first Emperor of the Wu dynasty in 229. See, for example, *BD* 1803; *TRD* V: 408.

[60]This common name results from writing the *yang* in Yangtze incorrectly. See Samuel Couling, *The Encyclopaedia Sinica*, Shanghai, Kelly and Walsh, 1917, p. 613.

[61]It was to be about 150 years after Ch'oe Pu's journey that Hsü Hung-tsu (1585-1643) discovered the source of the Yangtze to be not the Min Mountains, but the part of the Kun-lun Range that is on the Chinghai-Tibet-Sinkiang Border.

to our country. Did you know that?"

I said, "I have heard that a Han woman entered China, but that is all."

He said, "She was the one. This Han was a woman of your country who came to our country to be wet-nurse to the late Emperor. She is dead now, and her burial mound was put up at T'ien-shou Temple. This Commander is the one who took charge of burying the Han woman. That is the only reason he asked."

[We passed several places and came to Kuang-ling Station.]

23rd Day. Passing Yang-chou Prefecture. This day it rained.

At dawn we left Kuang-ling Station and passed the wall of Yang-chou Prefecture. The prefecture was the site of the old Chiang-tu of Sui, the great market of the lower Yangtze. The splendors of the ten *li* of pearled blinds, the twenty-four bridges, and the thirty-six banks were the greatest of all the prefectures. This was the land celebrated by the lines, "The spring breezes caress the city, and music fills the ears."[62] Passing by boat, we could not look about, and the only thing we were able to see was Chen-huai Tower, which was the south gate of the wall and had three stories.

[From there we went to Shao-po Transfer Station.]

The garrisons and places through which we had passed since the city of Hang-chou had sent centurions in relay to escort us. The Centurion from Yang-chou Garrison, one Chao Chien, said to me, "Six years ago a countryman of yours, Yi Sŏm, also drifted here and returned home. Did you know that?"

I said, "Yes." Then I asked for the whole story of Yi Sŏm's going adrift and returning.

Chien said, "In the beginning, Yi Sŏm was driven by winds to Chüeh-chiang Stockade, Yang-chou. The Fortress Commander, Chang Sheng, sent Centurion Sang K'ai at the head of troops to arrest him. They imprisoned him. A Patrol Commander said that he should be placed in Hsi-fang Temple to stay, and they took him there in the boat in which he had come. He stayed there about a month. His Excellency Kuo, Coast Guard Commissioner, saw Yi Sŏm's line, 'We spread ten sails but did not catch a wind,' and knew that he was a good man. He treated him like a visiting friend." Then he asked me, "How many *li* is it from the coast on which you landed to here?"

I said, "The road we took from Niu-t'ou-wai-yang to T'ao-chu Chiliad, Hang-chou, and Yang-chou was altogether over 2,500 *li* long."

Chien said, "When he came here, Yi Sŏm seemed to grieve because he was far from home. What saddens you now is many times [worse than what saddened] him."

I said, "Yi Sŏm was sad only because the road was long. What pains me is

[62]Again, Ch'oe suggests the splendor of a city by referring to poetry that has celebrated it. The ten *li* of pearled blinds and the twenty-four bridges, for example, appear in Su Tung-p'o's poetry. See *Su Tung-p'o chi, ch.* 3 (I: 2/36) for the former and *Su Tung-p'o shih chi, ch.* 35 (in *Kan-shi taikan*) for the latter. The thirty-six banks and the quoted lines may also be from Tung-p'o but do not appear in the usual indexes.

that my father died recently and has not yet been put into his coffin, and my mother is growing old in the house. I have neglected my filial duties, and the road to be traveled is very long; in my grieving heart, the world is black."

24th Day. Arrival at Meng-ch'eng Station. This day was fair.

From Shao-po Transfer Station [*Ti-yün-so*] we went [as far as Meng-ch'eng station].

25th Day. Passing Kao-yu Department [Chou]. This day was cloudy.

At cock-crow we left Meng-ch'eng Station and passed Kao-yu Department. The department had been the old Han-chou. Han-kou, also called Han River, curved round it, a strategic intersection in the north-to-south water route. The wall of the department overlooked a big lake, which was Kao-yu Lake. There, the scenery of the river and lake was splendid and the people numerous. It was another prosperous country, north of the Yangtze. In the time of Yü of Hsia [traditionally r. 2205-2197 B.C.], the Yangtze and the Huai were not yet connected. In *Yü Kung,* therefore, "They [tribute-bearers] followed the course of the Chiang and the sea, and so reached the Huai and the Ssu" [Legge, III: 112]. With King Fu Ch'ai of Wu, the Han-kou was first opened; when men of Sui widened it, boats first plied on it.

We then came to Hsi-ho Dike [and continued on as far as Chieh-chou Station].

Ch'en Hsüan had come as a military officer with Yang Wang. Since he understood a little about writing, Yang had appointed him scribe. Hsüan was extraordinarily greedy, and there was no one more deceitful. Now he became angry at Kim Sok, a soldier of mine, and accused him of several things to Yang. Yang had Sok seized and sentenced him to more than ten lashes. I ordered Chŏng Po to make a statement to Yang: "The Commander is supposed to escort us and nothing more. Is there any law by which on your own authority you may sentence and flog us foreigners? The soldiers I have are the same as the blind and the dumb. Even if they sometimes make mistakes, you ought to explain to them sympathetically. On the contrary, you beat them and hurt them. That is not the way for China to escort strangers."

Yang could not answer. Fu Jung said secretly to me, "Originally His Excellency Yang was from Peking, but he was transferred to Hang-chou Garrison. He is illiterate and ignorant. I have corrected him repeatedly, but he will not listen to us and continues to act presumptuously and contrary to principles. It is not worth the effort to bring charges against him."

We went on, into the rain, past Tzu-ying-ch'ien and along Chieh-shou Great Lake. On the edge of that lake, too, was a long embankment. We passed a police station and Huai-chüeh Tower and at night stopped in front of Fan-shui Stop.

26th Day. Arrival at Huai-yin Station. This day was cloudy.

[We went from Fan-kuang Great Lake to Huai-yin Station.] For the one hundred *li* and more between Fan-shui Stop and there, a long levee built on the east bank ran without break, either as stonework or as wooden palisades.

27th Day. Passing Huai-an Prefecture. This day it rained.

On the bank opposite Huai-yin Station, outside Ma-t'ou-ch'eng Gate, was P'iao-mu Shrine. North of it was K'ua-hsia Bridge, which was the place where Han Hsin ate another's food and was disgraced.[63] The station was opposite the transfer station keeper's storehouse, adjoining the transfer station.

From the station, we rowed the boats alongside Huai-an Prefecture. The prefecture had been the old Tung-ch'u Department, an important control point for the southeast. Inside the old wall were the prefectural capital, the seat of Shan-yang County, Huai-an Garrison, and various posts, for the Surveillance organization [*Tu-t'ang-fu*], Regional Command [*Tsung-ping-fu*], Censoring organization [*Yü-shih-fu*], and others. East of the old wall, a new wall had been built. The Ta-ho Garrison was inside the new wall, but other posts had not yet been established. There was a space between the new and old walls of about one *li*. The water of the lake flowed round the walls inside and out, but both the walls and the houses were on flat islands. We left from Nan-tu Gate and went north.

We came to the Huai River. In the interval had been [numerous structures and garrisons]. Garrisons for the regions south of the Huai and north and south of the Yangtze were gathered there to build boats, and they all had shipyards.

In general, for the four or five hundred *li* between the Yangtze River and the Huai River, the land has many big swamps and huge lakes. Of the lakes, the big ones like Shao-pu Lake, Kao-yu Lake, Chieh-shou Lake, and Pai-ma Lake seem to stretch endlessly in all directions.

This day we braved heavy rain and passed the Huai River, also called the Huang [Yellow] River. I asked Fu Jung about that: "According to *Yü kung,* the Huang River passes the Chi-shih, Lung-men, Hua-yin, Ti-chu, and Ta-p'ei mountains and then passes the Chiang-shui and Ta-lu, becoming the Chiu-ho and Ni-ho and entering the sea in the northeast. The Huai River passes the T'ung-po Mountains, joins the Ssu and I and enters the sea in the east.[64] Lin Chih-ch'i[65] thinks that the lower reaches of the [Huang] River lie in Yen and the lower reaches of the Huai in Hsü. Then the sources of the

[63]For Han Hsin (d. 196 B.C.), a great figure in the fighting before the establishment of the Han dynasty, see Burton Watson, tr., *Records of the Grand Historian of China,* New York: Columbia University Press, 1961, 2 vols., I: 208-232. A washerwoman provided food for Han Hsin in the hard days of his youth, but when he promised to repay her she took offense, not having expected any reward.

[64]*Cf.* Legge, III, pp. 132, 134, 139.

[65]For Lin Chih-ch'i (1112-1176), scholar and official of the Sung dynasty see *Sung shih* 433 (K'ai-ming ed. 5594.2). Some of his works exist, but I have not searched through them for his remarks on the rivers.

Huai and the [Huang] River are not the same, their courses not the same, and the places where they enter the sea not the same. How is it that now you put the Huai and the Huang River together?"

Jung said, "Under our Ming Court, we have channelled the bed of the Huang River and made it flow into the Huai; they flow into the sea together. The Huang River has lost its old course and is different from that in *Yü kung*."

The Huai River truly receives many waters. The Huang River and Huai River flow together as the West River. The Chi, T'a, and Wen rivers flow together with the Chu and Ssu rivers and then join the Pien River and to the east meet the I River to become the East River. The water of the West River is yellow, so it is called Yellow River. The water of the East River is green, so it is called Green River. The two rivers flow together there; combined, they are called Huai River. The river is more than ten *li* wide, it is bottomless, and the current is violent.

On the bank of the river was Keng-ch'i-kung-shen Shrine, and Mt. Kuei overlooked the river. Chao Chien said to me, "There is a god at the foot of that mountain. He looks like a Macacus monkey; he has a turned-up nose, high forehead, blue body, and white head. His eyes flash like lightning. The legend is that when the Great Yü channelled the waters, he bound that creature with a great rope and ordered him to live there and make the Huai flow quietly. Today, people who have pictures of that creature are spared trouble from wind and waves on the Huai."

I said, "There is nothing in the classics about this extraordinary tale; I cannot believe it." Chien was silent.[66]

[We went up the East River and stopped at night near Ch'ing-ho County.]

28th Day. Cloudy.

[We went past Ch'ing-ho-k'ou, up the Pai-yang River and beyond it.]

29th Day. Fair.

We set out at dawn and went [from Chang-ssu-chung Shoal to Ku-ch'eng Station].

30th Day. Passing Su-ch'ien County. This day was cloudy.

[We went from Ku-ch'eng Station past Su-ch'ien County to Chih-ho Station.]

1st Day. Third Month. Passing P'ei-chou. This day was cloudy.

From Chih-ho Station we [went to Hsia-p'ei Station]. The station was south of the prefectural wall.

P'ei-chou was the old Yen-tzu-kuo. East of the wall there is Yen-tzu Shrine,

---

[66]The story is told by Li Kung-tso (c. 770-850) as "Ku yüeh to ching." See the note on types of monkey tales in Chi-chen Wang, *Traditional Chinese Tales*, New York, Columbia University Press, 1944, p. 218.

which is the place where Confucius asked about government.[67] In the west there is Mt. Ai, which is the place where Lu Kung and Ch'i Hou met.[68] Pan-ho Mountain is also there, and on its top there is Yang-shan Temple. Then there is Resonant Stones [*Shih-ch'ing*] Mountain, which is six or seven *li* from the river bank. In *Yü kung,* under, "And the sounding stones that seemed to float near the banks of the Ssu" [Legge, III: 105, 107], a note says, "At Hsia-p'ei is Resonant Stones Mountain."[69] Perhaps in olden times it was considered a place where musical stones were gathered. I do not know whether it is true.

From Han-chou north the land had been quite flat, occasionally with distant mountains. From the Yangtze River north there had not been a single hill. We first saw some when we arrived there. Yet even those mountains were not big but like the Nam-san of our country.

The Director of P'ei-chou, named Li, and the Commander of P'ei-chou Garrison, named Han, came to see me. They met me courteously and presented to me one plate of wheat noodles, one plate of bean-curd, and two plates of vegetables and meat and fish delicacies.

From in front of the station, we [passed the wall of P'ei-chou and went to Hsin-an Station].

Since we had gone up the East River, the rivers had been broad and the banks on both sides high, and we had not been able to look about all the time.

2nd Day. Passing Fang-ts'un Station. This day there were light rain and high winds.

From Hsin-an Station we [went past Fang-ts'un Station] and came to Lü-liang Great Flood. The flood was in Lü-liang Mountains, and on both sides of it, scattered rocks jutted up sharply in the river bed. Some rose up high, and some were in low-lying clusters. The river twisted and turned, and when it came to those open banks it burst out free, angry and fuming, its voice like ten thousand claps of thunder. The hearts of those who passed pounded, and their spirits quaked. Boats occasionally met disaster. A stone levee that had been built on the east bank had been cut irregularly to check the force of the water, but even for tenders, it was necessary to use twisted bamboo rope and the power of ten oxen before they could be pulled up.

From in front of Ch'ing-shan-lung-shen Shrine, we went up the flood past [several places] and arrived in front of Shui-shou Shrine. The fastest part of the flood was eight or nine *li* long. Ch'en Hsüan said to me, "That was Lü-liang Flood. After the Great Yü did the dredging and channelling, there was a Ch'in Shu-pao who supervised the repairing of this flood."[70]

---

[67]Probably a reference to *Tso chuan*, Chao-kung 17/3.

[68]See *Ch'un ch'iu,* Yin-kung 6.

[69]Legge (III: 94-96) identifies the author of this note as Ts'ai Ch'en (1167-1230), a disciple of Chu Hsi.

[70]For Ch'in Shu-pao, or Ch'in Ch'iung, a great general at the time of the founding of T'ang, see *T'ang shu* 68 (K'ai-ming ed. 3315.2) and *Hsin T'ang shu* 89 (K'ai-ming ed. 3895.1). For notes on the Lü-liang Flood and the Hundred-Yard Flood to follow see (*T'ung-chih*) *Hsü-chou-fu chih* (25 *ch.,* 12 *ts'e*), *ch.* 11: 16r.-19r.

I said, "In *Yü kung* [after the passage], '[He] took effective measures at Liang and Ch'i' [Legge, III: 94], a note says, '"Liang" is Lü-liang Mountain.' Li Tao-yüan says, 'The rocks of Lü-liang rise up high. The flow of the river us turbulent and shakes heaven and earth.'[71] This flood must be none other than that one."

Hsüan said, "So it seems, indeed, but in *Yü kung* [it says], 'Lü-liang lies in Chi-chou.'[72] These rapids are in Hsü-chou, so it is somewhat puzzling."

3rd Day. Passing Hsü-chou. This day it rained, and there were high winds.

[We went from Chiu-nü-chung to Peng-ch'eng Station, two or three *li* southeast of Hsü-chou Prefecture.]

Hsü-chou was the old Ta-p'eng-shih-kuo. When Hsiang Yü called himself Dictator King of Western Ch'u, he put his capital west of that wall.[73] There is a levee to protect the wall, and there are the old foundations of the Yellow Tower, which was built when Su Shih was governor of Hsü. Su Che [wrote] a *Yellow Tower Fu,* praised to the present day.[74]

From the station we passed workers' quarters that were at the junction of two rivers and came to Hundred-Yard Flood. From the northeast the Ssu, Chu, Chi, Wen, and Pei rivers flowed together; and from the northwest the Pien and Sui flowed together. Arriving north of Hsü-chou wall, the Ssu, Ch'ing, Pien, and Cho converged and flowed south into this flood. The swift part of the flood, though not as long as that of Lü-liang, was extremely dangerous. Great numbers of rocks, like tigers' heads and deers' antlers, lay scattered in disorder. People called them the Boat-tipping Rocks. The water ran swiftly, twisting and turning past obstacles, turbulent with startling rushes, rumbling and shaking like thunder, and spuming like sleet and hail. It burst through some places and seeped through others, making it very hard for boats to pass.

From in front of Ch'ing-feng Hall, a local post of the Ministry of Works, it took over one hundred laborers, following the tow-paths on both banks, to pull the boats upstream with bamboo ropes that had been fastened to them. I, Fu Jung, and others climbed onto the bank and walked along the tow-path. I saw that the paving-stones were firm and in good repair, and I asked Fu Jung about them: "I imagine that the people who made this path must have bestowed a blessing on later generations."

Fu Jung said, "In olden times, this path was low and narrow. When the river rose a little, there was no path that could be used. When the water receded, the earth came away and the stones came out, and it was hard to walk. In recent

[71]Li Tao-yüan, comp., *Shui ching chu (Water Classic and Commentary)*, Changsha 1892 ed., 3/21r.

[72]Hsüan may be quoting from an edition different from the one Legge used, which does not make the point so directly. See Legge, III, 94.

[73]See Watson, *Records*, I: 59.

[74]Su Shih, who served at Hsü-chou from 1077 to 1079, took special pleasure in the Yellow Tower, which embellished an embankment he had directed to be built to protect the city against floods. He opened the tower with ceremony in 1078. See Lin, *The Gay Genius*, pp. 181, 192. Su Che's *Yellow Tower Fu*, celebrating his brother's achievement, may be found in his works, *Luan-ch'eng chi (SPTK* 1st series), ch. 17.

years, Kuo Sheng and Yin T'ing-yung in turn have repaired it.[75] They used stone slabs laid in layers, fastened them with iron bolts and cemented them with lime. That is why they are as strong and firm as they are."

At night we came to the junction of the Pien and Ssu and stayed there.

4th Day. Fair.

We pulled the boats and came to a transfer station, in front of which were Ch'i-feng Gate and Mu-yü Hall. Boats had been made into a bridge that spanned the river and was named Great Floating Bridge. Above and below the bridge, masts were like thorns. Two boats were removed from the bridge to let passing boats through, and when they had passed, the removed boats were put back and the bridge made again. My boats passed that bridge and Ta-ying workers' quarters and came to the river bank in front of Shui-tz'u Granary of Hsiao County, where we stopped.

5th Day. Passing Liu-ch'eng Market. This day was fair.

[We went from Chiu-li Mountain to Chia-kou Station.] The Station Master, whose name I have forgotten, did not go by what Ch'en Hsüan said and served us food lavishly. He presented a bushel of rice to Tu Yü. Hsüan struggled with Yü for it, and Yü hit Hsüan on the forehead.

From the station we came to Huang-chia Lock, on which was Mei Mountain Myriad Carriers Stone Marker [*Mei-shan wan-i pei*]. I ordered Chǒng Po to ask Yang Wang to let us look at it, but Yang was not willing to do so. He gave permission only after we had insisted. Briefly, the inscription on the stone said,

"Magnificent, the Exalted Emperor T'ai Tsu [1368-1398] of our ruling house rose, a dragon flying, from the region of the Huai and united the world. He built his capital at Nanking to watch over the Empire. With the succession to the great duties of our Cultured Emperor T'ai Tsung [1403-1424], he moved the capital to Peking. Then the Four Mountains, all the guardian mountains, and the Four Barbarians[76] paid tribute and taxes to the Court. Every year, they all gathered in the Imperial domains. But Tien, Shu, Ching, Ch'u, Ou, Yüeh, Min, and Che[77] sailed, by way of the Yangtze River, the Eastern Sea, following it north to Tientsin. They went up the Lu River[78] and reached the capital.

"The distances of the river and sea and the dangers of wind and waves made transporting [grain] and accumulating it at the capital hard. Our Cultured Emperor T'ai Tsung, therefore, mindful of the difficulty of transport in

---

[75]Kuo Sheng is noted as an official assigned to the local office of the Ministry of Works at the Hsü-chou floods in the *Ch'eng-hua* period. *Hsü-chou-fu chih, ch.* 6B: 3*r.* and *ch.* 11: 16*r.* I did not find Yin T'ing-yung.

[76]The whole subject of this sentence is literary language for all China and her tributaries; the Four Mountains would be the eastern mountain Tai, the southern mountain Heng, the western mountain Hua, and the northern mountain Heng; the Four Barbarians were the I of the East, the Jung of the West, the Man of the South, and the Ti of the North.

[77]These are literary names for parts of China south of the Yangtze and along its upper reaches, corresponding roughly to Yunnan, Szechwan, Hunan, Hupeh, Fukien, and Chekiang.

[78]The Lu River, connecting Tientsin and T'ung-chou, is also called the Pai River.

the Southern and Eastern seas, had his greatest ministers go to the Hsü, Yang, Huai, and Chi and survey the land and regulate the rivers. East from Kua-chou and west from I-chen they built embankments along them all to block them and keep them from leaking into the Yangtze. Making use of existing channels, they cut canals and led in streams to make a river, converging in the Yang. From the Yang it went to the Huai, from the Huai to the Hsü, and from the Hsü to the Chi.

"From the Chi south, rivers flowed south and joined the Huang River. That converged with the Huai and entered the sea. From the Chi north, rivers flowed north and joined the Wei River. That converged with the Pai River and also entered the sea. His Majesty, realizing that the land north and south, being of uneven height, dissipated the waters and kept none and that such a condition was not good in the long run, ordered those in charge to put up locks: in some places one lock every five to seven *li*, in others one every ten *li* or more, in order to catch the water and let boats pass. To the present day, that fountainhead [of benefits] has not been exhausted.[79]

"From then on, the gathering of tribute to the Court from the Four Mountains, the guardian mountains, and the Four Barbarians; the transportation and accumulation of military and civilian taxes; and all commerce and trade have come by way of it. For the first time, the advantages of water transport extend throughout the Empire to the benefit of the people. There will not again be danger from the wind and waves of the Yangtze and the sea.

"This act of our T'ai Tsung has truly carried on the virtuous accomplishments of Yü. It has made up a deficiency of Heaven. It has begun a glorious procedure for all ages and all alike.

"That is all the more so in that Hsü had been the old P'eng-ch'eng, a great prefecture of the east. It strategically dominated the Huai and Chi and was a controlling pass between the northern and southern capitals.

"North of Hsü and east of Huang-chia Village was a mountain stream that flowed south into a lock. Its force was torrential, and it had many whirlpools. Drifting sand having silted it up and made it shallow, boats passing there were constantly obstructed, and the people were extremely distressed by it.

"In the spring of *T'ien-shun wu-yin* [1458], the authorities drew up a memorial and laid it before the Court. Our Sagacious Emperor Ying Tsung [1457-1464] carried forward the tremendous and good work, adding much to the previous accomplishment. He ordered the authorities to set up locks and make a passage there, and he established an official to take charge of it. Thereafter, boats went to and fro, and there was no more of the previous distress."

The lock official opened the lock and ordered laborers to pull my boats up, and we passed. [We went from I-ching-huang-chia Stop to Hsieh-kou Lock.]

[79]For details of this work, see Wu Chi-hua, *Ming-tai hai-yün chi yün-ho te yen-chiu,* Institute of History and Philology, Academia Sinica, Special Publications No. 43, Taipei, 1961; especially pp. 76-82.

6th Day. Passing P'ei District. This day was fair.

[We went from Ku-t'ou Lower Lock to P'ei District,] which had been the native place of Han Kao Tsu [r. 202 B.C. -195].[80] Northeast of the district was a river, which was the P'ao. On its far bank was a high mound, in front of which a banner gate had been erected. It displayed the name Ko-feng Tower and was the place where Kao Tsu had sung of the great wind. Southeast of the district was Ssu-t'ing Station, which was the place where Kao Tsu had for a short time been head of Ssu-shang Pavilion. On the west bank of the river was I Bridge, which was the place where Chang Liang had got the shoe [that the old man had dropped].[81]

Fei-yün Lock was at the mouth of a river. We went up that river through the lock, looked at the stand, visited the bridge, and arrived in front of the station. The station was 150 feet from the river.

Fu Jung said to me, "Now that you see our great country's system, what do you think of it? Formerly there was no river route from south of the Yangtze to the northern capital. From the *Chih-cheng* period [1341-1367] there was for the first time a plan for a passage. With the reign of our T'ai Tsung, a Marquis of P'ing-chiang was established to carry it out.[82] He dredged the Ch'ing and Yüan, deepened the Chi and Pei, and channeled the Huai and Yin so that they passed into the Yangtze. Throughout the whole region for ten thousand *li,* streams interlace like veins. Boats are able to pass in safety because of the work. The people have received the benefits and will continue to do so forever."

I said, "If there were not this river passage, it would be our misfortune to hobble along by whatever means we could over a long, hard road. Now we lie at ease in the boats all the long way and do not know what it is to fall down. The benefits we have received are great, indeed."

This day we went from the station past Shui-mu-shen Shrine and on through the night.

7th Day. Alternately cloudy and rainy.

[We went from Miao-tao-k'ou to Ku-t'ing Lock.]

When we climbed the river bank and looked, we saw that in the vast spaces to the northeast were mountains, which were not very high. Fu Jung pointed to them and said, "They are the Ni-ch'iu Mountains, the birthplace of Confucius. Below the mountains are Confucius' village and the Chu, Ssu, and I rivers." We also saw in the northeast what appeared to be high mountains lying stretched out over several hundred *li* like clouds. Jung pointed to them and said, "Those are the T'ai Mountains, the old Tai-tsung Mountains. They

[80]For the biography of Han Kao Tsu see Watson, *Records,* I: 77-121.

[81]For Chang Liang see Watson, *Records*, I: 134-151. For retrieving the shoe and showing suitable respect for the old man otherwise, Chang Liang was introduced to the highest military arts.

[82]The title, as "Earl" *po* rather than "Marquis" *hou,* seems to have been conferred in 1402 on Ch'en Hsüan (1365-1433), who achieved enormous improvements in water transport. See *Ming shih* 106 (K'ai-ming ed. 7345); *TRD* IX: 49, 50; Wu Chi-hou, *Ming-tai hai-yün,* p. 48 *ff.*

are where Yü Shun [traditionally 2317-2208 B.C.] and the Chou emperors made eastern tours. If this group followed the land route by way of Ch'ü-fu District, Yen-chou, we could go through the Ni-ch'iu, cross the Chu and the Ssu, see Confucius' village, and look at the T'ai-shan from nearby."

We passed Yü-huang Shrine and came to Nan-yang Lock and stopped.

8th Day. Passing Lu-ch'iao Station. This day was cloudy.

From Nan-yang Lock we passed Tsao-lin Lock and came to Lu-ch'iao Station, in front of which was Lu-ch'iao Lock. There was a crossroads, going east to Ch'i and Lu, linking in the west with Chü-yeh, leading south to Huai and Ch'u, and reaching the capital in the north.

West of the lock was Black Ink-slab Lake, the water of which was black. An Overseer named Liu was there on his way to the capital to be enfeoffed. His multitude of flags, arms, armor, bells, drums, and musical instruments set the rivers trembling. Having come to that lock, he was wantonly shooting at boatmen with round shot. That was how depraved he was. Ch'en Hsüan said, "It is a eunuch who is behaving so wrongly in that boat."

Fu Jung asked me questions. He said, "Are there these overseers in your country, too?"

I said, "The eunuchs in my country are employed only in sprinkling and sweeping in the palace and conveying messages. They are not given charge of public affairs."

Fu Jung said, "The Emperor's father trusted eunuchs and gave them appointments. That is why those castrated for punishment, like that one, have great power as ministers close to the throne. All the civil and military officials toady to them."

Ch'en Hsüan said, "Which of the three Laws, Medicine, Taoism, or Buddhism, does your country respect?"

I said, "My country respects the Confucian practices. Medicine comes next. There are Buddhists, but people do not esteem them. There is no Taoism."

Ch'en Hsüan said, "The *Ch'eng-hua* Emperor [Hsien Tsung, r. 1465-1487] respected Taoism and Buddhism most. The new Emperor now strictly prohibits them."

I asked, "Now that it is the time of Great Ming in your country, why does everyone call it Great T'ang?"

Fu Jung said, "It is simply that the latter has become customary since Great T'ang times."

I then said, "Ever since I arrived here, all your countrymen have pointed at us and said, '*Ta-ta-ti-wu-yeh-chi.*' What kind of speech is that?"

Fu Jung said, "That is what the Japanese call eminent persons in our land. The people here suspect that you have come from Japan. That is why they use those words."[83]

[We went from Lu-ch'iao Lock to New Lock.] Fu Jung said to me, "This lock was built by Supervisor of Waterways Yeh-hsien Pu-hua.[84] When the Hui-t'ung River[85] reached here, sand and mud had silted it up. The stream had spread and could not carry boats. Sluice-gates were put in at both ends, from Hsin-tien to Shih-shih-chuang, but in shoals and [sections where the bottom was] rough, there were still difficult places. Every time a canal boat passed here, all the men, high and low, exhausted their strength, shouting through the day, gaining an inch and losing a foot, and being obliged to resort to carts on land for transport. Since this new sluice-gate was built, the movement of boats has acquired safety and regularity."

[We went on, noting landmarks.]

9th Day. Arrival at Chi-ning Department. This day was fair.

[We went from Shih-fu Lock to Hsia-hsin Lock,] which was more than one hundred feet in to the west from the mouth of the Yüeh River. To the east, the Yüeh River came close to T'ien-ching Lock and against the Hui-t'ung River on its north. The two rivers met at right angles. People going west on the river from the lock sometimes were overturned by the current, and those going up the Yüeh River had trouble towing against the current. The locks had been established below the two mouths to await the flooding or ebbing of the water to be opened or closed.

About twenty *li* northwest of the lock there was Huo-lin Knoll, which had been the place of "hunting and trapping unicorns in the west."[86] It is now the land of Chia-hsiang County.

We passed the lock and came to the wall of Chi-ning Department. To the northeast the Ssu from Ch'ü-fu and the Kung from Tsu-lai joined east of Lu Bridge and came into the Grand Canal to pass the Huai and enter the sea. Beyond the Huai was Nanking. To the northwest was Lake Chü, which in its eastern part received the Grand Canal and in its northern part, in Lin-ch'ing, put out the Wei River to pass to the sea. Beyond the sea was Peking. The two capitals stood over three thousand *li* apart.

All the rivers from outside divided in Chi-ning. The Kung River, bounding the east wall, and the Chi River, bounding the west wall, curved windingly round and joined below the south wall. In the two rivers were earthen dunes. The dunes started in the northeast and came undulating down for more than

---

[83] *Ta-ta-ti* has even recently been considered Japanesy Chinese for "very big," *Wu-yeh-chi (ki)* (K. *oyagi*) resembles the Japanese *oyaji,* "father" or "elder."

[84] A prominent statesman (d. 1309) of the Yüan dynasty. Among many assignments he supervised work on the Yellow River and other waterways. *TRD* I:281.

[85] A portion of the Grand Canal.

[86] *Ch'un ch'iu,* Ai-kung 14.

one thousand *li*.[87] On top of a dune there was Kuan-lan Pavilion, which had been built by Sun Fan.[88] From below the pavilion we came to T'ung-chin Bridge, which was on the road to the southern gate of the wall. South of the bridge was Ling-yüan-hung-chi-wang Shrine. We came to a stop on the river bank northwest of the shrine.

10th Day. Arrival at K'ai-ho Station. This day was fair, with high winds.

At dawn we left the wall of Chi-ning, went west past Fen-shui Lock and came to Nan-wang Lake. The lake was an endless expanse of water; only in the west did we see distant mountains. In the east were dense barriers of green grasses, which were the marsh in *Yü kung:* "The *lake of* Ta-yeh was confined within its proper limits" [Legge, III: 105]. Now it has become silted up, and in the lake a long stone levee has been built and named Public Dam.

[We went from Ma-chang-p'o to the Shrine of the Dragon King of the River Fork.]

A large river there came from the northeast, arrived in front of the shrine, and split into northern and southern branches. The southern branch was the one that we had come down, with the current. The northern branch was the one up which we were going to go, against the current. Because the shrine was at the fork of the two rivers, it had the name River Fork. I asked about the large river that came from the northeast, and someone said, "It is the source of the Chi River." I do not know whether that was so.[89]

Yang Wang and his staff entered the shrine, burned incense, and worshiped the god with sacrifices. They ordered us to pray, too. I said, "Sacrificing to mountains and rivers is a matter for the nobility; gentlemen and commoners sacrifice only to their ancestors. To overstep one's place is improper, and improper sacrifices make fawners of men and do not satisfy the gods. In my own country, therefore, I do not venture to pray to the gods of mountains and rivers. How could I possibly pray at the altars of foreign countries?"

Ch'en Hsüan said, "This is the altar of the Dragon King who once appeared here. For that reason, everyone who passes here sacrifices most respectfully before going on. Otherwise there would surely be trouble with the wind and waves."

I said, "One who has looked at the sea is not easily impressed by other

[87]Since the information on waterways in this entry is unclear, I have translated somewhat freely after consulting maps in *Chi-ning chih-li chou chih* (1840 ed., 10 *ch.*), just before the table of contents and *ch.* 3 and 4. The Yüeh River, which is not identified in the gazetteer's maps, presumably is the short-cut channel south of the Canal proper below the walls of the city. Although Ch'oe says that it crosses the Hui-t'ung River, the gazetteer indicates that the two streams meet, not cross, and I have translated Ch'oe's comment that way. None of the maps shows the Ssu meeting the Kung, but the gazetteer notes (*ch.* 4, 10*v.*) that sometimes they flowed together and sometimes not. Ch'oe has them meet near the wall or city of Lu (Lu-ch'eng), but the maps show a Lu Bridge (Lu-ch'iao), not a Lu-ch'eng, at the right spot. I have read bridge for wall. The gazetteer also speaks often of the characteristic silting of rivers in the region, accounting for the dunes in the Kung and Chi.

[88]The Kuan-lan Pavilion was less than ten years old. Sun Fan, a *Chin-shih* of 1464, while Director of the Department ordered it to be built. See *Chi-ning chih-li chou chih, ch.* 5: 6*v.*-7*r.*; *ch.* 7:42*r.*

[89]*SRCY* p. 231 notes that the course of the Chi has changed repeatedly, so that its parent stream might at any time be in doubt.

waters. I have passed through an ocean of tens of thousands of *li* and violent waves. The water of rivers like these, here in the land, is not enough to scare me."

Before I had finished speaking, Ch'en Hsüan said to Yang Wang, "This man will not pray, and we should not bend his will."

We passed K'an-ch'eng Stop and came to K'ai-ho Station. It was already the third watch of the night. What was called Public Dam went as far as K'an-ch'eng Stop and stopped. In it there were sluices, some eight or nine *li* apart, some over ten *li* apart, and fourteen in all. The dam itself was over one hundred *li* long.

11th Day. Fair.
[We went from K'ai-ho Market to An-shan Station.]

12th Day. Arrival at Tung-ch'ang Prefecture. This day was fair.
[We went from Pao-liang-ts'ang to Chin-hsien-cha Transfer Station.] In front of the station was Ching-k'uei Gate. From a house to the right of the gate hung a carved cage in which a bird was kept that was shaped like a pigeon. Its beak was red and long, the tip somewhat yellow and hooked, and its tail was ten or eleven inches long. Its eyes were yellow, its back green, and its head and breast inky. It was gifted with the ability to understand men's thoughts. Its speech was coherent and glib, and its songs were clear. If a person said something, it repeated it all. I went to look at it with Fu Jung and said to him, "This bird can speak; is it not a parrot?"

Fu Jung said, "It is."

I said, "This is a bird from Kansu, and I am a man from Korea. Kansu and Korea are tens of thousands of *li* apart; is it not a fortunate coincidence that we have come to meet each other here today! Traveling in a foreign country, I and the bird are alike. Thinking of our homelands we are alike. Anxious and haggard of appearance, we are alike. To look at this bird deepens my grief."

Fu Jung said, "This bird is spending his life in a cage, and in the end he will die in a foreign country. You, now, are returning safe and sound to your own country and will carry out your duties to your lord and parents. How can you call that the same?" The parrot also said something, as if he understooood us.

[We went from Shou-ch'ang County to Ch'ung-wu Station, in Tung-ch'ang Prefecture.]

Tung-ch'ang Prefecture was the Liao and She of the old state of Ch'i. The wall is three or four *li* up the river bank north of the station. Inside the wall are the prefectural capital, the seat of Liao-ch'eng County, a post of the Provincial Surveillance Office, the south post of the Provincial Administration Office, P'ing-shan Garrison, Yü-pei Granary, Hsüan-sheng Shrine, and the county school.

13th Day. Passing Ch'ing-yang Station. This day was fair.

[We went from T'ung-chi-ch'iao Lock past Ch'ing-yang Station to Tai-chia-wan Lock.]

14th Day. Fair.

We arrived in front of Kuan-yin Temple of Lin-ch'ing County. The temple was on a spit at the junction of two rivers. To east and west, four locks had been built to hold water. East of the temple a floating bridge had been built of boats to give passage into the county [seat]. The wall of the county was about a half *li* from the east bank of the river. Both the county seat and the Lin-ch'ing Garrison headquarters were inside the wall. It was an important junction between the two capitals, a place to which traveling merchants flocked. For several tens of *li* inside and outside the wall, the multitude of pavilions and towers, the flourishing of the markets, the wealth of valuable goods and the fleets of moored boats, though not equal to those of Su-chou or Hang-chou, were still the greatest in Shantung and famous everywhere.

[We followed the Ch'ing-ch'üan River north to Ch'ing-yüan Station and stopped there.]

15th Day. At dawn, a violent thunder-storm. In the afternoon, cloudy.

There were some men from Liao-tung — Ch'en Ch'i, Wang Chih, Chang Ching, Chang Sheng, Wang Yung, Ho Yü, and Liu Chieh — who had arrived there previously on commerce. When they heard of our arrival, they brought three pots of refined wine, one plate of sweetmeats, one plate of bean-curd, and one plate of large pancakes and served them to me and my staff. They said, "The site of our city of Liao-tung is adjacent to your country, and we are like a single family. We are fortunate today to have met you on our journey and venture to offer these crude things only as tokens of courtesy."

I said, "Your land was the former capital of old Koguryŏ, and Koguryŏ is now the land of my Chosŏn. Though the conditions of rule of the land have changed with the times, it is really the same country. Now, when I am panting from the closest brush with death and a voyage of ten thousand *li,* and no one I know is around me, to meet you and, moreover, receive your warm kindness are like meeting someone of my own flesh and blood."

Ch'en Ch'i said, "We started out in the First Month and arrived here on the first of the Second Month. In the first ten days of the Fourth Month we shall return home. I am afraid that we shall not be able to meet again. If you pass through my land ahead of me, ask inside An-ting Gate for Ch'en Ying, a Confucian scholar. He is my son. Be good enough to give him word of me." We took leave of each other and left. We poled the boats to [a point] in front of Hsia-chin-ch'ang and moored them there.

16th Day. Passing Wu-ch'eng County. This day was fair.

[We went from P'ei-chia-chüan Stop past Wu-ch'eng County to Chia-ma-ying Station.]

17th Day. Fair.

[We went from Cheng-chia-k'ou to Liang-chia-chuang Station and beyond.]

In the evening we arrived in front of Ku-ch'eng County and stopped. I said to Fu Jung, "The moon is bright tonight and the wind favorable. Why do we not leave?"

Fu Jung said, "Did you see the three corpses floating in this river?"

I said, "I saw them."

Fu Jung said, "They were all killed by bandits. This region has suffered successive famines, and many people have been driven into banditry. They do not know that you were set adrift and all your baggage lost. On the contrary, they will take it that as foreigners, you must have valuable things. All of them have greedy hearts. Then, too, on the road ahead settlements are few and scattered, and the bandits are many and reckless. That is why we do not leave."

I said, "On this journey, I have already met bandits from Ning-po Prefecture. The last person I want to meet in my life is a bandit."

Fu Jung said, "In general, the temperament of the Chinese in the north is forceful and violent. In the south it is mild and docile. The Ning-po bandits were men from south of the Yangtze; even though they were of the outlaw type, therefore, they plundered without killing people. That is what saved you. When these northerners plunder, they invariably kill the people. Either they put them in ditches or float them on rivers or the sea. That accounts for the floating corpses we saw today."

18th Day. Passing Te-chou. This day was fair; high winds blew up sand.

[We went from Meng-chia-k'ou to An-te Station.]

Ch'en Hsüan asked me, "Do the people of your country use tea to exchange drinks with their guests?"

I said, "They use wine, not tea."

Ch'en Hsüan said, "All my countrymen use tea for guests. For people from far away for whom they have deep affection, some may use wine."

I asked Fu Jung, "In China, what are the regulations for umbrellas, hats, belts and belt tablets?"

Fu Jung said, "For umbrellas and light silk gauze hats, there are no categories. As to *kai* umbrellas, the First and Second Ranks have yellowish-black gauze coverings, red raw silk linings, three tiers and silver spires. The Third and Fourth Ranks have the same, but the spires are red. The Fifth Rank has blue gauze coverings, red raw silk linings, two tiers and red spires. The Seventh, Eighth, and Ninth Ranks have blue, oiled, raw silk coverings, red raw silk linings, one tier and red spires.[90]

[90]The subject of the conversation is, of course, umbrellas of state. The Koreans had general guidebooks to the Ming system, but Ch'oe is attempting to establish the latest conventions. That small changes were introduced into the system from time to time is suggested by a comparison with official regulations. The difference between plain um-

"As to the belts, the First Rank has jade, the Second Rank rhinoceros [horn], the Third Rank inscribed gold, the Fourth Rank burnished gold, and the Fifth Rank inscribed silver, the Sixth Rank burnished silver, and the Seventh, Eighth, and Ninth Ranks horn.[91]

"As to tablets, all the civil officials from First to Ninth Rank have pewter tablets. On one side the office in which one serves is written in square style, and on the other side the four words 'Attached for all time,' are written in seal characters. Lictors carry them. All military officers for whom there are lictors and offices wear them."

I asked, "Sometimes do the Tatars make raids?"

Jung said, "Formerly they did, but now there are grand defending regional commanders on each border. The infantry and cavalry are constantly on guard, and [the Tatars], therefore, do not get in to raid."

At night we passed the wall of Te-chou. The river curved round west of the wall and then went north. The city had been the old P'ing-yüan-chün. It was a big place, crowded with people, and travelling merchants gathered there.

We came to a river bank, the name of which I do not know, and stopped. Fu Jung said to me, "A younger brother of the previous Emperor, being virtuous, was enfeoffed in Lu and entitled Lu Wang, with a territory of over three hundred *li* within the borders of this Te-chou. That is why men of the time called him Te Wang."[92]

I said, "Why did Te Wang live outside instead of inside the capital?"

Fu Jung said, "If princes of the blood were inside, disloyalty would be feared. When they are sixteen, therefore, they are all enfeoffed as princes and put outside."

I said, "With Te Wang in Shantung, he dominated a strategic area. Did he also on his own authority administer public affairs?"

Fu Jung said, "Officials of the offices of the Prince's Palace [*Wang-fu*] take charge of palace affairs only. There are an education official and a defense official. With them the Prince discusses literature and reviews archery and charioteering, but that is all. The Prince has nothing to do with administering public affairs, which are all directed from the Court."

19th Day. Passing Liang-tien Station. This day was fair.

[We went from P'i-k'ou Stop past Liang-tien Station to Lien-wo Transfer Station and stopped there.]

brellas and *kai* umbrellas is not clear. *Ta Ming hui-tien, ch.* 59, p. 2*v*.-3*r*., distinguishes between parasols and rain-umbrellas and differs from Fu Jung's description on the following points: (The words in brackets are translated from notes made in red ink in the Library of Congress copy by an anonymous reader and are here included as likely corrections.) After the description for the Third and Fourth Ranks and perhaps referring to Ranks 1-4, "For the above, all the parasols use black and yellowish-black, all the rain-umbrellas use [red], oiled raw silk." "The Sixth to Ninth Ranks have . . . blue raw silk coverings . . . two tiers . . . " "All the rain-umbrellas use oiled [paper]."

[91]*TMHT, ch.* 58, p. 1*v*., 2*v*., differs in a few places: Third and Fourth Ranks, plain gold; Fifth Rank, silver flowers; Sixth and Seventh Ranks, plain silver; Eighth and Ninth Ranks, raven's beak.

[92]More fully Te-chuang Wang. Enfeoffed in 1457, he occupied his fief in 1467. See *MS* 104.

20th Day. Fair.

,We went from Wang-chia-k'ou Stop to Hsüeh-chia-wo Village and stopped there.]

21st Day. Passing Ts'ang-chou. This day was fair.

[We went from San-chen-tao Stop to a workers' quarters of Ts'ang-chou.]

The wall of the department overlooked the east bank of the river. [The place] had been the Po-hai-chün of Han. At the edge of the river, a man's head fastened on top of a pole was displayed to all. Fu Jung said to me, "That is the head of a notorious bandit. Kung Sui of Han came to this land in a single carriage and subdued all the bandits.[93] There is a story that they sold their swords and bought oxen.

"The bandits here plunder much and kill people, and it has been so since olden times."

We passed Lien-fang, Ying-k'uei, and Ssu-chien gates, came to Ch'ang-lu Transfer Station, and stopped in front of it. I asked Fu Jung, "Ever since we passed the Huai River there has been a steady line of boats of officials from the various bureaus of the Ministries of War, Punishments, and Personnel. Why?"

Fu Jung said, "Because some of the ministers of the Court may have made small errors in what they did in former days, the present Emperor in his wisdom is dismissing them all. All those who are carrying pewter tablets and going the other way in the river are ministers of the Court who have been dismissed and are going to their homes. Even Huang Tsung, the Regional Commander who asked you about your past the other day at Shao-hsing Prefecture, has been dismissed and gone home."

I said, "If many court ministers are being degraded, why does [the Emperor] not dismiss the eunuchs instead of letting them have their way?"

Fu Jung said, "Eunuchs are also being executed and dismissed beyond number. All those now going to the capital on the river were commissioned by the previous Emperor. It is difficult to say what will happen to them when they go back. Both his Excellency Lo and His Excellency Nieh, the Overseers you met previously, have been degraded to the position of valet because they were slow in returning."

I said, "Now the Empire has got again a ruler like Yao and Shun. He elevates good men and dismisses wicked ones. The Court is calm, and the Four Seas are steady. Shall we not give praise?"

Fu Jung said, "Quite so, quite so. The ones our Emperor keeps at a distance are the petty men and the eunuchs. He attends the exposition of the Classics daily and discusses literature and government with the chief ministers and scholars. He keeps it up without tiring. On the 9th Day of the Third Month he attended personally the National University and sacrificed to Confucius,

---

[93]For a brief note on Kung Sui, a successful official of the 1st century B.C., see *BD* 1028.

which shows indeed that he honors the Confucian scholars and the Way."

Joking, I said, "Does the Emperor bow to a subject of a feudal state?"

Fu Jung said, "Confucius was the teacher of all ages; how could the Emperor treat him like a subject? But when the Son of Heaven attends the sacrifice to Confucius, a master of ceremonies says, 'His Majesty will bow.' The Son of Heaven is about to bow when from the side another master of ceremonies says, 'Confucius was Criminal Judge of Lu.' The master of ceremonies then calls out, 'His Majesty is excused from bowing.' He is supposed to bow but actually does not. Thereby the ceremony honors Confucius and the Son of Heaven with slight to neither."

I said, "Confucius' Way is greater than heaven or earth, brighter than the sun or moon, and more constant than the four seasons. It persists endlessly through all ages of the world. If the officials, gentry, scholars, and common people study his Way to train themselves; and the nobles study his Way to govern their states; and the Emperor studies his Way to put the world to order, all, from the Emperor to the common people, must pay homage through the Rite to Confucius. Why do you say the name 'Criminal Judge of Lu,' and, 'His Majesty need not bow?' If you use Criminal Judge to designate Confucius, that makes Confucius the secondary minister of a minor state. Then how can you humble the Emperor with such a sacrifice?" Fu Jung was silent.

At night Fu Jung came again and spoke to me. "Someone who recently came from the capital says that a minister [*shang-shu*] and a grand secretary [*hsüeh-shih*] were standing face to face and talking, it was not known about what. A captain of the police arrested them and reported it to the Emperor. They were ordered to be sent down to the Superintendent of the Imperial Bodyguard[94] for questioning on the subject of their talk. The grand secretaries are in the Cabinet [*Nei-ko*], and the Emperor discusses all matters, large and small, with them. When this one talked intimately with a minister, then, it was greatly feared that there might be collusion for selfish ends. That is why they were questioned."

22nd Day. Passing Hsing-chi County. This day was cloudy.

At dawn we passed An-tu-sai-k'ou Stop and Ch'ing-shui-wang-chia-k'ou Stop and came to Ch'ien-ning Station. The seat of Hsing-chi County was behind the station, in front of which was a huge house. Ch'en Hsüan said, "That is the private house of the new Empress, *née* Chang. At first, when the new Emperor was Crown Prince, the Directorate of Astronomy memorialized that the star of the Empress shone southeast of the Yellow River. The previous Emperor ordered that over three hundred daughters of good families southeast of the Yellow River be selected and assembled at the capital. The former Emperor and the Empress Dowager made a further selection, and Miss Chang was chosen and made Empress. The Empress's grandfather was Pre-

---

[94]*Chin-i-wei chien.* See Hucker, p. 60; *TRD* II: 289, VIII: 159-61

fect of Feng-yang Prefecture. Her father did not hold office but formerly was a student in the National University. Now he has been made a general."

[We went from Tso-wei Stop to Hsia-kuan-t'un and stopped there.]

23rd Day. Passing Ching-hai County. This day was fair.

Between 1 and 3 a.m. we pushed off the boats and passed Tiao-t'ai Stop, Nan-chia-k'ou Stop, and Shuang-t'ang Stop, and came to Feng-hsin Station, which was in front of the seat of Ching-hai County.

I said to Fu Jung, "I want to learn how water wheels are made."

Fu Jung said, "Where did you see something called a water wheel?"

I said, "Previously, when we passed Shao-hsing Prefecture, there were men on the shore of a lake turning water wheels and irrigating fields. Using little strength, they raised much water. That could be helpful to farming in droughts."

Fu Jung said, "The construction is known to carpenters. I am not familiar with it."

I said, "Long ago in the *Chia-yu* period [1056-1063], a man from T'o-lo Island,[95] which was subject to Koryŏ, drifted with the wind, his mast and boom broken, to shore. He reached K'un-shan County, Su-chou. The Magistrate of the county, Han Cheng-yen, served him wine and food and saw his old mast, which had been stood in the wood of the boat and could not be moved. He had a craftsman repair the mast and make a windlass and taught [the man] how to raise what had fallen. The man was so happy he clasped his hands and danced round.[96]

"T'o-lo is now our Cheju. I went to Cheju, was driven adrift, and came here; I am of the same type as that man. Make His Excellency Han's spirit your spirit, teach me how to make a water wheel, and I, too, shall clasp hands and be happy."

Fu Jung said, "The water wheel is used only for drawing water. It is not worth learning about."

I said, "In my country there are many irrigated fields, and frequently there is drought. If I study this method and teach the Koreans to improve their farming, your work of a few words can be an inexhaustible benefit to my Koreans for all ages. I should like to study the method carefully. If there is anything you do not know, you can ask the sailors and explain it to me clearly."

Fu Jung said, "Here in the North the land is mostly sandy soil, and since there are no irrigated fields, water wheels are not used. How can these sailors know their construction? However, I shall think about it."

While we were eating, Fu Jung told me briefly how the machine was built and turned. I said, "The ones I saw were turned with the feet. Yours is turned with the hands, and its shape, too, is a little different. How is that?"

[95]T'o-lo was an early name for Cheju Island. See, for example, *TRD* III: 332.

[96]Like Ch'oe's party these earlier castaways, more than 30 in number, won Chinese sympathy partly through signs that they belonged to the greater Chinese community. Their dress was in T'ang style, and they held documents in Chinese, connecting them with Koryŏ. See *Su-chou-fu chih, ch.* 145: 7*v.*, 8*r.*

Fu Jung said, "The ones you saw must have been treadwheels. They are not so convenient as this kind, which can be turned by a single man."

I said, "Can they be built of pine?"

Fu Jung said, "Pine is light and cannot be used to build them. For the upper and lower axles [*chi-t'ung*], we use cryptomeria. We use elm for the trough [*ch'ang-ku*] and camphorwood for the paddles [*pan*]. Bamboo strips are used to bind the spokes [*she-ch'ang*]. The four pillars in front and back must be big, but the central pillar, to the contrary, should be small. The dimensions of the wheels, spokes, and paddles are like this. If you cannot get cryptomeria, elm, and camphor-wood, you must use woods of tough, pliable grain; they will do."[97]

[We went from Tu-liu Police Station to Yang-liu-ch'ing Station and beyond.]

24th Day. Passing T'ien-chin [Tientsin] Garrison. This day was cloudy.

At dawn we passed Chih-ku. The name of the river by the wall was Ku River. We came to the wall of T'ien-chin Garrison.

The Wei River ran from south to north and was the river down which I had come, the Pei River ran from north to south and was the river up which I was to go, and the two rivers joined east of the wall to flow into the sea. The wall overlooked the junction of the rivers, and the sea was over ten *li* east of the wall. In olden times, all cargoes from the Yangtze, Huai, and places south of them sailed the open sea and reassembled there to reach the capital. Now, the benefits of canals cut, locks placed, and boats given passage reach throughout the Empire.

Inside the wall were garrison posts. The posts of the Left and Right Garrisons divided the administration of sea transport and other matters. East of the wall was a huge shrine overlooking the river bank, the inscription on its plaque so big that though I was far from it, I saw it. At the top was the word "Heaven" [*t'ien*] and at the bottom the word "Shrine" [*miao*]. There was a word in between them, but I do not know what it was.[98]

[We went from Ting-tzu-ku to Yang-ts'un Station.]

25th Day. Cloudy.

[We went from Shang-lao-mi Stop to Ho-hsi Station.]

Fu Jung said to me, "When the Three Authorities of Chekiang memorialized on your being blown adrift, their memorial was dated the 1st Day, Fourth Month. I brought the memorial with me, and I am afraid we may not meet the date. From this station I shall go by relay carriage ahead of you to the capital. Later, when we meet before the Ministry of War, do not greet me and show that we know each other. I say that because the laws of the new Emperor are strict."

---

[97]The words used here to translate the names of parts of the water wheel are largely surmised from pictures of water wheels and descriptions of them in *Ku-chin t'u-shu chi-ch'eng, ching-chi hui-pien k'ao-kung tien, ch.* 244, *shui-ch'e pu-hui k'ao chih* 2. Ch'oe Pu deserves the credit for introducing at least this kind of water wheel to Korea, as recorded in *Chōsen-shi* IV: 5: 616, Eighth Month, 4th Day: "Ch'oe Pu built a water wheel according to what he had seen and heard in Chiang-nan and presented it."

[98]No doubt "Consort" *fei*, as Professor Miyazaki suggests.

BOOK III

26th Day. Fair. High winds; dust and sand filled the sky, and we could not open our eyes.

[We went from Yao-erh-tu-k'ou to Hsiao-chia-lin Village and stopped there.]

In the place across from my boat were more than ten men on rafts that had shelters on top of them. They, too, had come and stopped. Bandits came to rob them, but the men on the boats were also strong and fought back. Ch'en Hsüan said, "That is how outrageously the bandits beat people and rob them. You had better warn your people to be on guard, and let us pass the night cautiously."

From T'ien-chin Garrison north, white sand lay flat as far as the eye could see. There was no grass in the waste land. The five grains did not grow, and settlements were few and far apart. When Ts'ao Ts'ao subjugated the Wu-wan, he sent his generals from Hu-t'o River into Lu-sha. Lu-sha was that place.[1]

27th Day. Fair. High winds.

[We went from Ho-ho Station to Chang-chia Bay,] which was the place at which the tax, tribute, and merchant boats from everywhere assembled.

28th Day. Arrival at Jade River House [Yü-ho-kuan], *Peking*. This day was fair.

[We left the boats and, at first riding donkeys and later walking, went from Tung-yüeh Shrine through T'ung-chou.]

T'ung-chou was Shang-ku-chün of Ch'in. Now it is under Shun-t'ien Prefecture. South of the department headquarters are T'ung-chou Garrison, Left Garrison, Right Garrison, Ting-pien Garrison, and Shen-wu Center Garrison.

Outside the west gate of the new wall we got on donkeys and passed Yung-chi Temple and Kuang-hui Temple and came to Ch'ung-wen Bridge. The bridge was outside the gates of Peking.

Yang Wang, Li K'uan, T'ang Ching, Hsia Pin and Tu Yü led us on foot through the Imperial City Southeast Ch'ung-wen Gate and to the Central Post Hotel [*Hui-t'ung-kuan*]. The capital was the place to which tribute was brought by the Four Barbarians; [consequently], in addition to the Main Building of the Central Post Hotel, an annex had also been built and called

[1]Ts'ao Ts'ao (155-220) destroyed Wu-wan power in northeast China *c*. 207. See, for example, *TRD* I: 203.

Central Post Hotel. That building, in which we were lodged, was also called Jade River House, because it was south of the Jade River.

29th Day. Going to the Ministry of War. This day was fair.

Yang Wang took us outside the gate of Jade River House. Over our shoulders we saw that on East Street there was a bridge, on both sides of which gates had been built. A plaque said, "Jade River Bridge." We walked along West Street past the Directorate of Imperial Parks, Nan-hsün Ward Stop, Imperial Academy of Medicine, Directorate of Astronomy, Court of State Ceremonial, and the Ministry of Works and came to the Ministry of War. Yü Tzu-chün, the Minister, was there, sitting in one hall. Left Vice-Minister Ho and Right Vice-Minister Yüan were sitting in a hall across from him.[2] Two Senior Secretaries and four Administrative Secretaries were sitting in a row in another hall. First we went to the Vice Ministers, next to the Minister, and afterwards to the hall of the Senior and Administrative Secretaries.

The Senior Secretaries and the others did not question me again on my drifting there. They pointed to the shadow of a Japan pagoda tree (*huai*) in the garden and ordered me to write a quatrain (*chüeh-chü*) on that subject. Then they ordered me to write an eight-line poem in the T'ang style on the subject "Crossing the Sea." Tai Hao, Senior Secretary for the Bureau of Maps,[3] took me up into the hall, on a wall of which a map of the Empire was hung. The places through which I had passed were clear at a glance. The Senior Secretary pointed at it and said to me, "Where did you start and where did you land?" I pointed out the place where the boat had gone adrift, the sea through which we had passed, and the island on which we had landed. Our course passed directly north of Great Ryukyu.

Senior Secretary Tai said, "Did you see Ryukyuan land?"

I said, "While drifting in the white sea, we met a northwest wind and went south. We saw vague mountainous shapes, and there was also an aura of settlement. I suspected that it was the shore of Ryukyu, but still I do not know."

He asked, "Did any of the men who accompanied you die?"

I said, "All forty-three of my men, trusting to an Imperial benevolence as great as the sea, kept alive."

He asked, "When you observe mourning in your country, do you use Wen Kung's *Chia li*?"

I said, "When my countrymen have children, they first teach them from the *Hsiao hsüeh* and *Chia li*. Even in the examinations, we choose those well-versed in it. It governs our mourning, and everyone follows it in daily life."

[2]For Yü Tzu-chün (d. 1489), *Chin-shih* of 1451, see *MS* 178 (K'ai-ming ed. 7502.3). Among men of sufficient political stature and named Ho, Ho Ch'iao-hsin (*MS* 183, K'ai-ming ed. 7515.4) seems most fitting as Left Vice Minister, but I have not found confirmation of him in that office. The Right Vice Minister was Yüan Ch'in, *Chin-shih* of 1454. He is mentioned in the biography of Yü Tzu-chün noted above.

[3]For Tai Hao, *Chin-shih* of 1478, see *CKJM* 1716; *LCLK*, *Ch'eng-hua* 14, 33r. For the Bureau of Maps, *Chih-fang ch'ing-li ssu*, see Hucker, p. 35.

He asked, "Does the King of your country like books?"

I said, "Our King receives the Confucian ministers four times a day. He never grows tired of learning, and he likes to select worthy scholars.[4]

When all had stopped asking questions, they served me tea and cakes. T'ang Ching took us back to Jade River House.

In the evening one Ho Wang, who understood our language somewhat, came and said to me, "Prime Minister An Ch'ŏ-ryang, an Envoy of Congratulations, and twenty-three men from your country came to this guest house and stayed more than forty days. They set out to return on the 22nd Day, Third Month."[5] I expressed sorrow that we had not met. Ho Wang said, "You will return to your country, too. Why do you grieve so much?"

I said, "I am suffering abroad, with no relatives anywhere around me. If I should see someone from my own country, it would be like seeing my father or elder brother. My father, moreover, has died recently, and my mother is in mourning. My younger brother is young and inexperienced. The family is poor and insecure from morning to night.

"I drifted out to sea, and whether I am dead or alive my family have not heard. They can only assume that in the mountainous, heaven-shaking waves of the great, endless sea, I must have blackened my name and buried myself in a fish's belly. My poor family will be observing double mourning. How great must be the grief of my old mother and weak, little brother!

"If I had met His Excellency An's party and returned home at the same time as he, I should have avoided mishaps on the road. If I had not returned with him but he had gone home first and kindly delivered word of me, it would have been possible to mitigate a little my mother's and younger brother's grief. Heaven has no pity on me; I have missed meeting an envoy from my own country by only seven days. How can I not have deep regret?"

1st Day, Fourth Month. Fair.

At dawn Li Hsiang,[6] Auditor [*Chu-pu*] of the Court of State Ceremonial, came and said to me, "Today the Ministry of War will submit your case in a memorial; put your mind at ease. Cases of drifting ought to be reported to the Ministry of Rites, but the Three Authorities of Chekiang reported directly to the Ministry of War and did not report to the Ministry of Rites. The Ministry of Rites, therefore, has put in a memorial charging them with fault. The Ministry of War, moreover, has flogged Commander Yang Wang twenty lashes." He also said, "An Envoy of Thanksgiving from your country is sure to arrive here within ten days. You can wait here and go back with him."

I said, "For me, going to my first mourning, one day as a traveler is like

---

[4]Apparently two characters of a four-character phrase have been left out here; the meaning would seem to be as given.

[5]An Ch'ŏ-ryang had been sent to China the 22nd Day, First Month, 1488. *Chōsen-shi* IV: 5: 601.

[6]Li Hsiang, a Korean interpreter, was the first to inform a Korean envoy that Ch'oe and his party were safe. *Chōsen-shi* IV: 5: 610.

spending three autumns. Please arrange for my speedy return." Li Hsiang nodded his head.

From Chekiang I had not met an interpreter until I arrived there and met that man.

2nd Day. Cloudy.

Li Chu, the Assistant Commissioner of the Central Post Hotel, came and said to me, "Since you forty-three men are not tribute-bearers for your own country, the daily ration a man will be only one quart of old rice. There will be no salt or other foods."

I walked out the gate of the house and happened to meet Fu Jung, and we talked at the foot of Jade River Bridge. I said, "Among the places that I have passed, there was a T'ung-chou in Chekiang, and Peking also has a T'ung-chou. Hsü-chou Prefecture had a Ch'ing-ho County, and so did Kuang-p'ing Prefecture. How is it that among the departments and counties of the country there are [different] places with the same name?"

Fu Jung said, "Though it happens that their names are the same, the public offices by which they are governed are different, and really no harm is done."

3rd Day. Cloudy; thunder, lightning, rain, and hail in the evening.

Li Hsiang came and said, "I am an interpreter for your Korea. For the past one or two days, the Ministry of War and the Palace have had things to do, and the memorial of your case, therefore, was not sent in. If it is not presented today, it will surely be tomorrow."

I answered, "Of all the unfortunates in the world, none is so ill-fated as I. My father is dead, my mother is old, my younger brother is delicate, and the family is poor. Everything needed to observe mourning is wanting. I, moreover, have drifted away, and they have not been informed whether I am dead or alive. How are my mother and younger brother to know that I have received great kindness from His Majesty the Emperor and have reached China alive? They must be mourning for me also; they must have boundless grief. Please petition the Ministry of Rites not to keep me here a long time."

Li Hsiang said, "Prime Minister An Ch'ŏ-ryang of your country has learned all about your arrival here alive and has turned back for home."

I said, "How did Prime Minister An know about it?"

Li Hsiang said, "The Overseer of Chekiang sent Commander Yang Lu speeding night and day by the land route to report your case. He arrived here the 12th Day, Third Month. His Excellency An copied the memorial and left. Between the end of the Fourth and the beginning of the Fifth Month, your family will know that you did not die at sea.[7] It is not worth grieving over. But the strain on you must be severe; truly I can sympathize with you. I

---

[7]On the 14th Day, Fourth Month, 1488, An Ch'ŏ-ryang reported that Ch'oe Pu and his party were safe and submitted copies of the memorial of the Chekiang Regional Commander (*Chōsen-shi* IV: 5: 609).

shall make known your anxiety to the Ministries of War and Rites."

4th Day. Fair.

Ho Wang took me to his house and served me food. I thanked him and he said, "You have drifted here from far away; I can pity your condition, and that is why I have served you. There is no need to thank me."

5th Day. Cloudy.

Yang Wang came and said to me, "The memorial was sent down to the Ministry of Rites on the 3rd Day."

6th Day. Fair.

Ryukyuans Ch'en Shan and Ts'ai Sai brought a feast of delicacies and served it to me and my staff. I was moved by their kindness but had nothing with which to repay them. I took, therefore, five quarts of rice from our rations and offered it to them, but they waved their hands and refused it.

At the time, Ryukyu had sent Ch'eng P'eng,[8] Doctor of Canonical Law, and twenty-four men to bring tribute. They were lodged in the rear house (*hou-kuan*), and Ch'en Shan and Ts'ai Sai were of that staff.

The Ministry of Rites sent Wang Min, a clerk, to summon Yang Wang. I asked what it was about, and Min said, "Your memorial has been returned; that is why I have come."

7th Day. Showers.

Cheng Ch'un and Li Ts'ung-chou, sub-officials [*li*] of the Ministry of Rites, came with a statement that the Ministry of War had sent to the Ministry of Rites and showed me the text:

"According to a report of the Three Authorities of Chekiang . . . "[9] At the end it said:

"In the case of that Ch'oe Pu, we instructed the Chekiang Administration Commissioner to send Assistant Commander Yang Wang on special commission to take charge of the escort and instructed the garrisons and transfer stations on the way to allot officials and troops to guard [the party] on the journey outside the capital, and to hold hearings and prepare reports.

"The officials of this Ministry received His Majesty's instructions: 'Let the proper ministry take note. Respect this.' Between the time that we respectfully copied that out and the time that we sent the authorities' decision, this Ministry continuously sent on whatever it received.

---

[8]Had ambassadors ranked by seniority, Ch'eng P'eng would probably have been the dean of the diplomatic corps serving Peking. He had been leading missions to China since 1470. See Wu Chuang-ta, *Liu-ch'iu yü Chung-kuo,* pp. 81-84.

[9]This abbreviated beginning probably means that the first part of the document is quoted from the previous one. I am grateful to Professor Chi-chen Wang for having pointed this out.

"According to the endorsement of the Chekiang Administration Commissioner, he has sent Commander Yang Wang to escort forward the aforementioned barbarian. Research has shown that in the Eleventh Month, *Ch'eng-hua* 6, the said Chekiang Grand Defender and other officials memorialized, [asking] to send forward Kim Maeng-hoe* and six other barbarians of Korea who had encountered winds. The Ministry memorialized and received permission to issue clothing against the cold and appropriate porters and rations and send them back to their country. Now, in the matter stated above, which has been sent to the Ministry, it is our view that though Ch'oe Pu and the forty-two other barbarians from Korea who encountered winds fall into the class of barbarians arrested by maritime patrols, the said Chekiang Grand Defender, Regional Inspector, and Three Authorities have met and judged that they are not spies, especially since the winds and waves have battered them all and they lacked clothes and food. Considering the general policy of the Court of bringing peace to distant areas, it is proper that they be treated with consideration. It is fitting that the matter not be transferred to the Ministry of Rites and that we allot a change of clothing to them. This Ministry will provide post horses and official rations to the official Ch'oe Pu and porters and rations to the other men. They will go with carriages, into which they will load their baggage, passing through the proper prefectures. We shall send one official to escort them to the Korean border and let them return home themselves. Since the case is one of managing the return to their country of foreign barbarians who have encountered winds, and since we have received the notation, 'Let the proper ministry take note,' we have not ventured to arrange matters on our own initiative alone.

"1st Day, Fourth Month, *Hung-chih* 1. Prepared by Yü, Senior Guardian of the Heir-Apparent and Minister [of War], and others.

"On the following day an edict was received by this Ministry, saying 'Respect this; carry it out.' In addition to setting the correct procedure, it is proper that we should refer the matter to your Ministry. Hence this communication."

I order Hyo-ja to barter some rations of rice for wine and offered it to Cheng Ch'un and the other. Cheng Ch'un said to me, "The two of us hoped to receive some gratuity, some cash or cloth or any kind of goods that we can take away to use. We do not intend to get drunk."

I said, "When I was drifting across the sea, my own limbs were not safe. I was barely able to survive; how can I have anything but what is on me? Look at my baggage. If there is a single thing there, feel free to take it away." When I considered their motives carefully, [I found] that they wanted the clothes I was wearing. I ordered Yi Chŏng to reduce the rations, exchange some for ten cash, and give them that. Li Ts'ung would not take it; he scattered it in front of me and left with Cheng Ch'un, very angry.

At night I happened to be talking with An Ŭi and Yi Hyo-ji: "In the Sung period a man from your Cheju drifted to the shores of Su-chou. In his boat were hemp seeds as big as lotus pods. A man of Su-chou got them and planted them, but in later years they grew small, like ordinary hemp seeds.[10] Do you have such hemp seeds in your land now?"

An Ŭi said, "That is a thing of the past. Now even ordinary hemp seeds are rare. That is why, when both nobles and commoners assemble tribute, they give coarse, arrowroot cloth, which is useless to the country and harmful to the people. If the tribute were governed by what is produced in the land, such as things from the sea, everyone would be benefitted."

8th Day. Cloudy.

Yang Ju-lin, Wang Yen, and Ch'en Tao, students of the National University, wearing black hats and blue collars round their throats, came and said, "Do the students in your country also wear these?"

I said, "All young students, even though they are in remote villages or secluded lanes, wear them."

They said, "In your country is there also 'specialization in Classics'?"

I said, "In the examinations in my country, those versed in the Classics and Books are passed. The students, therefore, study the Four Books and Five Classics thoroughly. Those who have mastered only one Classic do not attain the rank of full-fledged Confucian scholars."

9th Day. At Jade River House. This day was fair.

There were two brothers, Chang Yüan and Chang K'ai, whose house was opposite the guest house. They both came and chatted.

10th Day. At Jade River House. This day was fair.

Li Shu said to me, "The carriages, horses, and passports for your return home have come. You will not be here long."

11th Day. At Jade River House. This day was cloudy.

Li Hsiang came and said to me, "Why has the Envoy of Thanksgiving from your country not come by now?"

I said, "It is a long way; I cannot tell when he is moving and stopping or whether he is going fast or slow. All I think of is that my own coming here has nothing to do with affairs of state and that if only I receive the profound kindness of China and am returned home alive, I shall look up to Heaven and join my hands in prayer. But wasting away, loitering about, delaying for days and months, I shall not satisfy my desire to weep at the coffin and keep watch at the grave. It is that over which I grieve."

Li Hsiang said, "I have explained in detail to the Ministry of Rites what you say, and the Ministry has put in its memorial. You will soon be sent back; do not grieve."

[10]The hemp seeds were said to have arrived with the castaways who fell into the hands of Han Cheng-yen, mentioned on p. 207. See *Su-chou-fu chih, ch.* 145; 7v., 8r.

There was a man named Wang Neng who understood our language well. He said to me, "For generations my ancestors lived in Tung-pa-hu, Liao-tung, and they went to and fro between there and Ŭiju. I, too, am a man of Koryŏ. When I was thirteen, my father died, and I went with my mother and for thirty-one years lived in Liao. I and my mother were captured by Urianghai[11] and moved to Tatary. In the end we got back alive and have been living here. Whenever envoys have come from your country, I have always met them." He bought wine with cash that he had and comforted me and my staff. He said to me, "I have heard that none of your staff died; is that so?"

I said, "Yes."

Wang Neng said, "Wasn't that fortunate! Even ordinarily, among a large group of people over a period of time occasionally someone dies; how much more likely is that when violent winds are met and a great ocean crossed. Not to have a single death is rare in history. I imagine it must have been brought about by your amassing of virtue in ordinary life."

I said, "It is that the mantle of Imperial graciousness causes all things to take their place. We, too, therefore, survived."

12th Day. At Jade River House. This day it rained in the morning and was cloudy at noon.

There was one Li Hai who also understood our language. He came and said to me, "I have gone with envoys to your country and back six times. Is Prime Minister Sŏ Kŏ-jŏng still well?"

13th Day. At Jade River House. This day was cloudy.

One Chang K'uei was the youngest brother of Chang Yüan and was more perceptive than his eldest brother. He said to me, "How do you while away the days and months in this desolate house?" He brought vinegar and soy sauce and presented them to me.

14th Day. At Jade River House. This day was fair.

A man named Sun Chin said to me, "Long summer days like these are hard to pass; I am very sorry for you." He presented to me one peck of rice, a plate of vegetables, and one container each of salt, soy sauce, and vinegar. I ordered Chŏng Po to go and thank him, and Sun Chin said, "The fact that you are short of rations is the fault of the officials of this Central Post Hotel. How can the Emperor know that matters are like this?"

15th Day. At Jade River House. This day was fair.

An official came from the Ministry of Rites and asked my position and name

[11]The Urianghai were a tribe inhabiting the land between the Tatars and Jurchen in early Ming. Despite military arrangements meant to hold the northern barbarians back, the Urianghai penetrated to the northern borders of Ming. They were, however, later weakened by Tatars and others (*Tōyō-shi shōjiten*, Sōgen-sha, Osaka, 1953; p. 13).

and the names of the men who had come with me. He wrote them down and went back; I do not know why.

16th Day. At Jade River House. This day was fair.

One Sun Hsiung, Captain of the Dress Swords Post of the Rear Office of the Imperial Bodyguard [*Chin-i wei hou-so pan-chien ssu chiao-wei*], came. I said, "We have been lodged in this empty guest house with nothing to do, waiting and hoping, for more than ten days already. We do not know when we shall return home."

Sun Hsiung said, "After the Ministry of Rites has memorialized asking for awards, you may go back."

I said, "Our coming here had nothing to do with affairs of state. After being on the verge of death, we sought only to return home alive. Now, our dying breath has grown strong, our dried guts have softened, our hurt feet have healed, and our weak bones have hardened. That is all because the graciousness of the Emperor in caring for strangers is generous and great. I, without having served China in the slightest, have received that generous and great kindness. I am already embarrassed; why, then, should there be a giving of awards? What I want is to go home quickly, see my old mother, bury my dead father, and carry out my filial duties. How can the Ministry of Rites know what urgency this son feels?"

Sun Hsiung said, "Recently there has been some trouble in the Ministry of Rites, causing them to order your case to be delayed. I shall set all the circumstances concerning you before the Minister and later come see you."

17th Day. At Jade River House. This day there were showers.

The Ryukyuans Ch'en Shan, Ts'ai Sai, and Wang Chung came and announced that they were returning home. Then they presented to me two small fans and two floor mats and said, "Though they are poor things, our feelings truly go with them."

I said, "Our friendship is based on feelings, not things."

Ch'en Shan said, "Twenty years ago, the King of my country sent my father to your country and back. He was extended great love by numbers of people, and he always remembered their kindness. Is it not fortunate that I, now, have found so much in common with you?"

18th Day. Attending the Ministry of Rites. This day was cloudy.

Foreman Wang Huan, carrying a placard, came and summoned me. On the placard was written, "We summon Ch'oe Pu, the barbarian official of Korea who drifted across the sea, to come to this office in great haste."

I followed Wang Huan past the Nan-hsün Stop to Wen-te Ward. Inside the Cheng-yang Gate of the wall stood the Ta-ming Gate. To the left of the gate was Wen-te Ward; to the right Wu-kung Ward. Cheng-yang had three stories,

Ta-ming two. We arrived at the Ministry of Rites.

Li K'uei, Senior Secretary of the Bureau of Receptions, and Chin Fu and Wang Yün-feng, Administrative Secretaries, receiving commands from Minister Chou Hung-mo, Left Vice Minister Ni, and Right Vice Minister Chang,[12] said to me, "At dawn you will be taken to Court to receive awards of clothing. You should change your clothing to festive dress. When that is over we shall send you off to go back."

I replied, "When I was drifting at sea, I was overwhelmed by the wind and waves and let all my baggage go. I came here barely having saved these mourning clothes;.I have no festive dress. At any rate, I am afraid that to be festive when I should be in mourning would not measure up to what is proper. To enter Court in mourning clothes, moreover, could not loyally be done. I beg of your Excellencies to weigh the ceremony; would it be possible to change your instructions?"

Senior Secretary Li talked about. what I had said in detail and for some time and had the sub-official Cheng Ch'un say to me, "When you receive the awards tomorrow morning, there will not be an elaborate performance of ritual. You may order a subordinate officer to receive them for you. When you acknowledge the Imperial graciousness the day after tomorrow, you yourself will bow to the Emperor. You must take part in that." I returned to Jade River House.

In the evening, Sun Chin came again and presented to me two pecks of grain and one container of melons in soy sauce. A man drove a flock of sheep past the gate of Jade River House. One of the sheep had four horns, and two of them had hair so long it hung to the ground.

19th Day. Receiving Awards. This day was cloudy.

Sub-officials of the Ministry of Rites, Cheng Ch'un, Wang Min, and Wang Huan, came and summoned Chŏng Po and the other forty-odd men in my charge and went back. I stayed alone at the house. Chŏng Po and the others entered the Palace, received the awards, and came back. The things I had received were one undyed grass cloth gown, one inner red satin round-collar, one black and green satin lined gown, one blue satin money-bag, one pair of boots, one pair of felt socks, and two rolls of green cotton cloth. For each of the forty-two men from Chŏng Po down, there were one padded jacket, one pair of padded trousers, and one pair of Wu boots.

Li Hsiang demanded money and, with a man at the side of a market who wrote letters for money, wrote an account to report to the Court of State Ceremonial. It said, "In the matter of awards, the Koreans Ch'oe Pu and

---

[12]References for those who have been identified of this group are as follows: for Wang Yün-feng, *Chin-shih* of 1484, *CKJM* 123; *FSJW* 101: 27r.-30v.; *KCLC* 124: 16r., v. For Chou Hung-mo (d. 1490) *CKJM* 533; *FSJW* 108: 23v.,26r. For Left Vice Minister Ni Yüeh, *Chin-shih* of 1464, *MS* 183 (K'ai-ming ed. 7517.1). Right Vice Minister Chang is probably Chang Sheng, a *Chin-shih* of 1469 who later became Minister. For him see *MS* 184 (K'ai-ming ed. 7519.1).

others, having drifted across the sea to Chekiang and been sent to the capital, have now respectfully received awards of gowns, padded jackets, boots, and other things. It is fitting that their names be reported to the Court of State Ceremonial. On the morning of the 20th Day, Fourth Month, they will acknowledge the Imperial graciousness."

Li Hsiang said to Chŏng Po, "Inform your official that tomorrow morning he is to come in festive dress and give thanks for the Emperor's graciousness."

There was a ceremonies official, Hsü, whose given name I have forgotten, who came and inspected Chŏng Po and the others, putting on their hats and sashes and teaching them the order of prostrations. Although Hsü was called an interpreter, he did not understand our language well.

I ordered Chŏng Po to go with one gate-keeper to seek Li Hsiang's house and tell him how I felt: "Mourning for a parent is something that one must observe. To wear beautiful clothes is to be unfilial. I am human; how can I take off my mourning clothes and put myself in the position of being unfilial?"

Li Hsiang said, "I discussed that today with His Excellency the Minister of Rites. For the time being, mourning for a parent will be unimportant and Heaven's graciousness important. In the fourth watch of the night, all the necessary award clothing will come to the outside of East Ch'ang-an Gate. Do not cause delay."

In the evening, fifteen men and women from Ta-ning Garrison, Tatary,[13] came in flight from their country and lodged at the West Central Post Hotel.

20th Day. Acknowledging Graciousness in the Palace. This day was cloudy.

Between 1 and 3 a.m. Li Hsiang came from his house and said to me, "You will now put on the hat and clothes, go into Court, and acknowledge graciousness. You must not be slow."

I pointed to the mourning hat on my head and said, "in my mourning, if I wear brocade and a light silk gauze hat, will I be easy in my heart?"

Li Hsiang said, "If you were beside the coffin, your father would be important. Now you are here; know only that here is the Emperor. When the Emperor is gracious it is a great breach of ministerial courtesy if one does not go and thank him. That is why by our Chinese code of etiquette, if a prime minister goes into mourning and the Emperor sends a man with a funeral donation, though [the minister] is in deepest mourning, he must put on festive dress and hurry to the Palace to bow his thanks. Only after that may he change back to mourning dress.

"Imperial graciousness must be acknowledged. To acknowledge it, one must be inside the Palace. To get inside the Palace, one may not be in sackcloth. It is a matter of expediency, like giving a hand to a drowning sister-in-law.[14] If

---

[13]It may be a comment on the times that though Ta-ning-wei was one of the military units especially established in T'ai Tsu's reign to hold the barbarians in check, here it is said to be in Tatar territory, and refugees from there are arriving in Peking. The marauders may have been the Urianghai, mentioned earlier.

[14]As a rule, that is to say, one would not touch the hand of a sister-in-law, but if she is drowning, it is well to ignore the rule. *Mencius* IV A: 17.

you fall in with the festive mood now, you will be bowing to circumstances."

I said, "When the awards were received yesterday, I did not receive them personally. How would it be if now, at the time of the acknowledgement of graciousness, I again ordered my staff and those below them to go and bow?"

Li Hsiang said, "When you received the things, there was no elaborate series of bows, and it was all right to delegate someone. But now, the Ministry of Rites and the Court of State Ceremonial have discussed the matter of your acknowledging graciousness and have already put in a memorial that says, 'The Korean barbarian official Ch'oe Pu and others . . . ' You are at the head of the list. Can you afford to be absent?"

I could do nothing but lead Chŏng Po and the others behind Li Hsiang and walk to Ch'ang-an Gate. Still, I could not bear to put on festive dress. Li Hsiang himself took off my mourning hat and put on a light silk gauze hat. Not only that, he said, "When state business comes up, there is a way to rise from mourning and return to duty. You will now go in through this gate in festive dress; when you have finished the rite of acknowledgement and left through this gate again, you will change back to mourning dress. It will be only for that short while. There can be no complete regulation without exceptions."

By that time, the outer gates of the Imperial City had already been unlocked, and the ministers of daily attendance were entering in order. Compelled by circumstances, I put on festive dress and entered the Palace. We passed through a one-story gate and two large two-story gates. Then there was another big two-story gate, which was Wu Gate. Troops were drawn up smartly, lights burned brightly. Li Hsiang seated me in the central courtyard. Soon, drums were beaten at the left end of Wu Gate and bells struck at the right end. Three arched gates opened, and at each gate two big elephants stood on guard, their forms spectacular.

Just before daylight, the officials of the Court lined up by ranks in front of the gate. Li Hsiang led me to my place in the Court ranks and then led Chŏng Po and the others to form a separate group. They followed after the students of the National University.

After five genuflections with three kowtows each, we went through Tuan Gate and passed through the Gate of Ch'eng-t'ien, which was inside Ta-ming Gate. We went to the east, passing out through Ch'ang-an Gate again, and I put back on my mourning clothes. We passed Ch'ang-an Street and returned to Jade River House.

Yi Hyo-ji, Hŏ Sang-ni, and Kwŏn San came in the clothing that had been awarded them and visited me. They said, "Before this, men from Sŏnŭi under Junior Director Yi Sŏm also drifted here, but the Emperor did not graciously make awards. Next we come, and we alone receive these unexpected awards and bow before the Emperor. What good fortune we have had!"

I said, "Can it possibly have been by chance? An award is awarded for merit. What merit have you in China? Drifting to death you were saved and will be returned alive to your country; the Emperor has already been extremely gracious, the more so since you worthless bodies have been let inside the Vermilion Gate to receive those awards. Do you understand that? The Emperor's taking care of us and giving us awards are due to the virtue of our King, who fears Heaven and serves China, and not to you. Do not forget our King's virtue, do not treat Imperial gifts lightly. Neither damage them nor lose them; do not sell them to others. Let your descendants keep them as treasures forever."

21st Day. At Jade River House. This day was cloudy.

Centurion Chang Shu-tsu came and said, "I am commissioned by the chiefs [*tsung-ping lao-tieh*] of the General Headquarters of the Left Army[15] to escort you to Liao-tung. The documents of the Ministry of War and the Central Post Hotel have already been issued; you will set out in two or three days." He took the commission from his sleeve and showed it to me. The text said,

"The General Headquarters of the Left Army. A matter of maritime intelligence.

"The report of the Registry [*Ching-li ssu*] has been submitted, and permission has been granted. Identity cards of the Bureau of Maps of the Ministry of War have been received by the Ministry and sent successively on. The memorial of the said Ministry and the report of the said Registry have been taken by the Ministry and sent to the Headquarters [*Nei-fu*]; and copies of the memorial of Chang Ch'ing, Grand Defending Overseer for Chekiang, on the previous matter have been circulated.

"The Headquarters has commissioned one official to escort [the Koreans] by way of the military garrisons, adding and subtracting troops for protection. When they reach Liao-tung, the patrol and defense officials will be responsible for sending individually interpreters to escort them as far as the Korean border and letting them return home themselves.

"Because this concerns the management of the return to their country of foreign barbarians who have encountered winds, and because we have received and respectfully complied with [the Imperial order], 'Let the proper ministry act according to the principles and facts involved,' we have not presumed to act without authority.

"1st Day, Fourth Month, *Hung-chih* 1.

"Memorial drawn up by Yü Tzu-chün, Senior Guardian of the Heir Apparent and Minister, and others.

"The next day:

"We have received His Majesty's rescript: 'Let it be so. Respect this.' Besides making all general arrangements, we have sent to the Registry of the Headquarters a report for the Headquarters. This Ministry has memorialized

---

[15]*Tso-chün tu-tu fu*. See Hucker, pp. 57, 58; *TRD* VIII: 159-61.

and received [the instructions], 'Respectfully comply with the principles and facts of the matter. Resr ct this.' Accordingly, we have sent one appropriate official, commissioned t accompany [the party] as escort. Wei Lang, Grand Defending Overseer for Liao-tung, and Kou Ch'ien,[16] Regional Commander, will go with the party by way of the military garrisons. Let all public offices respect this. The successive posts should carry out these orders thoroughly.

"It is fitting that identity cards should be used for the advances forward. When the Registry of the General Headquarters of the Left Army reports that the staff has complied with this text, the identity cards will be issued. When the report of the case reaches the General Headquarters, they will make all arrangements. Besides making preparations for sending on the men and transferring despatches, they will draw up tallies.

"The basic task is to protect Ch'oe Pu and the other barbarians well and to escort them forward. Kou Ch'ien, Grand Defending Regional Commander for Liao-tung, will take care of handing them over to separately commissioned interpreters to be escorted away. Let the men not be lax or awkward. Let this be the necessary authorization."

22nd Day. At Jade River House. This day was fair.

From the 5th Day of this Month, I had had a headache. On the 17th Day it had improved, but this day I suddenly got a pain in the heart. My chest and diaphragm were both stiff, my hands and feet were numb, and there were chills throughout my body. My breath was short in my throat. Chŏng Po, Kim Chung, Son Hyo-ja, and Ko I-hok prayed for me without effect. The men we led were at a loss what to do. Yi Chŏng and Makkŭm wept at my side. There was one man—I do not know his name—who knew a little about treating sicknesses and saw that I was in danger. He punctured my ten finger tips with a big needle, and black blood spurted forth. The man said, "Very dangerous, very dangerous!"

Kim Chung and Chŏng Po hastened to inform the Bureau of Receptions of the Ministry of Rites; a report from the Central Post Hotel also reached the Ministry of Rites. They sent Chu Min, a Doctor of the Imperial Academy of Medicine, to come and treat my sickness. Chu Min felt my pulse and said, "This sickness is primarily because of injury to the seven affections and secondly because you have caught cold. That is why you have this sickness; you must take good care of it."

Chŏng Po said, "What medicine shall we use to treat it?"

Chu Min said, "Treat it with fragrant fire vitality tonic [*hsiang-huo-ta-ch'i-t'ang*]." He hurried to the Imperial Academy of Medicine and came back with a drug. It was seven spirits regulating tonic [*chia-chien-ch'i-ch'i-t'ang*]. He mixed it and simmered it with his own hands, made me drink it, and took his leave. In the second watch of the night, I vomited the medicine I had drunk.

[16]For Kou Ch'ien see *CKJM* 1525; *FSJW* 98: 43*v*. The latter source misprints his surname "Hou."

23rd Day. At Jade River House. The sky was cloudy, and there was thunder.

At sunrise Chu Min came again and took my pulse. He said, "Yesterday I found a pulse of three beats slow and two skipped. Today the pulse has regained vitality. We need only treat you." Then he simmered some ginseng digestive tonic [*jen-shen-yang-wei-t'ang*][17] and made me drink it. From the time that I drank the medicine, my body gradually recovered.

Toward evening Li Shu and Chang Shu-tsu came and said to me, "Early tomorrow morning your party will start back to your country, but if you are not well now, you may set out on the 26th Day. Which is better?"

I said, "I was on my way to the deepest mourning, [when] I drifted to another country. The circumstances are very pressing; the passing of a single day is like three autumns. Yesterday I was sick, today I am a little better; if I lie down in the carriage, I can go. Let us go."

Shu-tsu said, "In that case I shall call on the Shun-t'ien-fu [Peking] Transfer Station and order carriages, donkeys, and horses to come."

XXX The Exalted Emperor T'ai Tsu [r. 1368-1398] of our Great Ming established the capital at Nanking, which had been Chin-ling, the place at which capitals were established by the emperors and kings of the Six Dynasties. The Cultured Emperor T'ai Tsung [r. 1403-1424] moved the capital to Pei-p'ing Prefecture and made it Peking. But the administrative system of Nanking remains as before.[18] There are eighteen prefectures, Ying-t'ien Prefecture and others, in the Imperial domains of Nanking, with the departments and counties that belong to them. In the Peking Imperial domains there are eleven prefectures, Shun-t'ien Prefecture and others, and also the departments and counties that belong to them. The prefectures, departments, and counties of the Imperial domains of both capitals are controlled by the Six Ministries. The Empire is also divided into thirteen administrative regions called Shansi, Shantung, Honan, Shensi, Chekiang, Kiangsi, Hu-kuang, Szechwan, Fukien, Kwantung, Kwangsi, Yunnan, and Kuei-chou. They control the prefectures, departments, and counties. Regional military commissions, garrisons, and chiliads are also established to defend them. There are 149 prefectures, 208 departments and 1105 counties. There are also pacification, suppression, security, control, and other offices.[19] *XXX*

XXX The wall of the capital was the wall of the Great Capital of Yüan. It was enlarged and repaired in the *Yung-lo* period [1403-1424][20] and has

---

[17]One of three medicines mentioned here is found in *Chung-kuo i-hsüeh ta-tz'u-tien* (comp. by Hsieh Kuan, Shanghai: Commercial Press, 1954, 4 vols.), which says of ginseng digestive tonic that it is useful for external chills, internal cold feelings, headache, body pains, phlegm, dyspepsia, intermittent fever, and other symptoms.

[18]Offices at Nanking almost wholly duplicated those at Peking but with smaller staffs and duties directed mainly to the Nanking metropolitan region. See *Ming hui yao*, 1887 ed., 80 *ch.*; *ch.* 32: 1/22v.; and Hucker, p. 6.

[19]*Hsüan-wei ssu, chao-t'ao ssu, an-fu ssu, hsüan-fu ssu.* See Hucker, p. 48; *TRD* VIII: 152, 153.

[20]The wall was enlarged in *Yung-lo* only after it had been diminished earlier in Ming. At the beginning of the dynasty the northern side was rebuilt about five *li* south of the Yüan wall, and in the *Yung-lo* period the southern side was moved a bit, perhaps three *li*, farther south, leaving the area of the Inner City somewhat less in Ming than in Yüan times. At about the same time (1417), the wall was faced with brick (*TRD* VII: 498-501).

nine gates: at the south is Cheng-yang. To the right of Cheng-yang is Hsüan-wu and to the left Ch'ung-wen. At the east are Tung-chih and Ch'ao-yang, at the west Hsi-chih and Fu-ch'eng, and at the north An-ting and Te-sheng. Inside that wall there is also an Imperial Wall (*huang-ch'eng*), inside which are West Garden, T'ai-i Lake, Ch'iung-hua Island, Wan-sui Hill, She-chi Altar, and Great Shrine. South of Ch'ang-an Left Gate of the Imperial Wall, the Court of the Imperial Clan, the Ministry of Personnel, the Ministry of Revenue, and the Ministry of Rites stand successively to the south. Behind the Court of the Imperial Clan, the Ministry of War, the Ministry of Works, the Court of State Ceremonial, the Directorate of Astronomy, and the Imperial Academy of Medicine, are also in a line going south. South of Ch'ang-an Right Gate, the Central, Left, Right, and Forward General Headquarters of the Five Armies stand in a line to the south. The Rear General Headquarters is behind the Central General Headquarters. South of the Rear General Headquarters, the Messenger Office, the Court of Imperial Sacrifices, the Office of Transmission [*T'ung-cheng-shih ssu*], and the Imperial Bodyguard also stand in a line going south. The Color Guard [*Ch'i-shou-wei*] is behind the Office of Transmission. The Ministry of Punishments, Censorate, and Grand Court of Law are in Kuan-ch'eng Ward, standing in a line going south. The Hanlin Academy is west of Jade River, and the Office of the Imperial Tutor [*Chan-shih fu*] is east of Jade River. The National University is inside An-ting Gate, the Court of Banquets [*Kuang-lu ssu*] is inside Tung-an Gate, and the Court of the Imperial Stud is in Wan-pao Ward. There are also the Five Warden's Offices [*Wu ping-ma ssu*], four garrisons of Prefectural Forces, three *Yü-lin* garrisons, four *Chin-wu* garrisons, a left *Hu-pen* garrison, three *Yen-shan* garrisons, a left *Ta-hsing* garrison, two *Wu-hsiang* garrisons, two *T'eng-hsiang* garrisons, two *Yung-ch'ing* garrisons, three *Wu-kung* garrisons,[21] Chi-yang Garrison, Chi-chou Garrison, P'eng-ch'eng Garrison, the Four Barbarians Institute [*Ssu-i kuan*], and the Central Post Hotel. There are, in addition, the capital of Shun-t'ien Prefecture, the seats of Ta-hsing and Yüan-p'ing counties, and the shrines of Yüan Shih Tsu [Kubilai Khan, r. 1260-1294], Wen T'ien-shang,[22] the Jade Emperor, and others. All are inside the wall.

T'ien-shou Mountain is one hundred *li* to the north and is the guardian mountain of the capital. Below the mountain is Yung-an Wall, inside which there are Ch'ang-ling Garrison, Hsien-ling Garrison, and Ching-ling Garrison. The late *Ch'eng-hua* Emperor was buried there. Mt. Hsi, Mt. Chin, Mt. Chüeh, Mt. Ch'üan, Mt. Yang, Mt. Hsiang; and Lu-shih, P'ing-p'o, Han-chia, Shuang-ch'üan, Ch'i-p'an, Ts'ui-feng, T'an-chih, Yü-ch'üan, and Wu-hua mountains are all about thirty *li* northwest of the wall. Sheer and massive, they shield the capital, making it a sure bastion forever.

---

[21]The garrisons beginning with *Yü-lin* were parts of the Imperial Guard, the forces charged with defence of the Imperial precincts. See Hucker, p. 60; *Ming hui yao*, ch. 42: 7r.

[22]Wen T'ien-shang (1236-1283), heroic fighter for Sung against the Mongols.

Jade River rises in Jade Spring [Yü-ch'üan] Mountain, passes through the Imperial Wall and the Palace and goes out of the capital wall to the southeast, becoming the Ta-t'ung River. When it reaches Koryŏ Village, it enters the Pei River with the Sang-ch'ien River.

There are two lakes, one of which is three or four *li* west of the Imperial Wall. All the rivers from the mountains flow into it. The other is south of the wall and is a ground for the raising of game.

Otherwise, there are towers, such as P'i-yün; pavilions, such as Chung-hsin; guest houses, such as Yung-p'ing; and arbors, such as P'ao-kua, Yü-ch'üan and Nan-yeh. There are too many such things to be counted. *XXX*

XXX Peking was the land of Yu-chou of Yü. In Chou times [1122-249 B.C.], it was divided between Yen and Chi. From the Later Wei [386-534] on, it grew accustomed to northern barbarian ways. After that, Liao [916-1125] made it Nan-ching, Chin [1115-1234] made it Chung-tu, and Yüan [1260-1368], in turn, made it Ta-tu. Barbarian chieftains built capitals there one after another, and all their customs were customs acquired from the northern barbarians.

Now Great Ming has washed off the old dirt and made those who buttoned their coats on the left take the ways of hat and gown. That can be seen in the splendor of the Court ceremonial. But in the streets, they revere the Taoist gods and the Buddha, not Confucius. They work at business, not farming. Their clothing is short and tight, and men and women dress the same. Their food and drink are rancid. The high and the low use the same implements. There are still habits that have not been obliterated, and that is regrettable.

The mountains, moreover, are bare and the rivers filthy. Sand and dirt rise up from the ground, and dust fills the sky. The five grains are not abundant. In that setting, the numbers of people, the profusion of buildings, and the richness of the markets do not, I am afraid, come up to those of Su-chou and Hang-chou. Everything needed in the city comes from Nanking, Su-chou, or Hang-chou. *XXX*

XXX The Court, regarding us as barbarians who had drifted across the sea, ordered Liu Hsien and others, porters who kept the gate at the guest house, not to let us leave the house on our own if we had not received a clearly written authorization or summons from a superior official, and not to let brokers or vagrants into the house to hobnob with us. Liu Hsien, therefore, took strict precautions. Since, moreover, there was no interpreter, I was as if blind and deaf and was therefore not able to learn of anything done at court. *XXX*

24th Day. Setting out from the Central Post Hotel. This day was fair.

Centurion Chang Shu-tsu and his son Chung-ying ordered three carriages at the Shun-t'ien-fu Transfer Station and came. I mounted a horse, and my staff either sat in the carriages or got on donkeys. We went out Ch'ung-wen

Gate by way of Jade River Bridge, passed again through the new and old walls of T'ung-chou, and came to Lu-ho Station. Li Feng, an official of the station, boiled tea and served it to us.

25th Day. Cloudy.
[We went from the Pai River to San-ho County.]

26th Day. Cloudy.
Early in the morning, Wu, the Magistrate of San-ho County, Fan, the Vice Magistrate, and Yang, the Auditor [*Chu-pu*], (I have lost the given names of them all) brought a plate of rice, one catty of meat, one jar of wine, and a plate of vegetables and asked how we were.
[We went from there to Kung-lo Station.]

27th Day. Arriving at Yü-yang Station and Meeting an Envoy of Thanks-giving. This day was cloudy; at night there was heavy rain.
[We went from Pai-chien Stop to Yü-yang Station, about five *li* south of Chi-chou.]
Chi-chou had been the Yü-yang-chün of Ch'in and Han. When An Lu-shan of T'ang rebelled [755-763], he occupied it. Later it took the name of the old Chi-men Pass. P'an-lung Mountain is in the northwest and K'ung-t'ung Mountain in the northeast. Inside the wall are the prefectural capital and the headquarters of Chi-chou Garrison, Chen-shuo Garrison, and Ying-chou-yu-t'un Garrison. In the northwest corner of the headquarters is the shrine of Chang K'an. When K'an was Governor of Yü-yang, he taught the people to plant. A children's song says, "Two ears on each stalk of wheat . . ."[23] That is in memory of him. His shrine is kept like new.
When we were about to set out, a man rushed up and reported that an ambassador from Korea was coming. I talked it over with Chang Shu-tsu: "An envoy from my country is coming shortly. If we meet on the road, we must pass with no more than a bow. I should like to stay here a little and hear things about my homeland."
Chang Shu-tsu said, "All right."
That afternoon, Sŏng Kŏn, Chief Secretary in the Privy Council and Envoy of Thanksgiving,[24] First Secretary Yun Chang, Ch'oe Cha-jun, Wu Ung, Sŏng Chung-on, Kim Maeng-gyŏng,[25] Chang U-gi, Han Ch'ung-sang, Han

[23]For Chang K'an, famous minister of the first Emperor of the Eastern Han dynasty, see, for example, *BD* 77.

[24]For Sŏng Kŏn (d. 1496) see *CJM* 416. His embassy, though incorrectly associated with Sŏng Hyŏn, who led another embassy soon afterwards, reached Peking and was reported there over a month later. See *Hsiao Tsung shih-lu, ch.* 15: 1/6/10. Within a month of Ch'oe's return to Korea, Sŏng Hyŏn (1439-1504) was sent to China to thank the Emperor. (1st Day, Seventh Month, 1488; see *CS* IV: 5: 615.) His embassy was noted in China two months later. See *Hsiao Tsung shih-lu, ch.* 18: 1/9/3. For Sŏng Hyŏn see *CJM* 413, 414. These two missions together with two more that Ch'oe passes in his thirty-nine day journey from Peking to the Yalu River suggest the liveliness of official intercourse between Seoul and Peking.

[25]Kim Maeng-gyŏng served as a Chinese interpreter and had once impressed a Chinese ambassador with his poetry. See *CJM* 926.

Kŭn, O Kŭn-wi, Kim Kyŏng-hŭi, Kwŏn Hŭi-ji, Sŏng Chun-saeng, Yi Ŭi-san, Pak Sŏn, and Chŏng Hŭng-jo came and lodged at the station. When I called on the Envoy in the central garden, he came down the steps, returned my low bow, and said to me, "His Highness is well, the State is without incident. Your home district has also been spared misfortune. When His Highness heard that you had drifted to sea and not returned, he sent down instructions to the Board of Rites to order the governors of all the provinces to notify all officials along the coast to search thoroughly and report back quickly. Moreover, copies of these instructions were sent to Tsushima Island and the islands of Japan by earliest envoys.[26] Kyongjun, Right Receiver of the Royal Edicts, in turn made the instructions known accordingly. How impossible it is to measure His Highness's graciousness!"

I bowed and left. I said to Kim Chung and others, "We are little people. Like the life and death of cicadas and flies, our life is no gain to Heaven or earth, and our death is no loss. How wonderful that His Highness's thoughts should go out like that to little people! It has been by such royal sympathy that our lives have been saved from certain death as they have." Kim Chung and the others wept with emotion.

In a short while, the First Secretary and Ch'oe Cha-jun came to the place where I was staying and talked more fully about recent affairs at home. They said, "When we first heard the report that you had drifted away and drowned, everyone lamented your death. Sŏng Hi-an alone said loudly, 'I feel that Ch'oe Pu cannot die at sea. Sooner or later he must return alive.' Now we meet and prove the truth of what he said."

At dusk the Envoy invited me to sit with him. He offered me dinner and had some sent to my secondary officials, and I thanked him: "I am an unfilial son, my sins have been great: not having died myself, misfortune extended to my dead father. I have not yet beaten my breast or stamped my feet by the coffin; rather, I have been driven by a typhoon, my insides have collapsed, and I have thought I should not survive. I went east more than six thousand *li* and fortunately arrived at Min. Still, when I looked around me, I knew no one, and my speech was not understood. I have wanted to tell someone of my grief and suffering; meeting you now, therefore, is like seeing my father and mother."

The Envoy said, "I first heard that you had reached Chekiang and other places alive when I met His Excellency An's party at Tung-pa [Stop?]. I was weak with joy.[27] Is it not fortunate that I have met you unexpectedly today?" He then said, "A groom in this group of mine died on the way. It is certainly hard to keep everyone alive over thousands of *li*. Did some of the men who went with you also die?"

I said, "Fortunately, all forty-three of us survived. All of us have come here."

[26]Text unclear; meaning seems to be as given.

[27]On the twenty-fourth, only two days earlier, Sŏng reported home that he had received from Li Hsiang, the interpreter who appeared in Peking, notice that Ch'oe was safe in Chinese hands. See *CS* IV: 5: 610.

The Envoy said, "Heaven really saved you, really saved you. Not only saved you, but did it through His Highness's virtue. We can be happy for that."

I was then questioned by the Envoy and described in general the circumstances of my drifting and staying at places, the dangers of the ocean we crossed, the outstanding geographical sites, and the differences of custom. The Envoy said, "When my party passed some places, I thought we were doing great things. When I have seen what your eyes have beheld, there will be little left to impress me."

28th Day. The morning was rainy and cloudy.

The Envoy called me before him, served me breakfast and then presented to me ten pecks of ration rice, two rain hats, ten fans, twenty *li-chung* [pills],[28] and several kinds of food. He then called for the Centurion who was escorting us and said to him, "You are escorting my countrymen well, giving them your own protection and sympathy. I am extremely pleased." He then presented to him rain hats, fans, and other things. He distributed hats and fans to my secondary officials. The First Secretary also presented to me one summer gown and a pair of cloth slippers. Ch'oe Cha-jun and Wu Ung also each gave us two fans as farewell gifts.

The Envoy feasted my followers, each according to his rank, with wine and meat. He said to me, "The days are gradually getting hotter, and the way is long and dangerous. If you are even a little careless, sickness will cripple you. If you take pains to eat enough, you will return safely home to be filial to your mother." Just then Yi Chŏng, beside himself with gratitude for what the Envoy had given him, came suddenly to the very front and described the hardships of drifting at sea. I took my leave and went.

[We went from Yung-chi Bridge to Yang-fan Station.]

29th Day. Passing Yü-t'ien County and Meeting Imperial Envoys on the Road. This day was fair.

We passed K'ou-lun Stop and came to Ts'ai-t'ing Bridge, which spanned the Lan-shui River. Soon we came to Yü-t'ien County, entered the wall through Lan-t'ien Gate, and came to Lan-t'ien Transfer Station. Hsiao-ch'üan, Hsü-wu, and other mountains were twenty or thirty *li* to the northeast. The Yen Mountains were in the northwest, about twenty *li* from the wall. It is of them that it is said in Su Che's poem, "The Yen-shan are like a long snake,/ Separating Chinese from barbarians for a thousand *li*."[29]

I asked Chang Shu-tsu a question: "I have heard it said that this land was the land of Yu-pei-p'ing of Han. Where is the rock in which Li Kuang, shoot-

---

[28]Pills used to treat internal chills, vomiting, loss of appetite, painful bowels, excessive phlegm, and other symptoms (*Chung-kuo i-hsüeh ta-tz'u-tien*).

[29]From the poem "The Yen Mountains." See Su Che, *Luan-ch'eng chi*, ch. 16: 13*v*.

ing for a tiger, buried [the arrow] to the feathers?"[30]

Chang Shu-tsu said, "Thirty *li* northeast of here is Wu-chung Mountain, and at the bottom are the old site of Wu-chung-kuo and the ruins of the wall of Pei-p'ing. The wall was the place from which Li Kuang went out hunting and came upon a rock. On top of the mountain is also the tomb of Yen Chao Wang [traditionally r. 311 B.C.−279]."

We then passed the banner gate of Filial Son Li Mao and went out the east gate of the wall, which was the Gate of Hsing-chou-tso-t'un Garrison. When we had gone about two *li* past Han-chia Village, we met two officials, who rode up in sedan-chairs. They had tallies and halberds and pewter shields. The scouts shouted, "Dismount!" I dismounted.

The two officials called to me to come forward and said, "Who are you?"

Before I had answered, the senior official ordered me to write in the palm of his hand. Chang Chung-ying came up quickly and issued a statement of my name and the circumstances of my meeting winds, going adrift, and returning. The senior official turned and said to me, "Your countrymen already know that you reached China alive."

I bowed in thanks and left. When I asked who the officials were, Chung-ying said, "The one in front is Tung Yüeh, Chancellor of the Hanlin Academy, and the second one is Wang Ch'ang, a Supervising Secretary. Last month they received orders from the Emperor to go to your country with gifts, and now they are returning."[31]

We passed Liang-chia Stop and Sha-liu-ho Stop and came to Yung-chi Station.

30th Day. Passing Feng-jun County. This day was cloudy.

[We went from the Keng River past Feng-jun County to I-feng Station.]

1st Day, Fifth Month. Cloudy.

[We went from Luan-chou to Ch'ai-chia-ling Station.]

2nd Day. Arriving South of the Wall of Yung-p'ing Prefecture. This day was fair.

[From the Sha and Luan rivers we came to Luan-ho Station, near the wall of Yung-p'ing Prefecture.] The wall was two *li* north of the station, and a line of towers was built on top of it. One was Koryŏ-Lookout [Wang-kao] Tower. Inside the wall were the prefectural capital, the seat of Lu-lung County, and the headquarters of Yung-p'ing Garrison, Lu-lung Garrison, and Tung-sheng

---

[30]For Li Kuang (d. 125 B.C.), famous for his campaigns against the Hsiung-nu, see Watson, *Records*, II: 141-154. The story of his shooting the rock is on p. 146.

[31]For Tung Yüeh (d. 1502), a *Chin-shih* of 1469, see, for example, *FSJW* 69: 13v.-14v.; and "Chōsen-fu kaisetsu," in *Chōsen shiryō sōkan* 15: 1v. For Wang Ch'ang, *Chin-shih* of 1481, see *FSJW* 12: 15r.-16v. The two men came away from Korea with different impressions. When Tung Yüeh returned he wrote *Ch'ao-hsien fu* in celebration of the country. When Wang Ch'ang returned he reported indignantly that the King had offered him improper entertainments.

Left Garrison. The prefecture had been a Nan-ching of Chin.[32] Lu-lung had been old Fei-tzu-kuo and is the same Lu-lung that is often used to mean the land beyond the Wall. Lung, Tung, Shuang-tzu, Chou-wang, Ma-an, Yang, Hui, and Pi-chia mountains were there, linked one to the next and curving round in a natural barrier.

South of the station a mound dominated the scenery, and on top of it was a Buddhist temple. Pai Ssu-ching, the Station Master, said "This is K'ai-yüan Temple." At that time, an official of the Imperial Bodyguard, coming to arrest bandits, came to the office behind the station.

3rd Day. At Luan-ho Station. This day was fair.

Chang Shu-tsu ordered his son Chung-ying to return to Peking. Chung-ying left, taking with him by mistake the document by which the Ministry of War was to transfer us to the Overseer of Kuang-ning. Chang Shu-tsu sent a man after him, but since it was sunset when he returned, there was nothing to do but stay there.

At night there were heavy thunder, lightning and rain.

4th Day. Arrival at Fu-ning Garrison. This day was fair.

[We went from Tung-kuan Transfer Station to Fu-ning Garrison and stopped there.]

5th Day. Passing Yü-kuan Station. This day was fair.

We passed Ch'ing-yün-te-lu Gate and went out the east gate of the wall. We passed Hsing-shan Stop and Pei-shih Stop and came to Yü-kuan Stop. The stop had formerly been a pass which had now been moved to Shan-hai-kuan. East of the stop was the Yü River, and Lin-yü Mountain was above the river. When Koguryŏ was being brought to submission in the *K'ai-huang* period [581-600] of Sui, that was the Yü-kuan from which Han Wang Liang led troops.[33]

We went on, past Yü-kuan Station and Pan-shan Stop. Northwest of the road was the old wall of Hai-yang, north of which was Lieh-t'o Mountain. The mountain was high and majestic, the boldest among the mountains. We passed the Chang-ku-lao River and came to the Niang-tzu River. The day was already growing dark. On the river bank, where there were three or four houses, we borrowed utensils to make a meal. We passed more than ten villages and stopped the carriages at a road whose name I do not know.

6th Day. Fair.

We went on, coming to the Shih River. In the south was the wall of Wu-hua,

---

[32]Yung-p'ing was designated Nan-ching in 1123 and remained that briefly, while Chin was mounting its final attacks against Liao forces. See *Chin shih* 2 (K'ai-ming ed. 5861.4) and *Ta Ming i t'ung chih, ch.* 5.

[33]For Han Wang Liang, fifth son of Sui Wen Ti, and his part in the Koguryŏ campaigns see *Sui shu* 45 (Kai-ming ed. 2471.3).

which had been built by Hsüeh Jen-kuei[34] when T'ang T'ai Tsung was campaigning against Koguryŏ.

We came to Ch'ien-an Station, which was outside the west gate of the wall of Shan-hai Garrison. Southeast of the wall was Mt. Ku, overlooking the seashore. Mt. Chüeh was north of the wall, and at its very peak stood Shan-hai-kuan. There were some ten *li* between the mountains that pressed against the north and the sea that skirted the south. It was a strategic point between barbarians and Chinese. The Great Wall built by the Ch'in general Meng T'ien[35] was projected from the waist of Mt. Chüeh, passed as the east wall of the garrison, and extended to the sea. In the wall was Tung-men Transfer Station.

7th Day. Passing Shan-hai kuan. This day was fair.

We entered the west gate of the wall of Shan-hai Garrison by way of Tiao Bridge and came to Ju-hsüeh Gate. When I asked about what has been called the Shuang-wen Wells of the excellent water, everyone called them Shuang-feng.[36] We passed Pu-yün Gate, Chi-shih-fang, Ya-yüan Gate, and Ling-ying Shrine and came to No. 1 Northeast Pass, which was called Shan-hai-kuan. East of the pass was Chen-tung Official Guest House. One Administrative Secretary of the Ministry of War, in charge of military petty-officers, was regularly stationed in the guest house. Everyone going east or west was inspected and allowed or forbidden to pass. Everyone, even women drawing water or servants gathering firewood, was issued a pass to show for inspection. Chang-tsu wrote a list of our names and reported them to the Administrative Secretary, who passed us only after he had called out the names one by one and verified them.

We went out Kuan-tung-ch'eng Gate, on top of which Tung-kuan Tower was built. Outside the gate was Tung-kuan Bridge, which spanned a lake. Outside the pass were Look Homeward Tower and Husband-Lookout [Wang-fu] Tower. According to legend, Husband-Lookout Tower was the place from which Meng Chiang-nü[37] had sought her husband when Ch'in was building the Wall. We passed Tung-liao Stop 1 and Chen-yüan Stop. One *li* east of the stop was a small river, the name of which I do not remember. We passed the wall of Chung-ch'ien Chiliad, which was under the jurisdiction of the Ch'ien-t'un Garrison of Kuang-ning. East of the wall was another small river. We passed it and came to Kao-ling Station, which had a wall. From there on, walls were built round all the stations, and the transfer stations were inside the same walls.

---

[34]For Hsüeh Jen-kuei (614-683), a leader of T'ang forces against Koguryŏ, see *T'ang shu* 83 (K'ai-ming ed. 3345. 1); *Hsin T'ang shu* 111 (3934.4).

[35]For Meng T'ien (d. 210 B.C.) see Derk Bodde, *Statesman, Patriot, and General in Ancient China,* New Haven: American Oriental Society, 1940, pp. 53-67.

[36]The Shuang-wen Wells were famous as the only two sweet-water wells in Shan-hai Garrison. There were over 70 wells in all, but the others were brackish. See *Ta Ming i t'ung chih, ch.* 5. This source says nothing of the other name for the wells.

[37]For Meng Chiang-nü see G. Wimsatt and G. Chen, tr., *The Lady of the Long Wall,* New York: Columbia University Press, 1934.

8th Day. Passing Ch'ien-t'un Garrison. This day was cloudy.

The men of Kao-ling Station were exceedingly cruel and overbearing. When Munhoe, one of my soldiers, was urging his donkey forward, a man from the station struck him on the head with a stick, making blood spurt forth. Chang Shu-tsu went with us to the Ch'ien-t'un Garrison and complained to Sheng Ming, Commissioner for the Garrison Forces, [*Wei-kuan-chün tu-chih-hui*], who sent men to arrest the man at the station.

[We went on to a place west of Sha-ho Station.]

9th Day. Fair.

[We went from Chang-kung Tomb to Tung-kuan Station.]

10th Day. Fair.

[We went from Ch'u-ch'ih-ho Stop to Ts'ao-chuang Station.]

11th Day. Passing Ning-yüan Garrison. This day was fair with high winds.

[We went from Ts'ao-chuang Station past Ning-yüan Garrison to Lien-shan Station.]

12th Day. Fair.

[We went from Wu-li River to Hsing-shan Station.]

13th Day. Cloudy.

[We went as far as Ling-ho Station.]

14th Day. Fair.

The Hsiao-ling River was east of the wall of the station. We crossed the river, passed Ching-shan Stop, and came to the wall of the Chung-tso Chiliad of Tso-t'un Garrison. We went in through Hsi-ning Gate and out through Lin-ho Gate. Tzu-ching Mountain was west of the wall and Hsiao-yao Temple was north. Seven or eight *li* east of the wall was also the Ta-ling River. The two rivers were about forty *li* apart. Hsing-an Stop and Tung-yüeh Shrine overlooked the east bank of the river. For six or seven *li* northeast of the river there was a stretch of white sand, in which stood Sha-wo Stop. The white sand, winnowed by the wind, had drifted against the wall of the stop until only one or two feet of the wall were not buried in it.

We came to the wall of Thirteen Mountains Station. The Thirteen Mountains were in the east and were so named because they had thirteen peaks. The station also got that name from the mountains. The Hsiao-k'un-lun and Hsiung-feng mountains were also in the north.

An official arrived in a courier carriage (*jih*) with a thing in his travel bag the size of a gourd. In it was wine that one could drink after splitting it open. Chang Shu-tsu said to me, "That is coconut wine; Ling-nan produces much of it. If a man drinks it, it makes him productive. That was in a gift from the Kwangtung

Administration Commissioner to the Emperor. The Emperor, in turn, awarded it to the Overseer of Kuang-ning."

15th Day. Fair.

[We went from Shan-hou Stop to Lü-yang Station, south of the I-wu-lü Mountains.] I had heard that the great northern mountains that bordered the sea southeast from Yü-kuan were rugged and evil, without green cover, and that the chief mountains soared boldly into the blue sky. Those things could truly be said of the I-wu-lü.

16th Day. Arriving at Kuang-ning Station and Meeting an Envoy for the Imperial Birthday. This day was fair.

We passed Ssu-t'a Stop, two other stops, and Chieh-kuan Pavilion, and came to the wall of Kuang-ning Garrison. We went in through Ying-en Gate, the west [gate] in the wall, passed Chin-shih-fang, and came to Kuang-ning Station. Soon afterwards, Board Vice-President Ch'ae Su, an Envoy for the Imperial Birthday,[38] Kim Hak-ki, the Controller of Standards,[39] Chŏng I-dŭk, the First Secretary, Min Nim, Ch'ae Nyŏn, Pak Myŏng-sŏn, Yu Sa-dal, O Kye-mun, Chang Nyang, Yi Uk, Yi Suk, Yi Hyŏng-nyang, Hong Hyo-sŏng, Chŏng Ŭn, Sin Kae-son, Haeng Cha-gang, Yun Chung-nyŏn, Kim Chong-son, and Kim Ch'un came into the station. The First Secretary and the Controller of Standards came first into the place where I had been lodged and told me in a general way about news from home. I went and bowed to the Envoy, who took me to an upper seat and said, "It never occurred to me that I should meet you here today. Indeed, it was Heaven that set you adrift and rescued you, and the coast of China on which you landed was the Earth that saved your life." Then he asked me about strategic mountains and rivers and the densely populated [places] through which I had passed, and I described them roughly.

The Envoy, for his part, talked about river and mountain regions from Chekiang south as one would talk about places through which one had already passed. He said to me, "No one from our country in recent times has personally even seen the Yangtze River and the places south of it; you alone have passed through them and seen them as you have. How fortunate you are!" I left.

In the evening, the Envoy again sent a man to make an inquiry: "Since you drifted to a foreign country, your baggage and rations must want things. What do you need? I shall supply them."

I said, "I have repeatedly received the Emperor's generous graciousness and have reached here alive. After we pass here, it will not be many days before we reach our own country. His Excellency's party will take over seven months to return, and while abroad many things they have also will be limited.

[38]For Ch'ae Su, *Chinsa* of 1469, see *CJM* 1682. He was sent to China the 10th Day, Fourth Month, 1488. *CS* IV: 5: 608. The embassy was reported in Peking two months later. *Hsiao Tsung shih-lu, ch.* 15: 1/6/10.

[39]For Kim Hak-ki (1414-1488) see *CJM* 1094.

You should not give them away lightly." I ventured to refuse.

The Envoy summoned my followers and gave them as presents two pecks of rice and two bunches of green beans. He said, "He is a guest in mourning, and there is nothing he may eat. That is why I am giving you this."

At night the Envoy sat in the central garden in the moonlight and invited me to come before him. He served me wine to console me.

17th Day. At Kuang-ning Station. This day was fair.

The Envoy came with the First Secretary and the Controller of Standards to the place where I was lodged, talked a good long time, and left.

In the evening, Wei Lang, the Grand Defending Overseer, Hsü Kuan, a Censor-in-Chief,[40] His Excellency Hu Chung, of the Regional Military Commission, Regional Commander Kou Ch'ien, and Local Commander [*Ts'an-chiang*] Ts'ui Sheng, held a conference and, in view of the lamentable circumstances of our drifting toward death and regaining life, ordered Centurion Liu Yüan, the Station Master, to console us with a whole pig, four jugs of yellow wine, one peck of paddy, and twenty pecks of millet. I divided them among the secondary officials and soldiers to be eaten and drunk.

18th Day. At Kuang-ning Station. This day was cloudy.

Chang Shu-tsu announced his departure for Peking. He said to me, "I have accompanied you over one thousand *li,* and I feel great love for you. I am already sixty years old, and my legs are weak; how unlikely it is that I shall ever see you again! Yet it occurs to me that if you are a success in your own country, some day you will come with tribute. When you go to Court, my house is inside Shun-ch'eng Gate, opposite Master of Second Horses[41] Shih's house. I hope you will remember the feelings of this day and pay me a call." He took off his underclothing and gave it to O San, because on the way he had made O San his closest companion.

Local Commander Ts'ui Sheng ordered Chin Yü to invite us [to be entertained]. Yü was a man of Liao-tung and understood our language rather well. I ordered Chŏng Po and the others to go with him, and they were entertained lavishly, with an overwhelming service of wine and food.

19th Day. At Kuang-ning Station. This day it rained.

The Overseer, Regional Commander, Censor-in-Chief, Regional Military Commissioner, and Local Commander ordered Liu Yüan and Station Scribe Wang Li to bring clothing, hats and boots to the station and issue them to me and my followers. I received one bright blue round-collar, one white Chinese linen wrap, one white three-shuttle cloth gown, one big felt hat, one small gown, one pair of white deer skin boots, and one pair of felt socks. Each of the

---

[40]*Tu-yü-shih.* Basically the title was applied to the highest officials of the Censorate but more generally to others, such as regional military officers, whose authority might be enhanced by the title. Some such auxiliary usage may explain it here.

[41]*Fu-ma tu-wei.* A conventional title for Imperial sons-in-law.

forty-two men from Chŏng Po down received one white three-shuttle cloth gown, one small gown, one felt hat, one pair of boots, and one pair of felt socks. They also feasted us with one whole pig and two jugs of wine. Yüan said to me, "The three chiefs[42] say that when you return to your country you should report everything you have received today to your King."

In the evening Chŏng Po and the other forty-odd men knelt round me and said, "From olden days, even when boats that have gone adrift have not been wrecked, some of the people have been parched for water, some have fallen into the sea, and some have died of sickness. Half of every ten have died. We have had to endure hardships, but none of us has died or been hurt. That is one blessing. Of those who drift to foreign countries, some are suspected by coast guards, some are bound, some are imprisoned, and some are whipped and then examined and judged. We, now, have not suffered a single imprisonment. Everyone has treated us respectfully and given us plenty to eat. That is a second blessing. Before this, a great many of the men who went adrift with Junior Director Yi died. [The group] were also violently seized, and when they reached the capital, they were not awarded gifts. They suffered from hunger and thirst and were barely able to return alive. When we, now, reached the capital, the Emperor awarded us gifts; when we came to Kuang-ning, the Three Authorities presented to us clothing, hats, and boots. The soldiers came with empty hands and return heavily laden. That is a third blessing."

"We do not know what has brought about these three blessings."

I said, "They have all been brought about by the virtue of our sage Highness in benevolently caring for the people and sincerely serving China."

20th Day. Cloudy. High winds.
[We left the station and went as far as P'an-shan Station.]

21st Day. Fair but windy.
[We went from Yao-chan Stop to Sha-ling Station.]

22nd Day. Fair but windy.
[We went from Kao-tun Stop across the Liao River to Hai-chou Garrison, which was also a big market town.]

23rd Day. *Arrival at Liao-yang Station*. This day was cloudy, and there was thunder.
[We went from the wall of the garrison to Liao-yang-tsai-ch'eng Station, which was west of the wall of Liao-tung.]

24th Day. Fair.
A monk there, Chieh Mien, could understand our language. He said to me, "Originally my ancestors were Koreans, but my grandfather fled to this place.

---

[42]*San-t'ang lao-tieh*. They must be the Overseer, the Censor, and the senior military officer.

It has been three generations now. Since this region is near the border of the old country, a great many men from there come here to live.

"The Chinese are extremely cowardly. If they meet bandits, they all throw away their spears and flee. They have no good bowmen, moreover, and must seize immigrants from the old country and use them as vanguards, calling them picked troops. One man from our country is a match for ten or even a hundred Chinese.

"This region was the capital of our old Koguryŏ. It was taken into China over one thousand years ago, but the traditional customs of our Koguryŏ have not yet all died out. We have built a Koryŏ temple and use it as a center. We sacrifice regularly and do not forget our origins.

"I have heard, 'Birds fly home to die, and foxes head for their burrows.'[43] We, too, want to return to our country to live, but we are afraid that our country will consider us Chinese and send us back to China. Then we should be charged with having fled and lose our heads. Our hearts, therefore, want to go but our feet hesitate."

I said, "As an anchorite, you ought to be deep in the mountains. Why do you frequent the streets like a layman in a monk's hat?"

Chieh Mien said, "For a long time I was in the mountains; now I have been called out by the officials."

I said, "Why have you been called?"

Chieh Mien said, "The late Emperor respected the Buddhist law. Great monasteries were built all over the Empire, and there were more monks than people. We lay at ease, ate our fill, and did the Buddhist rounds.

"Since the new Emperor was Heir-Apparent, he has consistently hated the monks. When he took the throne, he was determined to do away with us. Now he has handed down an edict ordering all newly established temples and monasteries to be abolished. Monks who do not have official certificates are to be returned to the laity, and this is to be done in the greatest haste.[44] The Three Chiefs, therefore, ordered sub-officials to call out the monks. From now on the temples will be destroyed, and the monks will have to grow their hair. That is why I am like this."[45]

I said, "That way, the abolished temples become people's houses, the destroyed bronze Buddhas become vessels, and the heads that once were bald and now are hairy fill the army ranks. These actions are the deeds of a Sage Emperor, far superior to the ordinary sovereign.

"You people have prayed, saying, 'Long live His Majesty the Emperor.' If you so prayed for good fortune, and the late Emperor so respected Buddhism,

---

[43]The quotation is from *Ch'u tz'u*, Chiu chang, Ai-ying.

[44]It is not certain which edict is meant here, but one recorded by Delamarre (*Histoire*, p. 395, 396), for the Eighth Month, 1487 (the previous Emperor had died two months earlier) orders the abolition of the titles of the priests of two sects.

[45]Corrupt text; meaning unclear.

and the temples and priests so flourished, what good was your earnest praying when the late Emperor died before he was middle-aged?" Before I finished speaking, Chieh Mien made excuses and left.

25th Day. Fair.

Chiliarch Wang Hsien and Centurion Wu Hsi, the interpreters, came and talked with me: "The porters at the inn did not tell us that you would stay here several days, and not knowing, therefore, we stayed at home. That is why we are late in coming to see you."

Wu Hsi took Chŏng Po, Kim Chung, and others to call on the chiefs of the Three Authorities. Before them, they reported the whole story, from our going adrift to our arrival. The chiefs of the Three Authorities were Teng Yü, Regional Military Commissioner; Han Pin,[46] Deputy Regional Commander; Wu Yü, Administration Vice Commissioner [*Pu-cheng ssu fu-shih*]; and Ch'en Lin, Regional Inspector.[47]

In the evening, the General ordered an officer to bring us three jugs of yellow wine, one whole pig, one peck of rice, and ten pecks of millet for a feast.

26th Day. Fair.

Wang Hsien came again and said, "The road to your country and those to Hai-hsi, Mao-lin, and Chien-chou garrisons pass through here. Only Wu Hsi and I are here to receive the envoys of your country who pass to and fro. I am old now, and I dread the summer heat. The Regional Commander, therefore, has commissioned my colleague Wu Hsi to accompany you as escort. Wu Hsi is also a good man. Do not worry, you will get back safely to your country.

"Generally, during a long trip the body gets no rest, and sleeping and eating are irregular, so that one easily falls sick. That is why within a few months envoys from your country like Han Ch'an and Yi Se-p'il died one after another on the way. So hard is the journey! Yet you, now, have passed through mountainous seas and come all the way from south of Yüeh to north of Yen. You are going home safe yourself and your followers safe; from that it is evident that Heaven has made dangers to save you and calamities to bring you through them in good fortune."

I said, "My arrival safe and sound is entirely a gift of the Imperial graciousness. It must also be because my dead father's spirit has been giving me secret help."

27th Day. Cloudy.

Wu Hsi came and said, "The Regional Commander has commissioned me to escort you back to your country with forty-three horses and fifteen pack horses. One of the animals will be ridden by me. About how much baggage do you have?"

[46] For Han Pin, who became one of the most famous generals of his time, see *FSJW* 98: 42*v.*-44*r.*

[47] Possibly this Ch'en Lin is the *Chin-shih* of 1484. See *LCLK Ch'eng-hua* 20: 55*v*. With four men here described as the three chiefs, the first two, officers in the military organization, must stand for a single authority.

I said, "If we loaded together the baggage the forty-three of us had originally, it would not fill one or two packs. But the padded jackets and trousers we received as awards from the Emperor are winter clothes. There are also the gowns, shoes, and other things we received at Kuang-ning, and that is all."

Wu Hsi said, "If there is little baggage, the trip can be easy."

28th Day. Heavy rain.

Wu Hsi came again and said, "Today we were to pack the baggage and start, but it is raining hard; what shall we do?"

I said, "It is hard for me, impatient as I am, to delay a moment. I alone am distressed by the rain. There has been a severe drought this year; it has not rained since the Second Month. Now that we are fortunate enough to get rain, men and all things are happy. If Heaven truly has done it, what can I say?"

Wu Hsi said, "True, true."

XXX Liao-tung was the capital of our old Koguryŏ. It was taken and attached to China by T'ang Kao Tsung [r. 650-683]. Originally in the Five Dynasties period, it was held by the overlords of Po-hsieh.[48] Later it was absorbed by Liao, Chin, and Barbarian Yüan.

Inside the wall are the Regional Military Commission, the Office of Surveillance [*Ch'a-yüan*], the Provincial Administration Office, the Local Office of the Imperial Stud, and the Inspectorate of Horses.[49] There are also Left, Right, Center, Forward, and Rear garrisons. From Sheng-p'ing Bridge west of the wall to Su-ch'ing, Ying-en, Ch'eng-ch'ing, Yang-wu, Wei-chen, and Ssu-lu gates; and between Chin-shih-men-pa-tso and Koreatown, the houses can be called dense. By standards south of the Yangtze, [the city] can be pitted against Chia-hsing Prefecture. But outside the wall of Chia-hsing Prefecture, villages stretch one after another; outside the wall of Liao-tung, neither the crowing of cocks nor the barking of dogs is to be heard. Along the Hai-tzu Road, there is nothing but great altars stretching like beads on a string. The wall of Tung-ning Garrison is built separately east of the city. Mt. Shou, Mt. Ch'ien; Mu-ch'ang, Lo-t'o, T'ai-tzu, and Hsing-hua mountains circle the city to the east, south, and west. To the north is a flat, endless plain. *XXX*

29th Day. Setting out from Liao-tung. This day was fair.

Wu Hsi and Chiliarch T'ien Fu came to the station and set out, leading us. Less than one *li* outside the east gate of the station wall was the wall of Liao-tung. Kuan-wang Shrine was between the two walls. We passed Urianghai House, T'ai-ho Gate, and An-ting Gate and came to our Korea House. In front of the house stood a plaque with the (four) words, "Dread Heaven, Defend the State."

---

[48]Also called Po-hai, a state (*ca.* 700-926) in eastern Manchuria and northern Korea founded on T'ang institutions. Five capital cities, one at Lung-ch'üan Prefecture. See *Tōyō-shi shōjiten*, p. 109 and *TDC*, plate 15.

[49]*T'ai-p'u fen-ssu* and *Yüeh-ma ssu*. The latter may be an error for *Yüan-ma ssu*. See Hucker, p. 35.

[We went from Shih-ho-erh to Hsien-te-chai Village, where we stopped.] There were three or four houses in the village.

Under cover of dusk, villagers stole my hat box. I had packed light silk gauze hats, satchel pulls, and the manuscript of a poem presented to me by a man south of the Yangtze in the box. Chŏng Po reported it to Wu Hsi, who questioned the villagers but did not get it. Wu Hsi said to me, "Carelessness in putting things away teaches others to steal. Who is at fault?"

1st Day, Sixth Month. Fair. An eclipse of the sun.[50]

[From Hsien-te Range we came to Lien-shan Pass.] Tung Wen, the Pass Chiliarch, invited me, Wu Hsi, T'ien Fu, Fang Hsiang, Chang Yung, and Shen Jung [to join him]. He had food prepared and served to us. Fu, Hsiang, Yung, and Jung; and Wang Sheng, Ma Tsung, Hung Chieh, Wu Hsi, Chin Ch'ing, and Chou Tuan, with thirty centurions, over two hundred soldiers, and ten porters from the inn, were men who had been commissioned by the Regional Commander of Liao-tung to escort us.

We went up the Lien-shan River and at sundown stopped at people's houses at Pai-chia Village.

2nd Day. Fair.

[We went from Watershed Range to Li-hai-t'un, where] a villager said, "Last night escort soldiers commanded by Chiliarch Ma Tsung came here ahead of you. A tiger seized and wounded one of the horses they had been riding. We have not had that trouble since long ago; that is why everyone who passed here would walk in the mountains and sleep out of doors. Now that this has happened, there is reason to be afraid again."

We passed the Hsieh-shao-t'un River. The water was then a flooding torrent, racing violently downstream. Ko Pok, a soldier, slipped and fell into the stream. Wu Hsi happened to be bathing and saw him drowning and rescued him.

We came to Li-sheng-t'un.

3rd Day. Fair.

We passed Hsieh-shao Great Range and came to Eight Crossings River, which was named for its eight ferries. Some called it Halfway River. It was so named because it was exactly halfway between Ching-ch'eng [Seoul] of our Korea and Peking of China. We passed [several places] and came to Feng-huang-shan-tung-ning Garrison. Military laborers had been sent out and were just then building a wall there. Wu Hsi said to me, "That wall is being built to protect the road along which envoys from your country pass."[51]

[We went from K'ai-chou Wall to Hai-ch'ing Mountain.]

[50]Confirmed by Father P. Hoang, *Catalogue des Éclipses de soleil et de lune relatées dans les documents chinois et collationées avec le canon de Th. Ritter v. Oppolzer, Variétés sinologiques* No. 56, Shanghai, 1925, p. 83.

[51]The Korean envoys' road to Peking was a dangerous one, as the size of the escort assigned to Ch'oe's party suggests, and in 1480 the Koreans had requested a more southerly route, but the Chinese Ministry of War refused to give its permission, saying that the new route would be too long (*SYC ch.* 1, p. 14v,). At that time, the Korean envoy who made the request said that every embassy was attacked by Jurchen on the way.

4th Day. Crossing the Yalu River. This day was fair.

At dawn we passed T'ang-shan Stop and two small rivers, whose names I do not remember, and came to Chiu-lien Wall. The wall was in ruins; there were only the old foundations made of earth. It was also called P'o-so-pao. A river in front of it was the Feng-p'u. We crossed the Wu-yeh River in boats. The two rivers rose together, split, and then reunited; together they were called the Ti River. We crossed the Yalu River in boats. The Prefect had sent Yun Ch'ŏn-sŏn, a military officer, to comfort me at the river bank. In the evening we crossed the T'anja River in boats. These two rivers, too, split from a single one and flowed together again downstream.

Hurrying, we entered the wall of Ŭiju in the third watch of the night. The wall was squarely at a crossroads for passing Chinese and barbarians. It was of skimpy dimensions, and it was in ruins. The streets inside the wall were desolate and depressing.

XXX [A summary list of the stations between Ning-hai and Peking, and a list of stations on an alternate land route from Yang-chou to Peking.]

On water there are red boats and on land relay horses. All envoys, tribute, and commerce come and go by water. If either the water in the locks and rivers is too shallow because of drought to let boats pass or there is a very urgent matter, the overland route is taken. The fact is that Yang-chou Prefecture is near Nanking, only three stations away. All the roads from Fukien, Chekiang, and places to the south, moreover, go through it to reach the capital. For that reason, its stations are big and the roads wide.

Some of the land stations are sixty *li* apart, some seventy or eighty *li*. As to water stations, the thirty *li* from Wu-lin to Wu-shan and the forty *li* from the Lu River to the Central Post Hotel are land passages within the water route. Those intervals, therefore, are short. Otherwise, some [stations] are sixty or seventy *li* apart, some eighty or ninety *li* apart, and some as much as over one hundred *li* apart. Between stops the intervals are sometimes ten *li* and sometimes twenty or thirty *li*. After Yang-chou, shoals have also been made at the water's edge, some six or seven *li* apart, some over ten *li* apart, to mark the distances. Altogether, the distance over which I passed from Niu-t'ou-wai-yang to T'ao-chu Chiliad, Hang-chou, and the Peking Central Post Hotel was approximately six thousand *li* or more.

[From the Central Post Hotel we passed more stations, coming to Liao-tung.] The intervals between stations were sometimes thirty or forty *li,* sometimes fifty or sixty *li*. Altogether they exceeded 1,700 *li*. Inside Shan-hai-kuan, beacon towers had been built every ten *li* to hold signal fires. Beyond the pass, too, small earth mounds had been put up at intervals of five *li,* and on them signs had been stood to mark the distance.

From Liao-tung we passed T'ou-kuan, T'ien-shui, T'ung-yüan, Pao-hsieh-li, K'ai-chou, T'ang-chan, and other stops (*chan*) and came to the Yalu River.

That was another three hundred *li* or more.

From Shan-hai-kuan east, another long wall had been built and earthwork strongholds put up to guard against nomads. All the stations and transfer stations had walls and were of the same type as defense points. Prefectures, departments, and counties had not been established, but garrisons and chiliads (*wei-so*) had been put up. The officials who manned them, though like those of the stations and transfer stations, were all military.

I also heard it said that from Three Branch River there was another road, which passed Hai-chou Garrison, Hsi-mu-ch'eng, Hsiu-an-ch'eng, Ying-na-ho-t'un, Lao-fang, Lin-tzu-t'un, and P'u-lu-hu-t'un and reached the Yalu River in a mere two hundred *li* or so. It was also a main road. To the left of the road were the foundations of an old wall that, abandoned, had become An-shih Village. According to legend, it was the place where the T'ang troops had been resisted.

In the *Hung-wu* period [1368-1398] of Great Ming, another long wall had been built to ward off the Mongols. It started from the Great Wall of Ch'in and came east. I do not know its exact course from Three Branch River west, but from there east[52] it went north past Ch'ang-ching, Ch'ang-ning, Ch'ang-an, Ch'ang-sheng, Ch'ang-yung, Ch'ang-ying, Ching-yüan, Shang-yü-lin, and Shih-fang-ssu places. It then went east past P'ing-lo-po-pao as far as the wall of P'an-yang [Mukden?]. Then it went north past P'u-ho, I-lu-hsien, Fan-ho, T'ieh-ling, and Wei-yao-chan towns and came to the wall of K'ai-yüan. It then went east, passing south of the wall of Fu-shun-so and, touching Tung-chou-ma, Ken-tan, Ch'ing-ho, Hsien-ch'ang, Ai-yang, and Shih-ch'a-k'ou places, reached the Yalu River. Altogether it curved round several thousand *li* and made secure the twenty-five garrison and patrol stations left of the Liao. There is another road—but I cannot know that for certain. *XXX*

XXX From Feng-hua County south, many high and steep mountain ranges with fantastic cliffs and scattered rocks line the coast. Rivulets and mountain torrents wind sparkling among green growth. From the Yangtze River south, the land is often soft, miry, and watery; but the T'ien-t'ai, Ssu-ming, K'uai-chi, T'ien-mu, and T'ien-p'ing mountains lie helter-skelter across it. From the Huai River south, the land has many lakes and swamps. From there north, the land is often rolling. The Grand Canal within its banks is higher than the plain. It erodes [the banks] and shifts its course, land and water exchanging places.

North of Chi-ning Department is Watershed Shrine. From the shrine south all waters flow south; from there north all flow north. From Wu-ch'eng County north the land is frequently muddy and sandy, as at Ch'ang-lu and other places. It is salt land, with much brackish water; the land of *Yü kung*'s [statement], "Near the sea were wide tracts of salt land" [Legge, III: 102]. From T'ien-chin Garrison north, all the waters flow south to Chang-chia-wan. Flat sands stretch

---

[52]Possibly the wall he traces is that shown in *TDC*, plate 22 (*Ch'ang-cha*).

endlessly, streaming and shifting with the wind. At Peking, the T'ien-shou and other mountains curve round in the north. Their western branch joins the Ta-hsing and Wang-wu mountains and extends to the border of Honan. Their eastern branch runs east past San-ho and Chi-chou and, as the Yen-shan, reaches north of Yü-t'ien County. It continues east past Feng-jun County and reaches Chen-tzu Market. It then splits into two branches, of which the southern branch goes east past Luan-chou and Ch'ang-li County to Chieh-shih Mountain and directly reaches the sea; and the northern branch joins the Yen-shan range, goes east past Ch'ien-an and Yung-p'ing to east of Fu-ning and directly reaches Shan-hai-kuan. Outside the pass it wriggles about and goes east to northwest of Kuang-ning Garrison as the I-wu-lü Mountains. The mountains from Peking there are bare of green growth.

In that space, from the Yangtze River north, Ta-hsing east, and Yen-shan and I-wu-lü Mountains south, everywhere for thousands of *li* a fine, level plain reaches east to the ocean. It extends east of Kuang-ning, west of Hai-chou Garrison, and north of Liao-tung as a great plain, that which is called Hao-yeh.

There were the An Mountains for the first time east of Hai-chou Garrison. They twisted round toward the south as the Ch'ien Mountains. After that, peaks rose in range after range, like a screen of ranks of halberds. They extended to the Yalu River in the southeast and crossed the nomads' boundaries in the east.

South of Liao-tung was a Watershed Range. From the range north, all waters flowed north, and from there south, all flowed south.

From Shih-men Range south, the mountains were many, the woods thick, and the streams clear and blue. From Peking to the Yalu River, everything named river (*ho*) was a small stream (*ch'uan*). All of them flooded in rains and dried up in droughts. Only the Luan River and Three Branch River were big; after them were such rivers as the Pai River, Ta-ling River, Hsiao-ling River, and T'ai-tzu and Eight Crossings rivers.

From the Yangtze River south were many places with soft stone. Everywhere on land the stone was cut and laid on roads or across mud and salt flats. There were many places, such as Ning-hai and Feng-hua County, where it capped mountain ridges. Everywhere on water arched gates and bridges were built up of the stone. There were many places, such as Wu-chiang County, where levees against rivers and lakes were built of it.

From the Huai River north, there was not a single stone bridge. Either boats were made into floating bridges or wooden bridges were put crudely up. Along the roads, sand and dust filled the sky.

After Lien-shan Pass, the winding roads were like threads. Wild grass grew on all sides. Travellers, their faces bitten by mosquitoes and gadflies, suffered cruelly.

From the Huai River south were many irrigated fields, rich with paddy, and grain was cheap. From Hsü-chou north, there were no irrigated fields. From Liao-tung east, the weather was hot in the evening and cold in the morning, and the five grains did not thrive. Only glutinous, panicled millet (*shu*) grew there.

In olden times, all water transport from Chekiang and Fukien south met at the Yangtze River and sailed by sea, passing up the Lu River to reach Peking. The Grand Canal was first dug in the period of the barbarian Yüan Shun Ti [r. 1333-1367]. Levees were built and locks put into place to let the transport pass. In our *Yung-lo* period [1403-1424], the Huang River was opened into the Huai, and the Wei River was led into the Pai River. There was much enlarging and rebuilding. Where water overflowed, dams were put up to prevent it. Where water brought silting, levees were put into place to resist it. Where water was shallow, locks were established to hold it. Where water was swift, floods were laid to hinder it. Where wood jammed, wedges were placed to split it.[53]

The plan for embankments: At the nearest point between two bodies of water, dams are built on both the inner and outer sides. Two stone posts are stood on top of each dam. A wooden beam is laid like a gate across the posts and a large hole bored in it. Then a wooden post is inserted into the hole of a cross-beam so that it can be turned. Irregular holes are bored along the post. The boat is fastened to the wooden post, split and twisted bamboo being used for line. A short wooden pole is forced into an irregular hole and turned, and the boat is pulled up. It is hard to move it up the embankment, there being resistance; it is easy to let it down, there being gravity.

The plan for locks: On both banks, stone levees are built so as to allow one boat to pass between them. Then the current is blocked with wide planks and the water held. The number of planks depends on the depth of the water. A wooden bridge is set up on top of the levees to let people pass. Two posts are also implanted at both ends of the bridge, as in the plan for embankments. When boats come, the bridge is removed, and they are tied to the posts. After the wide planks have been drawn up with hooks and [the water] let flow, the boats are pulled past. When the boats have passed, [the river] is again blocked.

The plan for floods: Again, dams of stone are built on both banks. Tow-paths are laid on top of the dams, and bamboo line is used again for the pulling. It takes over one hundred laborers or ten oxen to pull one boat. At all embankments, locks, and floods are officials who gather laborers and oxen to be ready for the boats.

All dams and wedges are built of stone. There are also some that have wooden palisades.

When the Chekiang Grand Defender commissioned Yang Wang to escort

---

[53]What I have called a flood is a place where the banks of a stream open out to form a wide section that slows the current. A wedge is presumably a mole or two laid in a river so as to shunt debris into the banks. An embankment, discussed subsequently, being an incline over which boats slide, might also be called a ramp.

us to the capital, he set a time limit of the 1st Day, Fourth Month. Yang Wang, therefore, led us forward night and day. In favoring winds we set sail, in head winds we pulled the boats. If the water was shallow we poled the boats, if the water was deep we rowed them. At the stations we were issued rations, and at the transfer stations we changed boats. The traffic of all envoys and tribute was like that. *XXX*

XXX Generally, there are different manners and customs within a hundred *li*; how much more is that so in the Chinese Empire. It is impossible to discuss the customs and manners of the whole. I shall consider them in broad outline, taking the Yangtze River as the boundary between north and south:

As to the prosperity of the settlements, they are elegant and beautiful beyond words in all the prefectural towns, counties, and garrisons from the river south. Whether it is market town, police station, chiliad, fortress, station, stop, village, or embankment post, sometimes for three or four *li*, sometimes for seven or eight *li*, sometimes for over ten *li*, and often for as much as twenty *li* around them, village gates crowd the ground, markets line the roads, towers look out on other towers, and boats ply stem to stern. The product — pearls, jade, gold, silver, and precious things — ; the riches — rice, kaoliang, salt, iron, fish and crabs — ; the animals — sheep, geese, ducks, chickens, pigs, donkeys, and cattle — ; and the things — pines, bamboos, vines, coir palms, longans, lichees, oranges, and pumelos — are first in the Empire. It was because of that that men of old considered the land south of the river a beautiful land.

From the river north, both Yang-chou, Huai-an, and from the Huai River north; and Hsü-chou, Chi-ning, and Lin-ch'ing, are handsome and prosperous, the same as places south of the river. Lin-ch'ing is the most thriving. There are other places, such as among the walled towns governed by public offices, that are also prosperous and thronged. But among the market towns, fortresses, stations, stops, villages, markets, wedges, storehouses, bays, banks, locks, embankments, and camps, the settlements are not very thriving, and the streets are desolate. From T'ung-chou east, the settlements gradually become fewer. After Shan-hai-kuan, one can go one hundred *li* and barely find a single village altar and not more than two or three houses with thatched roofs. There are, however, animals — sheep, chickens, pigs, donkeys, camels, and horses — ruling the wild plain. Willows, mulberries, and jujubes grow thickly, their branches intertwining. The land from Eight Crossings River south is a plain without houses.

As to houses, south of the river they are roofed with tile and paved with brick. All steps are built of stone, and sometimes stone pillars are also erected. All [the houses] are spacious and beautiful. North of the river, about half the houses have thatched roofs and are low and small.

As to dress, south of the river all the people wear big, black jackets and trousers. Many things are made of silk gauze, raw silk, and satin. Some wear wool hats, black satin hats, or horse-tail hats. Some wrap their heads in turbans, either cornerless black turbans or cornered black turbans. Officials have light silk gauze hats. Mourners have white cloth turbans and coarse cloth turbans. Some wear boots, some leather boots, Wu boots, and straw sandals. There are some who bind their legs in cloths *(chin-tzu)* instead of socks. Everything worn by women is buttoned to the left.

As to the head-dress, from Ning-po Prefecture south, it is curved, long, and large. Pretty ornaments are attached to the ends and the middle. From there north, it is curved and pointed like an ox's horn. Some wear Kuan-yin caps decorated with gold and jade and dazzling to the eye. Even white-haired old women wear earrings.

Dress and ornaments north of the river are generally of the same sort as south, but north of the river short, narrow, white gowns are often worn. Three or four of every ten are threadbare and ragged. The women's headdress is also curved and pointed like a chicken's beak. From Ts'ang-chou north some women button their clothes on the left and some on the right. From T'ung-chou on, everyone buttons his on the right. From Shan-hai-kuan east, the people are rough and their clothing ragged. In Hai-chou, Liao-tung, and other places, some of the people are Chinese, some are from our country, and some are Jurchen. From Shih-men Range south to the Yalu River, all the people are emigrants from our country. Their clothing and speech and the women's head-dress are the same as those of our country.

As to the temperament of the people and the manner and customs, south of the river they are peaceful and compliant. Brothers, paternal first cousins, or paternal second cousins live together under one roof. In some places from Wu-chiang County north, there are fathers and sons living separately. All the people frown on this. The people, whether male or female, young or old, sit on their beds and chairs and do their work.

The people north of the river have violent dispositions. From Shantung north, those of a single family do not defend each other. Quarreling voices clamor endlessly. There are apt to be many bandits and murderers. From Shan-hai-kuan east, the people's passions are most explosive. There is a strong barbarian influence.

People south of the river, moreover, read books. Even village children, ferrymen, and sailors can read. When I came to their region and wrote questions to ask them, they understood everything about the mountains, rivers, old ruins, places, and dynastic changes and told me about it minutely.

North of the river, the unschooled are many. That is why when I wanted to ask them something they would all say, "We do not understand the characters." They were illiterate.

The work of the men south of the river is the mastery of the waters. Hundreds and thousands of them get into small boats carrying bamboo baskets and catch fish with traps. North of the river, I did not see fishing equipment except at Nan-wang Lake, Chi-ning Prefecture and some other places.

None of the women south of the river goes outside the house. Some go up red towers, roll up the pearl-embroidered screens, and look out, but that is all. They do not walk in the streets or work outside. North of the river they work fields, row boats, and do other labor themselves. At some places, such as Hsü-chou and Lin-ch'ing, they make themselves up and sell their charms. They demand money, on which they live.

Some of the people called officials south of the river do tasks themselves like servants. Some, their caps and belts without insignia, sit in armchairs without regard for rank as if they had lost all decorum. But at the office, their behavior is correct and serious. In the army, orders are strict, and the regular ranks fall into formation, not presuming to complain. When a command is given a clang is heard, and [the men] gather like clouds from near and far. There are no laggards. That is so north of the river also, but from Shantung north, a command given can never be effected without whips or sticks.

Weapons south of the river are spears, swords, lances, and halberds. The word "valor" *(yung)* is branded into all the helmets, armor, and shields. But there are no bows, arrows, or war horses. There were first men with bows and arrows north of the river. From T'ung-chou east and in places in Liao-tung, the men occupy themselves with bows and horses. The shafts of the arrows are made of wood.[54]

South of the river, people pay much attention to their appearance. Both men and women carry mirror cases, coarse and fine combs, and toothpicks.[55] North of the river there is the same [liking], but I did not see anyone carrying those things. South of the river, gold and silver are used in the markets; north of the river, copper cash are used.[56] Children for sale south of the river have their arms braceleted with tin; those north have their noses pierced with lead. [People] work hard at farming, manufacturing, and commerce south of the river. North of the river there are many wastrels. Travelers by land south of the river use sedan-chairs; those north use horses or donkeys. There are no good horses south of the river; the horses north of the river are as big as dragons.

When people die south of the river, some of the great families put up shrines and banner gates. Most people simply use coffins and do not bury them but simply leave them by the water.[57] At such places as Shao-hsing Prefecture, white bones make piles beside the wall. At such places as Yang-chou north of the river, burial mounds are made at the edge of a river, between fields, or at a village gate. Mourners and priests south of the river sometimes eat meat but

---

[54]He has in mind the famous metal-shafted Korean arrows.

[55]Or perhaps a kind of toothbrush?

[56]For comments on the historical development of these different metallic currencies, see Miyazaki, *Tōyō-teki kinsei*, p. 46-50.

[57]This statement disagrees with others like, for example, C. R. Boxer's note that coffins were left unburied only as a last resort of the very poor, or because of bad omens (*South China*, p. 147).

not garlicky or oniony plants. North of the river, everyone eats such plants and meat.

Those are differences north and south of the river. As to similarities, [the people] honor gods and demons and revere the Taoist gods and the Buddha. When they talk, they always wave their hands. When they are angry, they always purse their lips and slaver. Their food is coarse. They eat with chopsticks at a common table and from common bowls. They always chew their lice. They use stone for all their laundry blocks and beaters. To turn mills they use donkeys and oxen. The shops are marked with signs and pennants. Travelers carry baggage across their shoulders but not on their backs or heads. Everyone does business; even some successful officials and men from powerful families carry balances in their own sleeves and will analyze a profit of pennies. The usual punishments of the public offices are those like the "bamboo strips," "flogging," "pressing the fingers," and "carrying stones."[58]

There are other things, such as mountains, rivers, strategic places, towers, pavilions, and old ruins known to all. Even if I were to wear all the hair off my brush, I could not record them all, nor could one see them all, even if one had a thousand years. I, moreover, did not care to go sightseeing or to pick out scenic spots while I was in mourning. I merely ordered my four secondary officials to look at honors lists and inquire about localities every day. I have noted a little and missed much. I have recorded only a summary.

The End

[58]Since the finger press, at least, was generally used to extract confessions from people arrested by the authorities, Ch'oe's list may refer to tortures rather than to formal punishments. *Cf.* Boxer's discussion of usual forms of punishment (*South China*, p. 185). The standard Five Punishments are discussed in detail in Niida Noboru, *Chūgoku hōsei-shi*, Iwanami Zensho 165, Tokyo, 1952, pp. 82-87.

BIBLIOGRAPHY

Boxer, C. R., ed., *South China in the Sixteenth Century*. Being the Narratives of Galeote Pereira, Fr. Gaspar da Cruz, O. P., Fr. Martín da Rada, O.E.S.A. (1550-1575). Hakluyt Society, Second Series No. CVI, London, 1953, 388 p.

Brunnert, H. S., and V. V. Hagelstrom, *Present Day Political Organization of China*. Shanghai: Kelly and Walsh, Limited, 1912, 572 p.

Bodde, Derk, *Statesman, Patriot, and General in Ancient China*. New Haven: American Oriental Society, 1940.

Cammann, Schuyler, *China's Dragon Robes*. New York: The Ronald Press Company, 1952, 230 p.

Changnŭng chi, by Sŏnnyŏng namhak myŏngja, (tr. by Hosoi Hajime), 77 p., in *Chōsen sōsho*.

Ch'ao-hsien fu, by Tung Yüeh, reproduced from a Chinese printing of 1531 as *Chōsen shiryō sōkan*, No. 15, Keijō: Chōsen Sōtokufu, Chōsen-shi Henshū-kai, 1937, 1 fascicle.

Che-chiang t'ung-chih. Shanghai: Commercial Press (Reprint of 1899 ed.), 1934, 4 vols.

Chi-ning Chih-li chou chih, by Shêng Pai-êrh. Ed. Wang Tao-hêng, 1785, 34 *ch.*

Choe Sang-su, "Korean Annual Custom and Festival," *Koreana Quarterly* IV: 1 (Autumn, 1962), pp. 134-150.

Chŏmp'ilje sŏnsaeng munjip, by Kim Chong-jik, 1892 ed., 10 *ch.*

Choo Young-Ha, *The Education in the Yi Dynasty*. Seoul: The Soodo Women's Teachers College, 1961, 181 English & 119 Korean pages.

Chōsen jimmei jisho, comp. by Oda Shôgo and others, Keijō: Chōsen Sōtokufu Chūsūin, 1937, 2012 p.

Chōsen kosho mokuroku, Keijō: Chōsen Kosho Kankōkai, 1911, 245 p.

Chōsen rekidai jitsuroku ichiran, comp. by Suematsu Yasukazu. Keijō: Keijō Teikoku Daigaku, 1941, 224 p.

Chōsen sōsho, ed. Hosoi Hajime. Tokyo: Chōsen Mondai Kenkyūsho, 1936, 3 vols.

"Chōsen to Ryūkyū no kankei," by Chong Tong-yu, (tr. by Shimizu Kagiyoshi), in *Chuya-p'yŏn*, ch. 1, p. 40-44, *Chōsen sōsho*, vol. I.

Chōsen tosho kaidai. Keijō: Chōsen Sōtokufu, 1919, 708 p.

Chōsengo jiten. Keijō: Chōsen Sōtokufu, 1910, 983 p.

Chōsen-shi. Keijō: Chōsen Sōtokufu, Chōsen-shi Henshū-kai, 1932-1938, 34 vols.

Chōsen-shi, by Hatada Takashi, Iwanami Zensho 154. Tokyo: Iwanami Shoten, 1951 (4th ed.), 299 p.

Chōsen-shi taikei, Jōsei-shi, by Oda Shôgo, Keijō: Chōsen-shi Gakkai, 1929, 239 p.

Chōsen-shi taikei, Kinsei-shi, by Seno Makuma. Keijō: Chōsen-shi Gakkai, 1927, 318 p.

Ch'ou hai t'u pien, by Hu Tsung-hsien, 1562, 13 *chüan*.

Ch'üan T'ang shih. Ed. Ts'ao Yin. Peking: Chung-hua shu-chü, 1960, 12 vols.

Chūgoku hōsei-shi, by Niida Noboru, Iwanami Zensho 165. Tokyo: Iwanami Shoten, 1952, 363 p.

Chūgoku-shi gaisetsu, by Wada Sei, Iwanami Zensho 120. Tokyo: Iwanami Shoten, 1950, 2 vols.

Chung-kuo i-hsüeh ta tz'u-tien, by Hsieh Kuan. Shanghai: Commercial Press, 1954, 4 vols.

Chung-kuo jên-ming ta tz'u-tien. Shanghai: Commercial Press, 1927, 1808 p.

Chung-kuo wên-hsüeh nien-piao, comp. by Ao Shih-ying. Peiping: Li-ta shu-chü, 1935, vol. 1 of 4.

Cordier, H., *Histoire Générale de la Chine.* Paris: Librairie Paul Geuthner, 1920-1921, 4 vols.

Dai Kan-Wa jiten. Ed. Morohashi Tetsuji. Tokyo: Taishū-kan shoten, 1955-60, 12 vols.

Delammare, L. C. (tr.), *Histoire de la Dynastie des Ming Composée par l'Empereur Khian-loung.* 1ᵉ partie, Comprenant les dix premiers livres (1368-1505). Paris, 1865, 448 p.

Demiéville, Paul. "Les Versions chinoises du Milindapañha," *Bulletin de l'École Française d'Èxtrême-Orient* XXIV: 1-258.

Dugout, Le P. Henry, S. J., *Carte de la province du Kiang-sou au 200,000ᵉ. Variétés sinologiques* No. 54. Shanghai, 1922, 8 leaves and index of 40 p.

Edwards, E. D., *Chinese Prose Literature of the T'ang Period, A.D. 618-906.* London: Arthur Probsthain, 1937, 2 vols.

Fairbank, J. K. and S. Y. Têng, "On the Ch'ing Tributary System," *HJAS* VI (1941-1942): 135-246.

Fairbank, J. K. and S. Y. Têng, "On the Transmission of Ch'ing Documents," *HJAS* IV (1939): 1, pp. 12-46.

Feng-hua-hsien chih, 1908 ed., 40 *ch.*

Fung Yu-lan, "The Rise of Neo-Confucianism and Its Borrowings from Buddhism and Taoism," tr. by Derk Bodde, *HJAS,* VII: 2 (July 1942), pp. 89-125.

Gernet, Jacques, *Daily Life in China on the Eve of the Mongol Invasion 1250-1276.* Tr. H. M. Wright. New York: Macmillan, 1962.

Gibert, Lucien, *Dictionnaire historique et géographique de la Mandchourie.* Hongkong: Sociétés des Mission-Étrangères, 1934, 1040 p.

Giles, Herbert A., *A Chinese Biographical Dictionary.* London and Shanghai, 1898, 1022 p.

Goodrich, L. C., "Korean Interference with Chinese Historical Records," *Journal of the North China Branch of the Royal Asiatic Society* LXVIII (1937), pp. 27-34.

Goodrich, L. C., "Sino-Korean Relations at the End of the XIVth Century," *Transactions of the Korea Branch of the Royal Asiatic Society,* XXX (1940), pp. 33-46.

Haedong chamnok, 6 *ch.* vols. 4,5 in *Taedong yasŭng.* Keijō: Chōsen Kosho Kankō-kai, 1909-1911, 72 *ch.,* 13 vols.

Hanguk kohwalcha kaeyo (English title: *Early Movable Type in Korea*), by Kim Won-yong. National Museum of Korea Series A vol. 1. Seoul: Eul-yu Publishing Company, 1954, 36 p. +26 plates + 15 English pages.

Hazard, B. H., Jr.; James Hoyt; H. T. Kim; W. W. Smith, Jr., *Korean Studies Guide.* University of California, Berkeley and Los Angeles, 1954, 220 p.

Henderson, Gregory, "Korea Through the Fall of the Lolong Colony," *Koreana Quarterly,* I: 1 (Autumn, 1959), p. 147-168.

Hoang, Le P. Pierre, *Catalogue des Éclipses de soleil et de lune relatées dans les documents chinois et collationées avec le canon de Th. Ritter v. Oppolzer. Variétés sinologiques* No. 56. Shanghai, 1925, 169 p.

Hōtō shika no kentō, by Hosoi Hajime. Chōsen Kenkyū sōsho, No. 7. Tokyo, 1921, 81 p.

(*T'ung-chih*) *Hsu-chou-fu chih.* 25 *ch.,* 12 *ts'e.*

Huang Ming shih-lu. See *Ta Ming Hsiao Tsung Ching Huang-ti shih-lu.*

Huang Ming ssu i k'ao, by Cheng Hsiao (1499-1566). Peiping: Kuo-hsüeh wen-k'u, No. 1, 1933, 147 p.

Huang Ming ta cheng chi, by Lei Li. Ming *Wan-li* ed., 25 *ch.*

Hucker, Charles O., "An Index of Terms and Titles in 'Governmental Organization of the Ming Dynasty,'" *HJAS* XXIII: 127-151.

Hucker, Charles O., "Governmental Organization of the Ming Dynasty," *HJAS* XXI: 1-66.

Hyeon Sang-yun, "A History of Thought in Korea," *The Journal of Asiatic Studies* III: 2: 261-312 (Part I); IV: 1: 299-355 (Part II).

I Ching or Book of Changes, The. tr. Richard Wilhelm, rendered into English by Cary F. Baynes. Bollingen Series XIX. New York: Pantheon, 1950, 2 vols.

Kan-shi taikan. Ed. Saku Misao. Tokyo: Seki shoin, 1936-1939, 5 vols.

Kim Hyontay, *Folklore and Customs of Korea.* Seoul: Korea Information Service, 1957, 132 p.

Kinsei Chōsen-shi, by Hayashi Taisuke, Tokyo: Waseda Daigaku, 420 p.

Kinsei Kangaku-sha chojutsu mokuroku taisei, by Seki Giichirō and Seki Yoshinao. Tokyo: Tōyō tosho kankō-kai, 1941.

Kiong, Le P. Simon, S. J., *Quelques mots sur la politesse chinoise. Variétés sinologiques* No. 25. Shanghai, 1906, 117 p.

Korea: Its Land, People and Culture of All Ages. Seoul: Hakwon-Sa, 1960.

Ku-chin t'u-shu chi-ch'eng, Ch'in-ting, comp. by Chiang T'ing-hsi and others. 1725, 10,000 *ch.*

Ku-chin t'ung-hsing-ming ta-tz'u-tien, comp. by P'eng Tso-chen. Hao-wang shu-tien, 1936, 1239 p.

Kuo ch'ao ching-sheng jen-wu k'ao. See *Pen-ch'ao fen-sheng jen-wu k'ao.*

Kuo-ch'ao lieh-ch'ing chi, by Lei Li. Ming ed., 165 *ch.*

Kuo-ch'ao lieh-ch'ing nien-piao, Lei Li. Ed. of period 1567-1619, 139 *ch.*

Kyongguk taejon. Keijō: Chōsen Sōtokufu Chūsūin, 1934, 600 p.

Lan-t'ai fa-chien lu, by Ho Ch'u-kuang. Ming *Wan-li* ed., 20 *ch.*

Latourette, K. S., *The Chinese, Their History and Culture.* New York: The MacMillan Company, 1938, 2nd Edition, 2 vols. in 1.

Lattimore, Owen, *Inner Asian Frontiers of China.* American Geography Society Research Series No. 21. New York: Capitol Publishing Company and American Geographical Society, 1951, 585 p.

Lee Man Kyoo (Yi Man-gyu), *Chosun Kyoyook Sa.* Seoul: Ulyue Munhwa Sa, 1947, 2 vols.

Legge, James, *The Chinese Classics, with a Translation, Critical and Exegetical Notes, Prolegomena, and Copious Indexes.* London: Henry Frowde, 1898, 7 vols.

Legge, James (tr.), *The Sacred Books of China, The Texts of Confucianism.* Part II. The Yî King; in *The Sacred Books of the East,* ed. by F. Max Müller, vol. XVI. Oxford: Clarendon Press, 1882.

Lin Yutang, *The Gay Genius, The Life and Times of Su Tungpo.* New York: The John Day Company, 1947.

Lin-hai-hsien chih, comp. by Hung Jo-kao. Preface dated 1683, 15 *ch.*

Li-tai chih kuan piao, comp. by Chi Yün and others under Imperial order of 1780. 72 *ch.*

McCune, George McAfee, *Notes on the History of Korea: Early Korea.* Research Monographs on Korea I: 1. Korean Research Associates, Hamilton, N.Y. ?, 1952.

de Mailla, *Histoire Générale de la Chine.* Paris, 1777-1785, 13 vols.

Makita Tairyō. *Sakugen nyūmin-ki no kenkyū.* Kyoto: Hōzōkan, 1955 & 1959, 2 vols.

Mayers, W. F., *The Chinese Government.* 2nd ed. rev. by Playfair. Shanghai: Kelly and Walsh, 1886, 158 p.

Miam ilgi-ch'o, by Yu Hŭi-ch'un. *Chōsen shiryō sōkan,* No. 8. Keijō: Chōsen Sōtokofu, Chōsen-shi Henshū-kai, 1936, 1937, 2 vols.

"Min no jidai-sei ni tsuite—Taiso no tōji hōshin o chūshin to suru—," by Tamura Jitsuzō, in *Shirin* XXX (1945): 2, pp. 1-12.

"Min no kōbō to seiryoku no tōzen sōsetsu," by Wada Sei, in *Sekai bunka-shi taikei, Min no kōbō to seiryoku tōzen.*

"Min no kōbō to tōa shokoku," by Ishihara Michihiro, in *Shichō* X (1940): 3, 4 (Special issue: *Tōa bunka-ken no rekishi-teki kenkyū*), published 1941, p. 93-119.

"Min-chō kōbō shikan," by Shimizu Taiji, in *Shigaku zasshi* LII (1941): 11, pp. 123, 124.

"Min-dai So-Shū chihō no shitaifu to minshū," by Miyazaki Ichisada, in *Shirin* 1954 No. 3, pp. 219-251.

"Min-Shin jidai no Soshū to keikōgyō no hattatsu," by Miyazaki Ichisada, in *Tōhō-gaku* 2, 1951.

Ming Ch'ing liang-ch'ao li-k'o t'i-ming pei-lu, comp. by Li Chou-wang and others. No date, 14 *ts'ê.*

Ming hui yao, comp. by Lung Wên-pin. Yung-huai-t'ang ed. of 1887, 80 *ch.*

Ming lü chi-chieh fu li, ed. by Kao Chü. Hsiu-ting Fa-lü Kuan ed. of 1908, 30 *ch.*

Ming shih, comp. by Chang T'ing-yü and others. Po-na-pen ed., 332 *ch.*

Ming shih kao, comp. by T'ang Pin. 1668 ed., 20 *ch.*

Ming shih-lu. See *Ta Ming Hsiao Tsung Ching Huang-ti shih-lu.*

"Ming-tai wo-k'ou shih chi-chih mu," in *Yü kung (Pan-yüeh k'an)* II: 4, 6.

Monzen sakuin. Comp. Shiba Rokurō. Tōdai kenkyū no shiori, Special No. 1-3. Kyoto: Jimbun kagaku kenkyūsho, 1957-1959, 3 vols.

Moule, A. C., "The Bore on the Ch'ien-t'ang River in China," *T'oung Pao* XXII, 135-188.

Moule, A. C., "Marco Polo's Description of Quinsai," *T'oung Pao* XXXIII (1937): 2, pp. 105-128.

Moule, A. C., *Quinsai with Other Notes on Marco Polo.* Cambridge University Press. 1957.

Moule, A. C., "The Ten Thousand Bridges of Quinsai," *The New China Review* IV (1922): 1, pp. 32-35.

Moule, A. C., "A Version of the Book of Vermilion Fish," *T'oung Pao* XXXIX (1949): 1-3, pp. 1-82.

Needham, Joseph, *Science and Civilisation in China.* Cambridge: University Press, 1954-, vol. I-IV[1].

Nihon-shi jiten. Kyoto Daigaku Bungaku-bu Kokushi Kenkyū-shitsu. Osaka, 1954, 983 p.

Ning-po-fu chih. 1846 ed., 36 *ch.*

Nisshi kōshō-shi kenkyū, by Akiyama Kenzō. Tokyo: Iwanami Shoten, 1939, 693 p.

Nisshi kōtsū-shi, by Kimiya Yasuhiko. Tokyo: Kinshi Hōryū-dō, 1928, 2 vols.

Osgood, Cornelius, *The Koreans and Their Culture.* New York: The Ronald Press Company, 1951, 387 p.

Pa-shih-chiu chung Ming-tai chuan-chi tsung-ho yin-te, comp. by T'ien Chi-tsung. Harvard Yenching Institute Sinological Index Series No. 24. 1935, 3 vols.

Pen-ch'ao fen-sheng jen-wu k'ao, also *Kuo-ch'ao ching-sheng jen-wu k'ao,* by Kuo T'ing-hsün. Ming ed., 115 *ch.*

Po Chü-i, *Po-shih chang-ch'ing chi. SPTK,* 1st series.

Reischauer, Edwin O., tr., *Ennin's Diary, The Record of a Pilgrimage to China in Search of the Law.* New York: The Ronald Press Company, 1955, 454 p.

Reischauer, E. O., *Ennin's Travels in T'ang China.* New York: The Ronald Press Company, 1955, 341 p.

Reischauer, E. O., "Notes on T'ang Dynasty Sea Routes," *HJAS* V (1940): 2, pp. 142-164.

Rockhill, W. W., *China's Intercourse with Korea from the XVth Century to 1895.* London: Luzac and Company, 1905, 60 p.

des Rotours, Robert, *Traité des fonctionnaires et Traité de l'armée.* Traduit de la Nouvelle Histoire des T'ang (Chap. XLVI-L). Bibliothèque de l'Institut des Haute

Études chinoises, vol. VI. Leyde: E. J. Brill, 1947, 1948, 2 vols.

Sentetsu sōdan, by Hara Zen and Tōjō Kō. Tokyo: Shōei-dō shoten, 1899.

Serruys, Henry, *The Mongols in China during the Hung-wu Period (1368-1398).* Ann Arbor: University Microfilms No. 12, 321, 1955, 415 p.

Shih tung jih-lu, by Tung Yüeh. Ed. of Ming *Cheng-te* period, 1 *ch.*

Shina gakugei dai-ji-i, by Kondō Moku. Tokyo: Ritsumeikan Shuppan-bu, 1940, 1446 p.

Shina rekidai chimei yōran, by Aoyama Sadao. Tokyo: Tōhō Bunka Gakuin, 1939, 721 p.

Shu yü chou tzu lu, comp. by Yen Ts'ung-chien. Peiping, 1930 ed., 24 *ch.*

Sinjŭng Tongguk yŏji sŭngnam, ed. by Yang Sŏng-ji and No Sa-jin, rev. by Yi Haeng and others. Keijō: Chōsen-shi Gakkai, 1930, 4 vols.

Sŏye sŏnsaeng munjip, by Yu Sŏng-nyong. 1633, 20 *ch.*

Sprenkel, van der, O. Berkelbach, "The Chronological Tables of Lei Li: An Important Source for the Study of the Ming Bureaucracy," *Bulletin of the School of Oriental and African Studies,* (University of London) XIV (1952): 2, pp. 325-334.

Sprenkel, van der, O. Berkelbach, "High Officials of the Ming: A Note on the Ch'i Ch'ing Nien Piao of the Ming History," *BSOAS* XIV (1952): 1; pp. 87-114.

Sprenkel, van der, O. Berkelbach, "Population Statistics of Ming China," *BSOAS* XV (1953): 2, pp. 289-326.

Ssu-ma Ch'ien, *Shih chi.* In *Erh-shih-wu shih,* K'ai-ming shu-tien ed.

Su Che, *Luan-ch'eng chi. SPTK,* 1st series.

(T'ung-chih chung-hsiu) Su-chou-fu chih. 81 *ts'e.*

Su Shih, *Su Tung-p'o chi. Kuo-hsüeh chi-pen ts'ung-shu* ed., Shanghai: Commercial Press, 1958, 3 vols.

Ta Ch'ing i t'ung yü t'u, comp. by Yen Shu-shen. 1863, 32 *ch.*

Ta Ming Hsiao Tsung Ching Huang-ti shih-lu, (Ch'eng-hua 23.8 — Hung-chih 18.5), comp. by Li Tung-yang, Chiao Fang and others. MS copy of Tōyō Bunko and photo-offset ed. of Library of Congress, 224 *ch.*

Ta Ming hui-tien, ed. by Hsü P'u and others. 1511 (1st edition), 180 *ch.*

Ta Ming hui-tien, ed. by Shen Shih-hsing and others. Palace edition and 24 *ts'e* edition of 1587, both 228 *ch.* The copy of the Palace edition consulted at the Library of Congress was incomplete, with 204 *ch.*

Ta Ming i t'ung chih, comp. by Li Hsien and others. 1713, Japanese ed., 90 *ch.*

Ta Ming i t'ung ming-sheng chih, comp. by Ts'ao Hsüeh-ch'üan. Ming edition, 207 *ch.*

Taedong yŏjido, by Kim Chŏng-ho. Keijō: Keijō Teikoku Daigaku, 1936, 1 box with 22 plates.

T'ai-chou-fu chih, rev. and ed. by Chang Lien-yüan. 1722 ed., 18 *ch.*

(Chiang-su) T'ai-tsang chiu-chih wu-chung. Kuang-hsü ed., 8 *ts'e.*

T'ang shih chi-shih. Comp. Chi Yu-kung. *SPTK,* 1st series.

Tchang, Mathias, *Synchronismes Chinois. Variétés Sinologiques* No. 24. Shanghai, 1905.

Tōa-shi kenkyū (Manshū-hen), by Wada Sei. Tōyō Bunko Ronsō No. 37. Tokyo: Tōyō Bunko, 1955.

Tōyō dokushi chizu, Yanai Wataru and Wada Kiyoshi *(sic).* Tokyo: Fuzambō, 1943, 33 plates and 64 p.

Tōyō rekishi daijiten, Heibonsha, 1937-1939, 9 vols.

Tōyō-teki kinsei, by Miyazaki Ichisada, Osaka: Kenkyū Taimususha, 1950, 208 p.

Trigault, Nicholas, S. J., *The China That Was, China as Discovered by the Jesuits at the Close of the Sixteenth Century.* From the Latin of Nicholas Trigault. Translated by L. J. Gallagher, S. J., Milwaukee, 1942.

Tsunoda, Ryūsaku, tr., *Japan in the Chinese Dynastic Histories; Later Han through Ming Dynasties.* Ed. by L. Carrington Goodrich. South Pasadena: P. D. and I. Perkins, 1951, 187 p., maps.

Wagner, Edward W., "The Recommendation Examination of 1519: Its Place in Early Yi Dynasty History," *Chōsen Gakuhō* 15 (April, 1960), pp. 1-80.

Waley, Arthur, *The Life and Times of Po Chü-i 772-846 A.D.* London: George Allen and Unwin, 1949.

Wang, Chi-chen, *Traditional Chinese Tales.* New York: Columbia University Press, 1944, 225 p.

Wang Yi-t'ung, *Official Relations between China and Japan, 1368-1549.* Harvard-Yenching Institute Studies IX. Cambridge, Massachusetts: Harvard University Press, 1953, 127 p.

Wan-li Shun-t'ien-fu chih, comp. and ed. by Shên Ying-wên and Chang Wên-fang. *Wan-li* ed. 6 *ch.*

Watson, Burton, tr., *Records of the Grand Historian of China.* New York: Columbia University Press, 1961, 2 vols.

Weems, Clarence Norwood, ed., *Hulbert's History of Korea.* New York: Hillary House, 1962, 2 vols.

(Hsü) Wen-hsien t'ung-k'ao. In *Shih t'ung,* Commercial Press ed., 1936.

Werner, E. T. C., *Myths and Legends of China.* New York: Brentano's, 1922.

Wild, Norman, "Materials for the Study of the Ssŭ I Kuan," *BSOAS* XI (1943-46), pp. 617-640.

Wilkinson, W. H., *The Corean Government: Constitutional Changes, July 1894 to October 1895.* Shanghai: The Inspectorate General of Customs, 1897, 192 p.

Wimsatt, Genevieve and Geoffrey Chen, tr., *The Lady of the Long Wall.* New York: Columbia University Press, 1934, 84 p.

Wu Chi-hua, *Ming-tai hai-yün chi yün-ho te yen-chiu.* Institute of History and Philology, Academia Sinica, Special Publications No. 43. Taipei, 1961.

Wu Chuang-ta, *Liu-ch'iu yü Chung-kuo.* Shanghai?: Cheng-chung shu-chü, 1948.

Wu pei chih, comp. by Mao Yüan-i. Ed. of period 1621-1627, 240 *ch.*

Yang, Key P. and Gregory Henderson, "An Outline of Korean Confucianism," Part I: *Journal of Asian Studies,* XVIII: 1 (November 1958), pp. 81-101. Part II: *JAS* XVIII: 2 (February 1959), pp. 259-276.

Yijo sillok. Keijō: Keijō Teikoku Daigaku, 1933-1934. Photolithographic reproduction of annals 1392-1864 and printing of annals 1864-1910; 900 fascicles.

Yŏllyŏsil kisul, by Yi Kŭng-ik. Keijō: Chōsen Kosho Kankō-kai, 1912, 33 *ch.*

Yŏnsan-gun ilgi. 63 *ch.,* in *Yijo sillok.*

Youn, L. Eul sou, *Le Confucianisme en Coŕee.* Paris: Paul Geuthner, 1939.

Yu-mun soe-rok, by Cho Sin. In *Taedong yasŭng.* Keijō: Chōsen Kosho Kankō-kai, 1909-1911, 72 *ch.,* 13 vols.; vol. I, pp. 405-425.

INDEX